The Which? Guide to Getting Married

Elizabeth Martyn

CONSUMERS' ASSOCIATION

Which? Books are commissioned and researched by
Consumers' Association and published by
Which? Ltd, 2 Marylebone Road, London NW1 4DF
Email address: books@which.net

Distributed by The Penguin Group:
Penguin Books Ltd, 27 Wrights Lane, London W8 5TZ

Acknowledgement to Virginia Wallis for 'Financing your wedding' in Chapter 3, 'Having a
dress made' in Chapter 8, and Chapters 18 and 19.

First edition April 1999
Reprinted 2001

Copyright © 1999 Which? Ltd

British Library Cataloguing in Publication Data
A catalogue record for this book is available from the British Library

ISBN 0 85202 760 5

For a full list of *Which?* books, please write to Which? Books, Castlemead, Gascoyne Way,
Hertford X, SG14 1LH or access our web site at www.which.net

Cover and text design by Kyzen Creative Consultants
Cover photograph by Robert Harding Picture Library

Typeset by Saxon Graphics Ltd, Derby
Printed and bound in Great Britain by Clays Ltd, Bungay, Suffolk

Contents

Introduction 7

1 Getting engaged 11

2 What kind of wedding? 20

3 Your wedding budget 30

4 Getting organised 49

5 Principal players 60

6 Wedding guests 66

7 Wedding gifts 77

8 Wedding outfits 82

9 Flowers 94

10 Transport 103

11 Music and readings for the ceremony 108

12 Wedding cake options 116

13 Photographs and video 120

14 Religious ceremonies 129

15 Civil ceremonies 143

16 Organising the reception 149

17 At the reception 170

18 Insurance 184

19 Financing your future 191

Appendix: Wedding Law 203

Addresses★ 214

Index 220

★An asterisk next to the name of an organisation in the text indicates that the address can be found in this section

Introduction

No longer is the traditional church wedding the norm in Britain. Civil ceremonies have outnumbered religious ones since 1992. In addition, couples in England and Wales are no longer restricted to choosing between a church wedding and a simple ceremony in a register office. Since 1995, following the Marriage Act 1994, venues such as hotels, stately homes, restaurants, castles, sports grounds, schools and even zoos have been able to apply for a licence for the solemnisation of marriage. This change has enabled couples to have a civil ceremony that mirrors a church ceremony in all but religious content. They can now personalise their ceremony by adding readings and music (as long as they are secular). Some couples take this a step further by arranging their wedding to reflect their surroundings – for example, by marrying in a castle in medieval dress or in a hotel in Bath with dress and conveyance etc. in the style of a Jane Austen novel.

An increasing number of couples are choosing to get married abroad. This option enables them to escape the stress that can accompany a wedding at home, perhaps arising from family arguments or problems connected with divorced parents and step families. Other couples simply like the idea of getting married somewhere exotic, while many choose to get married abroad because they can save money by having their wedding and honeymoon in the same place.

Those who want something a bit different might opt for, say, a quiet civil wedding in a register office followed by an alternative ceremony elsewhere, perhaps in their garden or on the shores of a lake or beside the sea. The choices open to these couples are unlimited because alternative ceremonies carry no legal weight and are therefore not subject to any restrictions (for example, a civil or religious ceremony in England and Wales must, to be legal, be held indoors).

So why are couples breaking away from tradition? One reason is probably age-related. People are marrying later in life: the average age of a bachelor on his wedding day was 28.9 in 1996 and the average age of a spinster was 26.8, compared with 26 and 23.8 respectively in 1985. Over two-thirds of couples have lived together before marriage, and rarely are they two youngsters leaving their parents' home for the first time. These couples are more likely to decide on a civil wedding. Those having a religious ceremony are more likely to have lived apart before their wedding. The number of second marriages is increasing in comparison with first-time marriages, and divorced couples are currently not allowed to remarry in church. Many couples who are not religious feel that it would be hypocritical to have a traditional wedding in church; instead, they might opt for an elaborate civil wedding in, say, a stately home. Other couples want more freedom to personalise their wedding and it is easier to do this with a civil wedding in an alternative venue than in a church. Finally, traditional weddings call for family unity: for example, parents are expected to sit together in church, stand together in a receiving line and sit together at the top table at the reception. An untraditional wedding, followed by an informal reception, where etiquette is not as rigid, can alleviate the tension of a traditional wedding format for couples whose parents are divorced and perhaps have remarried.

Preparing for marriage

No one marrying in the late twentieth century can be unaware that in Britain over two marriages out of every five end in divorce. Second marriages fail at an even higher rate than first ones. A more pragmatic attitude towards marriage is being by adopted by some engaged couples, and by the government, with moves in England and Wales to legalise pre-nuptial contracts, introduce post-nuptial contracts and even allow couples in future to decide on just how committed they want to be, with different 'levels' of marriage being proposed.

Another response to the high divorce rate is to try preventative measures – to help couples avoid becoming a statistic by encouraging them to consider more carefully what they are entering into. Relate* (formerly the Marriage Guidance Council) has introduced marriage preparation courses to help engaged couples do just this. They are asked to think about the major events that might happen during their marriage, such as parenthood, loss of employment or serious illness, and consider how these might impact on their relationship. The courses stress the importance of good communication (the lack of which is acknowledged to be at the root of most marital problems), and couples are shown how to achieve it. They are also made aware of the sorts of arguments that are likely to arise and are shown how best to contain and deal with these. Among the major causes of rows identified by Relate are money (number 1 on the list), attitudes to child-raising, arguments over the frequency of sex, and difficulties in agreeing over who does what around the house.

What this book covers

As couples are marrying later and have often already set up home together, an increasing number of them are arranging and paying for their wedding themselves. So the advice given in this book is aimed at the couple, rather than just the bride and her mother.

For the event to go without a hitch, detailed planning is crucial. Whether your wedding takes place in a village church, a synagogue, a register office or a Gothic castle, and whether you invite 50 or 150 guests, the organisation calls for strategy and forward thinking. As soon as you have agreed to marry, events take over and it is vital to keep on top of all the arrangements, to say nothing of the costs. This book will help you to plan every last detail, and checklists and budget sheets for you to copy and complete are provided throughout to help you to monitor your arrangements and spending. In addition, the book gives information to those getting married for the second time, covers several different ceremonies (including Church of England, Church of Scotland, Roman Catholic, Quaker, Jewish, Muslim, Hindu and Sikh), and suggests possible alternative wedding venues.

The guide goes beyond explaining how to arrange the ceremony and reception. It also gives advice about how couples can finance their wedding, and their future as a couple, with advice on tax, savings, investments, wills, pensions, life insurance and bank accounts.

Wedding etiquette

If you opt for a traditional white wedding, you need to be aware of the associated etiquette, from the wording of invitations to organisation of the seating plan and content of the speeches. All of it is in these pages but none of it is carved in stone, and you can mix the old rules with the new as you wish. Perhaps the bride wants to give a speech, or the groom would like his sister to act as 'best woman'. It can be done. Perhaps you are in a situation where traditional etiquette does not fit. Couples marrying for the second time, those whose parents are divorced or those who just want a very informal and personal occasion are at liberty to throw the rulebook to the winds and redesign the etiquette to suit themselves. After all, what do you give a couple who have already set up home and have lived together for some time? Where do you seat your step children at the reception? And who stands in the receiving line when the bride's mother is there with her new husband and neither of them is on speaking terms with the bride's father? These questions, and many others, are answered in this guide. But all these factors pale into insignificance beside the real purpose of your wedding day, which is simply to make a public declaration of your mutual love and commitment.

Chapter 1

Getting engaged

For most people, becoming engaged to be married is a big step, not to be taken lightly. Whether you will be leaving your parents' home for the first time, you have been living with your partner for years or you are marrying for the second time, the decision to tie the knot is a momentous and exciting one. Although some couples dispense with any trappings of formal engagement, for most the time leading up to the wedding is one when they can enjoy making plans together and start getting used to the idea of a long-term shared future.

Announcing the news

Courtesy and tradition demand that you should first tell the bride's parents, who will, after all, probably make a financial contribution to the wedding. Ideally, you should visit them together unless long distance means that a phone call is the only option. The man does not need to ask his fiancée's father for permission to marry her, although he might like to do so as a mark of respect and consideration for his future father-in-law, if it seems appropriate. Whether you ask permission or not, the bride's parents will welcome a chance to talk to you together about your plans for the future. Next, you should tell the groom's parents – again, in person if you can. After that other family members and friends can be notified by phone or letter.

Formal announcements

An announcement in the local paper or in one of the nationals is a good way to spread the news. Ring the 'Births, Deaths and Marriages' column a week or so before you want the announcement to appear.

Traditionally, the bride's parents announce their daughter's engagement, but couples who live independently of their parents, or who are marrying for the second time, might prefer to make the announcement themselves. Standard formal wording is as follows, but you will see other versions in the engagements columns in any newspaper.

Mr G R Evans and Miss L A Thompson
The engagement is announced between Graham Ralph, younger son of Mr and Mrs Anthony Evans of Guildford, Surrey, and Lesley Anne, only daughter of Mr and Mrs Malcolm Thompson of Reigate, Surrey.

In the version below, the groom's father is deceased and his mother has not remarried:
. . . between Graham Ralph, younger son of the late Mr Anthony Evans and Mrs Martha Evans of Guildford, Surrey . . .

In this version, the groom's mother has remarried:
. . . between Graham Ralph, younger son of the late Mr Anthony Evans and Mrs Martha Morgan of London . . .

If the bride's parents have divorced but neither has remarried, it would say:
. . . Lesley Anne, only daughter of Mr Malcolm Thompson of Reigate, Surrey and Mrs Susan Thompson of Winchester, Hampshire.

If the bride's parents have divorced and the mother has remarried, it would read:
. . . Lesley Anne, only daughter of Mr Malcolm Thompson of Reigate, Surrey and Mrs James Wallace of Winchester, Hampshire.

An informal announcement (usually in a local newspaper), made by the couple themselves, could be:
Mr G R Evans and Miss L A Thompson
Graham Evans and Lesley Thompson are delighted to announce their engagement.

Engagement party

You might like to have a party or gathering of some kind to mark your engagement and to introduce your fiancé(e) to friends and family who have not yet met him or her. This could take any form you like, from a drinks party or a sit-down dinner to a night out at a club. You could also use it as an opportunity to announce your engagement, if you can arrange the party before the news gets around. Whether you have a party or not, you will probably receive some engagement gifts, and you should send a thank-you letter for these immediately from you both.

Introducing the parents

If the two sets of parents have not already met, then you should do your best to set up a meeting as soon as possible. You could arrange a lunch, dinner, or even a weekend stay if they live far apart. If you are planning a lavish wedding you will almost certainly be looking to both sets of parents for financial help, and this initial meeting would be a good time to start the all-important discussions about the wedding budget and who will pay for what (see pages 34–5). However, if a meeting is impossible, then an exchange of letters between the two sets of parents would help to reduce any feeling that they are meeting as strangers on the wedding day.

Choosing engagement and wedding rings

An engagement ring, though not compulsory, is a symbol of love and commitment that many couples enjoy choosing together. The range of styles is enormous so you should first decide on a price limit, then browse round a few jewellers' windows to get an idea of what is on offer.

The classic engagement ring, with a diamond solitaire, is still the most popular style. The cut of the diamond (the number of facets) is important because the more facets the diamond has, the more it will sparkle. The 'carat' value, which in diamonds is a measure of weight, is reflected in the price, and the heavier and larger the diamond, the more expensive it will be. The very finest, and most expensive, diamonds are completely clear and flawless, but stones with tiny flaws, visible only under magnification, can still be very beautiful and are cheaper. However, you do not need to restrict your choice to diamonds. The other precious stones – emeralds, rubies and sapphires – as well as a wide range of semi-precious stones, from agates and aquamarines to topaz and turquoise, are all beautiful and can either be set alone or in combination with diamonds. Some brides choose an engagement ring which incorporates their birthstone.

Birthstones

Month	Stone	Meaning
January	garnet (dark red)	constancy
February	amethyst (clear purple)	sincerity
March	aquamarine (pale blue/green) or bloodstone (green, flecked red)	courage (bloodstone)
April	diamond	love, innocence
May	emerald	happiness, hope
June	pearl	health and beauty
July	ruby	love and contentment
August	peridot (greenish yellow) or sardonyx (white/yellow layers)	married bliss (sardonyx)
September	sapphire	wisdom
October	opal (milky white/multi flecks)	hope
November	topaz	fidelity
December	turquoise	harmony

Gold and other metals

When used in rings, gold, which in its pure form is too soft for daily wear, is alloyed with other metals. The 'carat' value of gold refers to its purity, so 18-carat gold is purer and darker in colour than 9-carat, but also less durable. Most wedding rings are made of 18-carat gold, but people who do heavy work may choose a tougher 9-carat ring. White gold, which is alloyed with silver, is another popular choice, and rings are also available in matt gold and rose gold as well as in combinations of colours.

Platinum, a beautiful silver-coloured and very hard-wearing metal, is also available and is more expensive than gold. Silver is cheaper than either gold or platinum but is less hard wearing. It tarnishes and will start to wear thin over the years and show signs of knocks and scratches.

What type of design?

The choice is wide, and you may well be able to find exactly what you want in a high-street jeweller's, particularly if you are looking for a traditional setting. If you do not see anything you like, you can have a ring made for you. You can either choose one of the jeweller's existing designs or have one made up to your own specification, using the stones and metals you particularly want, although this is a more expensive option. Antique rings can be very attractive and often have dainty settings and unusual combinations of stones. Go to a reputable antique dealer and get the ring checked by a valuer before buying it. One other option is to wear a family engagement ring. If it is too large or small, a jeweller can adjust it to fit you.

Almost all women, and 80 per cent of men, wear a wedding ring, and the traditional plain gold band, which comes in a variety of widths, colours and cuts, remains highly popular. For something different, however, look for engagement and wedding ring sets, where the two rings are designed to match, and may interlock. A plain band studded with diamonds or other gems can double as engagement and wedding ring; or you could choose a Russian wedding ring, with three interlinked gold bands of different colours, a cladagh (clasped hands) ring or signet ring.

Rings can be engraved inside with your wedding date, initials or any short wording you choose. This usually takes four to six weeks.

Tips for choosing the perfect rings

- Remember, you will wear the rings for the rest of your life. A high-fashion ring might seem like fun now but could look sadly dated in 20 years' time.
- Try on lots of different rings to find the weight and style that suits you. Something that looks great in the jeweller's window may look quite wrong on your finger.
- Choose engagement and wedding rings that are made of the same metal and carat, otherwise they may wear each other down as they rub together.
- Make sure the rings fit well. If you buy on a hot or cold day your finger measurement may not be a true gauge of fit.
- Take time to choose and keep an open mind. The right rings will give you daily pleasure, so it is worth taking care when you choose.

Q   *Can a man wear an engagement ring?*

A   Yes he can wear an engagement ring, an engagement/wedding ring set to match the woman's, a signet ring or any other sort you choose. Otherwise, you could give him a wedding ring that can be worn on a different finger until the wedding day. Some men do not like wearing rings, in which case he could have another item that he can wear all the time, such as a neck chain or watch.

Caring for your rings

Engagement rings with intricate settings can quickly pick up grime and grease, and stones lose their sparkle with daily wear. When buying the ring, check with the jeweller which is the best way to clean it, as some stones are particularly delicate and should not be immersed in cleaning liquids. Always be gentle when cleaning and have the settings checked occasionally. Some jewellers will steam-clean your ring while you wait.

Many people like to wear their wedding ring all the time, but engagement rings should be taken off when doing rough chores to avoid damaging them or scratching delicate surfaces in the home. Rings with 'rub-over' settings, where the gems are set flush with the band rather than standing proud, can take more everyday wear and tear than some other designs.

Remember to add your rings to your household insurance (see Chapter 18). A costly ring could be worth more than the single-item limit, which in many policies is £1,000, and should be itemised separately on the policy and covered at all times, not just when in your home. When you buy your ring, ask for a valuation certificate and keep it safely, together with a photograph of the ring(s) if possible, as it will be needed if you ever need to make a claim. Valuations need to be re-done every three to five years, otherwise insurance companies may not accept them.

Alternatives to engagement rings

If you do not want to wear an engagement ring, you could choose another piece of jewellery, such as a necklace, locket or bracelet, instead, or spend the money on something for your home. Remember, though, if it is cost that is putting you off, that it is not the price of the ring that is important, but what it stands for. The ring may have been inexpensive but will still be a potent and treasured reminder of your partner and your relationship.

Pre-nuptial contracts

Pre-nuptial agreements, once the province of the rich and famous, have become widely used in Europe and the USA and are due to become legally binding in England and Wales on the grounds that they could help to cut down on costly divorce litigation. Until then a pre-nuptial contract will be taken into account by a court in the event of a divorce but may ultimately be ignored. The longer the marriage has continued (or if there are any children of the marriage), the less weight the contract will carry. The prime function of a pre-nuptial contract is to itemise the division of assets in the event of a divorce, but it can also include expectations in regard to sharing the responsibilities of housework, child care and so on.

Those in favour of pre-nuptial agreements argue that although it is painful to contemplate splitting up before you are even married, two in five marriages end in divorce and it is better to be prepared.

They believe that broad principles may be better detailed now, when both partners can think rationally and discuss matters harmoniously, rather than later when they are tackled in the throes of an acrimonious divorce. However, the Church has criticised the plan, saying that such agreements weaken, rather than strengthen, marriage by encouraging couples to view divorce as an option when they should see marriage as a life-long commitment.

Every couple will have to decide for themselves whether some kind of pre-nuptial agreement has any place in their relationship. It does not have to be a formal, written agreement (although this would be required if the law were called upon to enforce your contract in the future), but all couples would be well advised to discuss the way they see their future lives together taking shape. Talking over questions such as whether you both want children, how you plan to manage spending and saving, who will take responsibility for what in the home and for the care of any children, can help to clarify differences of attitude and might avoid problems later on.

While many people are happy to marry in the expectation of a life-long tie, where problems will be resolved as and when they occur, others find that discussion (or even making a written agreement) will help to focus their thoughts and highlight exactly what is involved when entering into a marriage.

The Lord Chancellor's department is also currently considering making post-nuptial agreements (similar in content to pre-nuptial agreements) legally binding.

If the engagement is broken off

However upset and embarrassed you may be about breaking off an engagement, remember that it is easier to unpick a wedding than it is to unravel a marriage. It is very common to have occasional doubts as the wedding approaches; almost everyone suffers from last-minute nerves or the urge to escape from the pressure. But if your fears are more serious and persist even during the enjoyable parts of the preparations, it is far better to talk your concerns over with your partner and halt the proceedings, even if only for a short time.

If you do decide to break off the engagement, you do not need to give any explanations. Relatives and friends can be informed quietly, and if you originally placed an announcement in the newspaper, a brief notice of cancellation is all that is needed, simply stating your names and the fact that the marriage will not now take place.

Traditionally, if the woman breaks off the engagement, she should return her ring to the man. If he breaks the engagement, then she may keep the ring, although she may prefer to return it. Any presents the couple have received should be returned to the givers.

Chapter 2

What kind of wedding?

One of the first decisions you need to make is whether you would like to have a civil or religious ceremony. Couples with a religious background who want their church's sanction on their marriage will naturally choose a religious ceremony, as will those who want a traditional wedding. However, there are many reasons why over 50 per cent of the British population choose a civil ceremony, and these are discussed on page 22. You may have to take the thoughts and feelings of your families into consideration but ultimately you should choose the type of ceremony you both want.

Once you have made your choice, you can go on to consider where the wedding will take place. As a result of the 1994 Marriage Act the range of options for civil marriages in England and Wales has increased beyond the register office to include a wide selection of other approved premises (see page 23). However, if you are having a religious marriage then your choice will probably be limited to either of your parish churches. How informal/formal you want your wedding to be and roughly how many guests you want – and can afford – to invite will both influence the sorts of places you can choose for the ceremony.

Religious weddings

The religious ceremony is imbued with ritual and tradition, the surroundings are solemn and often beautiful, and the wording of the religious ceremonies encompasses ideas of mutual love, fidelity, harmony and stability.

In the Anglican church you have the right to marry in your parish church as long as neither of you has a former marriage partner still living and one of you lives within the parish boundaries. Most ministers will expect you to attend services and preparation sessions to ensure that you understand the religious significance of the marriage service.

In England and Wales a religious ceremony may be conducted only in a church. In Scotland, however, it is the celebrant who is licensed, not the premises, and a religious ceremony may take place anywhere – at your home, on a river bank, in a historical building – as long as the minister agrees that the surroundings are suitable.

A Roman Catholic priest will expect you to be confirmed and may insist on a lengthy period (usually six months) of notice of your intention to marry as it is regarded as essential for you to prepare properly for such a serious commitment. (See the Appendix for legal requirements.)

Interfaith marriages

Some religions do not allow marriage to members of different religions. If you suspect there may be a problem make enquiries immediately, since if no compromise can be found you may be forced to have a civil ceremony.

- There is no objection to marriage between people of different religions if you belong to the **Church of England, Church of Scotland, Church in Wales** or **Nonconformist (or Free Church)**, such as **Methodist, Baptist or United Reformed**.
- A **Roman Catholic** must acquire a special dispensation from his or her priest in order to marry a baptised Christian from another church. A priest's dispensation is also needed if the marriage is to take place in a non-Catholic church. If a Roman Catholic wishes to marry a non-baptised Christian, or someone who has no faith, then a bishop's dispensation will be needed; your priest will know how to obtain this. The couple may be required to take a course of instruction on marriage and agree to do everything in their power to bring up their children in the Roman Catholic faith.
- In the **Jewish faith**, if either the bride or groom is not Jewish, he or she must convert before getting married. This could take two years or more, depending on whether the conversion takes place

under the Orthodox, Reform or Liberal/Progressive authority. Conversion is complicated and demanding, involving instruction and an examination.

- **Quakers** require that a non-member who wants to marry a Quaker meet with at least two members of the Religious Society of Friends,★ so that they can assess whether the person has sufficient understanding of the religious nature of the society for the marriage to be allowed.

Civil weddings

Over half of all weddings are civil ceremonies, that is those which take place in a register office or other authorised place (see opposite). Although the wording differs from that used in a religious ceremony, a civil wedding can be just as solemn and meaningful as a religious one (see page 144 for full details of the civil marriage service).

You might choose a civil wedding because you have no religious beliefs and feel that marrying in church would be meaningless or hypocritical. Perhaps your beliefs differ from each other's to the extent that a religious wedding would be impossible. If one or both partners are divorced, then arranging a church wedding may be difficult (see page 24 for details). Some people opt for a civil ceremony because they want a quieter, less lavish service, although this is not to say that civil weddings have to be low-key.

Some religious ceremonies, for instance Hindu and Sikh, usually take place in premises that are not licensed for the solemnisation of marriages, so the couple must by law have a civil ceremony as well. (See the Appendix for legal requirements.)

Register offices

Most civil weddings take place in register offices. To find out where your local register office is, look under 'Registration of Births, Deaths and Marriages' in your phone directory. You are not tied to your local office, however, and can marry in any register office in England or Wales, provided you live in either country. Some register offices are in beautiful buildings and are much more appealing than others, so if this is important to you hunt around before deciding.

Approved licensed premises for the solemnisation of marriage

A civil wedding in England and Wales does not have to take place in a register office. Over 2,000 venues have been licensed, and you can marry in a hotel, country inn, stately home or castle, or even in the boardroom of a football club, in a museum or at a zoo. However, this is not the case in Scotland, although there are moves to bring legislation in line with that in England and Wales in the future. At the moment, however, your only option for a civil wedding in Scotland is in a register office.

Your local register office should be able to tell you about approved premises in your immediate area, or a list of them all is available from the Office for National Statistics.★ For more details of each place, including capacity and catering arrangements, refer to *Noble's Wedding Venue Guide* (see Publications, page 219).

Restrictions on approved premises

More venues are becoming licensed all the time. To gain a licence the premises must:

- be open to the public (so your own home could not be licensed)
- be indoors (so weddings cannot take place in the open air)
- be fixed (so a ship, for instance, would have to be permanently moored. It is not possible to marry on board a ship while it is at sea)
- be suitably solemn.

If your chosen venue does not meet these criteria – perhaps you want to marry beside a lake, in a ruined abbey or simply in your own garden – then you could consider having a civil ceremony in a register office, followed by an 'alternative' ceremony (see page 28) at your chosen venue.

Advantages of a wedding at an approved venue

- Where register offices are generally small and can seldom accommodate more than a handful of guests, approved premises tend to be larger, and some can hold up to several hundred people, so all your family and friends can be present at the ceremony.

- The ceremony and reception can take place at the same venue, so the proceedings are not interrupted while people travel from one to the other.
- Approved premises offer more flexible hours than register offices, and you should be able to book them for a whole day on a Saturday, and even on a Sunday or Bank Holiday, although you would need to persuade the registrars to attend.
- You will probably be able to personalise your ceremony to a greater extent at an approved venue than at a register office, by adding readings, music, and even your own words to the service (see page 113–15 for more details), although do check that this is possible before you book. You must remember, however, that in either setting no religious content is allowed

---

Themed weddings

Your wedding could be themed to suit the setting, for example, a castle or country house could provide the perfect backdrop for a medieval, Victorian, or Jane Austen-style wedding. You could either restrict the costumes to the bridal party or encourage your guests to join in by dressing up too. Other options are to pick a simpler theme and let a particular colour combination run through the day, making it easier for guests to take part; or let the season dictate the mood of your wedding and have a Christmas or springtime theme, with decorations, music and a cake chosen to tie in.

Second marriages

In 1996, 42 per cent of marriages were not the first for one or both partners. While the Church of England is happy to marry widows or widowers, the question of whether or not a divorced person may marry in church is a cloudy one. Church regulations currently forbid it, but it seems that some ministers flout this rule and will agree to marry people who are divorced, especially if they consider that the people involved are not to blame over the collapse of their first marriage.

There is a move in the Church of England to rethink the ban on remarriage for divorcees, but for the time being, if it is your second marriage, your best option may still be a civil ceremony followed by a church blessing (see page 141). Talk to your vicar before making any arrangements, as some do not approve of hymns, bridesmaids, flowers and traditional bridal dress at a blessing.

In Scotland divorcees may marry in church at the discretion of the minister, who will want to know something of the circumstances of the breakdown of any previous marriages before agreeing. See the Appendix for further details on remarriage.

Getting married abroad

Tying the knot in an exotic foreign location is becoming increasingly popular, with about 17,000 couples a year marrying abroad. Many people who get married abroad do so because they want a quiet ceremony without the stress that accompanies a wedding in the UK. Also, if the ceremony and the honeymoon are in the same place, the cost is much less than the average UK wedding. The choice of destinations is wide, and many major tour operators now have dedicated wedding brochures and telephone numbers (see page 217). Although it is possible to organise a wedding abroad yourself, most people use a tour organiser, who can offer a complete package. You can either stay on at your wedding resort for your honeymoon or choose a two-centre package, if you prefer.

Exotic wedding venues

If you would like a beach wedding, your choice of destinations could include: the Caribbean, Kenya, Mexico, Sri Lanka, the Seychelles, Mauritius, Hawaii and Thailand. In the USA you could get married in a chapel of love in Las Vegas – with an Elvis look-a-like singing during the ceremony – or have a fantasy wedding in Disneyland, with Micky Mouse as a guest. The truly adventurous might like an underwater wedding at Key Largo or marriage in a helicopter 1,000 feet above Orlando. Other options include a slope-side wedding in a ski resort, a ceremony in a game reserve in Africa or even a marriage on the Equator.

The legal requirements vary from country to country with regard to minimum residency required, documents needed and so on. See page 212 for preliminary guidance on this, but be sure to check carefully with the tour operator, who will be able to give you a detailed checklist of what is needed. Some countries will not marry people of certain denominations or those who have been divorced, so do check carefully before making any bookings. A marriage performed abroad in accordance with local law is valid in the UK as long as you would both have been legally entitled to marry in the UK. Check on the availability of a marriage certificate, as you may have to take steps to register your marriage in the UK in order to get a duplicate certificate, should you ever need one. Your travel company should be able to advise on this.

Limitations of getting married abroad

Although wedding packages are very popular, they can be basic. The standard package usually offers all the paperwork, a simple ceremony, a bottle of sparkling wine, a posy of flowers and a few photographs. If you want something more lavish, choose a company that offers a good range of extras, which might include special transport, floral decorations, extra champagne, a video and more photographs, and a celebration dinner, but be prepared to pay extra for all of these.

- If all you want is a simple ceremony with no extras, and you would have taken a foreign honeymoon anyway, getting married abroad can be an inexpensive choice, with the basic ceremony package ranging from £300 to £700, excluding the cost of the holiday.
- In popular resorts there may be several weddings each day, and you may have to queue for a licence. Tour operators can advise on less busy destinations.
- A beach ceremony can be very simple and brief; this is fine if that is what you want and you know what to expect.
- Although you might be longing for a quiet wedding with none of the hassle of guest lists and seating plans, your family and friends may feel left out. Some companies will organise a special deal for guests who want to travel with you and will even arrange to put them up at a different hotel so that you have some privacy. Alternatively, you could organise a blessing (see pages 141–2) or a celebratory party when you return home.

- Photographs taken at a wedding abroad may not be of such a high standard as those you would get at home.

Marrying a foreigner

If one of you comes from a country other than the UK, you will have to take various steps when organising the wedding. These will depend on the country in which you plan to marry (check with the relevant consulate).

An Anglo-Japanese wedding

Mark and Yumiko met in Osaka while he was travelling round the world before going to university. After living together for 18 months they returned to England and later went back to Japan to get married.

Yumiko's parents did all the organisation for the wedding. First, the couple were driven to a Japanese register office for a civil ceremony, which would be recognised under UK law. After this they were taken to a specialist dresser, who arranged Yumiko's hair in a traditional style, applied white make-up to her face and helped both Yumiko and Mark to dress in traditional kimonos. They were then taken to a Shinto temple for the traditional ceremony conducted by a Shinto priest. This was in Japanese, but Yumiko's mother had arranged for a translator to be present so that the English guests could understand what was being said. The couple sat side by side in the centre, with eight members of Mark's family – who had flown to Japan for the occasion – on one side. As a sign of courtesy towards Mark's family, only eight members of Yumiko's family sat on the other side. The couple did not have to do or say anything during the ceremony.

After the ceremony the two families went back to a nearby hotel where the couple got changed into more comfortable clothes before sharing an elaborate meal with their guests.

In the United Kingdom
A foreigner will generally be asked to produce a passport as identification when applying to marry in the UK. He or she should take steps to ensure that a UK marriage will be valid in his or her country of origin; the consulate will be able to advise on this.

In a foreigner's country of origin

To be married in a foreign country under the law of that country, a UK subject may be required to give notice of the intended marriage in England, Wales, Scotland or Northern Ireland, if that is where he or she is resident, or to the marriage officer of the country in which he or she lives, and then apply for a certificate saying that no impediment to the marriage exists. It is important for the individual to check with the consulate that the marriage will be recognised in the UK. The rules on this vary widely from country to country, so check carefully.

Alternative ceremonies

Those who find a religious service inappropriate and the civil ceremony uninspiring might like to consider an alternative ceremony. These are not legally binding, so you would need to have a civil ceremony as well, but the alternative service could be the main part of the wedding, to which most guests are invited, and could take place in any setting you choose.

Among the possibilities are Pagan, Druid, New Age, Viking, Spiritualist and Humanist ceremonies, or you could create a ceremony that is entirely your own. A number of books give plenty of ideas for you to think about (see publications, page 220). For more details of what form an alternative ceremony might take, see page 146–8.

One couple wrote their own wedding promises

Jane and Michael had a very quiet register office wedding, followed by a reception for friends and relatives. They had worked out between themselves a list of ten 'wedding promises' and after the speeches they stood side by side and read these out alternately. The final promise was 'never to argue when tired'. A relative had produced a decorative copy of the promises on her computer and had it framed as a wedding present for the couple; it now hangs in their kitchen and is a daily reminder of the promises they wrote and made together.

Celebrating gay and lesbian relationships

Although the law in the UK – unlike in Denmark, the Netherlands, Norway and Sweden – does not recognise same-sex marriages, gay and lesbian couples can mark their relationship with a special ceremony. The Lesbian and Gay Christian Movement★ can provide details of ministers who are willing to conduct blessing ceremonies for lesbian and gay couples. The Unitarian and Free Christian Churches★ has a tradition of supporting civil and religious liberty, and can put you in touch with a minister who could organise a service for you. For a non-religious ceremony, the Pink Triangle Trust★ can arrange an affirmation ceremony which gives the couple the opportunity to make pledges of love and committment and exchange rings.

Chapter 3

Your wedding budget

Getting married usually involves major expenditure, with the average cost of a traditional white wedding being about £11,000 (including the honeymoon). So before you start spending, decide how much you can afford and plan your budget carefully. If you do not, you will almost certainly find that you overrun your limit.

Financing your wedding

You will need to pay a deposit for most wedding services, such as the reception venue, catering, wedding dress and photographs, as soon as you book them but you will not have to pay the rest until a week or so before the wedding.

The cheapest way to pay for your wedding is with savings. However, if you do not have any – or you do not have enough – you should consider saving a certain amount every month during your engagement period. Before you set your wedding date, work out how much money you can afford to save each month; you may find that you want to postpone your wedding for two or three months to give you a chance to save enough money to pay for it.

If you cannot meet the whole cost with savings you will either need to look at ways of reducing the costs or borrowing the money. But before deciding to borrow, think about how you will feel if you are still paying for your wedding in, say, five years' time and think hard about the sorts of financial commitments you are likely to have in the future. For example, are you likely to have children by then? Are you going to be paying a large amount of money into your pension each month? If you think your financial commitments are likely to be quite hefty in a few years' time, you should consider paying back more money per month over a shorter period.

For the sums involved, it is unlikely that an overdraft on your current account is going to be sufficient, and you certainly should not consider this option without first talking to your bank. Because an overdraft is better for short-term dips into your finances, your bank may well suggest that you take out a personal loan instead – but do not take it until you have compared what is on offer from other lenders – see below. With this sort of loan, you decide how much you want to borrow. Your lender (which does not have to be your bank) gives you the lump sum, which you then repay by making fixed monthly payments for a certain number of years (you decide this when you take out the loan).

The advantages of a personal loan are that you know what your monthly payments are going to be for the entire time that you are paying it back and you can choose a monthly amount that best suits your budget. The disadvantages are that the smaller the monthly repayment, the longer you will take to pay back the loan and the greater the total cost of borrowing. Another disadvantage is that if you want to repay the loan early – with money you have been given as a wedding present, for example – you may have to pay a penalty charge.

How to compare loans

Once you have decided how much you need to borrow, comparing the cost of loans from different lenders is quite straightforward. First compare the APR (annual percentage rate of charge), making sure that you are comparing loans of the same amount and for the same number of monthly repayments. Do not be taken in by the headline APR (which you may see on the front of literature about the loan): this is nearly always for the biggest loan on offer, which may not be the amount you want to borrow (the bigger the loan, the lower the APR).

Looking at the APR helps you to whittle down your choice of loans. The next thing to look at is the cost of the monthly repayments, which tells you which is the cheapest. But again, make sure that you are comparing like with like: a loan repaid over 24 months is always going to look more expensive (in monthly terms) than a loan repaid over 36 months.

Typical monthly cost of a personal loan of:	APR (%)	1 year	2 years	3 years	4 years	5 years
£2,000	18.5	£182.50	£98.98	£71.40	£57.81	£49.81
£5,000	13.3	£445.70	£236.83	£167.56	£133.20	£112.80
£10,000	13.3	£891.41	£473.65	£335.13	£266.41	£225.61
£11,500	13.3	£1,025.12	£544.70	£385.40	£306.37	£259.45

Monthly repayments are for a loan without loan payment protection insurance.

The other thing to watch out for is the extra cost of loan payment protection insurance. This sort of insurance is usually quite restrictive when it comes to paying out and can push up the price of borrowing quite considerably. A common ploy in personal loan literature is to make the repayments with insurance look far more attractive than those without it or to hide the repayments without insurance over the page.

Other ways to borrow

Another type of loan, which has a lower rate of interest than a personal loan but is more risky, is a secured loan. For this you would increase the size of your mortgage and so increase your monthly mortgage payments accordingly. This is advisable only if your mortgage is significantly less than the value of your property. If it is not, you might find that your mortgage becomes more than your property is worth.

If your mortgage lender is not willing to give you a loan against your mortgage you could go to another lender (a bank, for example) and ask for a loan secured against your mortgage. Again, your house is at risk if you fall behind with your payments.

Another option is to borrow against an investment-type life insurance policy (endowment or bond) if you have one. If you do, you should ring your insurer and ask if you can borrow money against the policy, what the interest rate is and how long you have to repay the loan. If you do not have one of these policies you can take out a personal loan.

Paying for your honeymoon

It is a good idea to pay for your honeymoon on credit card because of the extra protection you get from the Consumer Credit Act. If you have a problem with anything you pay for by credit card (between £100 and £30,000) and your supplier won't help, you can seek compensation from your credit card issuer. For example, if your honeymoon is a disaster because your hotel was a building site and you cannot get redress from the tour operator, you can claim the money from your credit card company. You are often charged a fee for paying for the whole of your holiday by credit card so to avoid this you could pay the deposit for it (minimum of £100) by credit card and the rest with cash (if possible). If you do this you will still be covered by the Consumer Credit Act.

'I did babysitting jobs to help pay for my daughter's wedding'

Barbara and Graham's daughter and her fiancé had set their hearts on a large white wedding, with a reception for over 100 guests at an Elizabethan manor country hotel. The estimated cost was between £8,000 and £9,000. The couple was able to contribute £3,000, and Barbara and Graham agreed to pay the rest.

'We had about £2,500 in savings and decided to take out a bank loan for £4,000 over two years. The repayments worked out at just over £200 a month. So the only problem was where to get the money to repay the loan. A colleague then told me that she had been babysitting for a number of families and that there was plenty of work in the area. This struck me as a good way to earn some of the money to repay the loan and I was able to charge £3 per hour.

'It wasn't long before I was babysitting regularly and earning up to £50 per week. In the weeks leading up to Christmas and at New Year I was working every evening and once or twice stayed the night so that the parents could stay out longer.

'I babysat for about 18 months and earned £3,800. After that I worked less often and eventually stopped altogether once I had earned all the money I needed.'

The preliminary budget

If you take the time to plan your budget carefully, you will almost certainly save money. Make a long list – or copy and use the one in this book – of every conceivable item that will be needed for your wedding day. Be it large or small, put it in your preliminary budget and write a figure against it. Phone round suppliers, browse through wedding magazines, trawl the shops, compare estimates (but remember, these are not binding) to get an idea of how much each item costs (we give a guideline in this book, see pages 44–8).

When you have some idea of what to allow for each item, add it all up and include a contingency amount of 5 to 10 per cent of the total cost for unforeseen expenses. It is important to include this sum since it will almost certainly be needed and should not be viewed as an optional extra. For example, if your absolute top limit is £10,000, you should work to a budget of £9,000, allowing for a 10 per cent contingency of £1,000.

At this point, if the total is more than you can afford, you may have to rethink your plans and cut out some items to meet your limit. For example, you could have two bridesmaids instead of six, opt for a paying bar at your reception instead of providing all the alcohol yourselves, or invite fewer guests. Do not be tempted to underestimate deliberately.

Who pays for what?

You will also need to work out who is going to pay for what. The traditional responsibilities are shown in the box opposite but nowadays few families stick rigidly to tradition, and instead apportion the cost to suit themselves.

In a great many cases the couple themselves foot a sizeable proportion of the bill, although the bride's family is still likely to pay for more than the groom's family. Try to sit everyone down together as soon as you have a rough idea of the amounts involved and work out where each cost will be borne. This may not be as easy as it sounds, and you may have to use considerable diplomacy to arrive at a point where everyone is happy and no one feels unfairly burdened with his or her share of the cost.

Traditional responsibility for payment

The bride's family pays for:

- engagement announcements (in the newspapers)
- invitations and all other wedding stationery
- the bride's clothing
- the bridesmaids' outfits (but often the bridesmaids, or their parents, will pay)
- flowers in the church and at the reception
- photographs/video
- transport to church/wedding venue and reception for the bridal party
- wedding cake
- the reception

The groom (or his family) pays for:

- engagement and wedding rings (bride pays for groom's ring)
- cost of licence or registrar's fee
- all church expenses
- transport to church/wedding venue for groom and best man
- bride's and bridesmaids' flowers, buttonholes
- gifts for attendants
- hotel for first night
- honeymoon

The final budget

Once you have agreed on the limit for expenditure on your wedding (and the cost of individual items), you can start placing firm orders.

- Wherever possible get **written quotations** – which are legally binding – and ask for them to be made out in as much detail as possible. If you change your mind about anything you have asked for, confirm in writing.
- Keep careful **records of all expenditure**. File away all bills, receipts and so on and do not throw anything away. Keep notes

of any deposits paid, when the final balance is due and how much it is.

- Consider opening a **wedding bank account**, so that all cheques come from a single source.
- It is very **easy to overrun your budget**. Keep yours on a tight rein by being aware that any extras – and you will be offered dozens – will add to the cost, and a few relatively small amounts can add up to a sizeable total.
- Naturally, you will change your mind about things and discover **items that were not in your original budget**. Look at the impact on the overall budget before adding anything.

'The hotel tried to overcharge'

When Susanna and Andrew booked their reception, months before the wedding, they were told that payment in full was expected a few days before the event. When the final bill came, it included a charge of £450 for the use of the (big) room. Fortunately, during their original visit Susanna had taken a checklist and against 'separate room charge?' she had recorded 'no'. The new hotel manager was not happy (remember that staff can change between the booking and the actual occasion – another good reason for keeping detailed records) but was forced to accept the situation. However, it was a stressful and unpleasant incident, which the couple could have done without just a few days before their wedding.

Negotiating discounts

It is quite often possible to get a discount on items for your wedding. Try offering the full amount at the time of ordering, in return for, say, 10 per cent off, but be aware that if the company runs into financial problems before delivering, your money could be at risk. The late autumn, winter and early spring are relatively quiet for many wedding suppliers, who may be more willing to consider giving a discount in order to secure your business at these times than in the busy summer months.

Q *If I have to cancel the wedding, where do I stand financially with suppliers?*

A In this situation you will be in breach of contract and will usually forfeit any deposit paid. You may also have to pay compensation to, say, a caterer for any financial loss suffered as a result of your breach of contract. This would normally amount to any profit element the firm loses on your deal. However, the caterer does have a responsibility to keep losses to a minimum. The more notice you can give of cancellation, the better the chance that suppliers' losses will be small. If you pull out at the last moment, they will be unlikely to get another booking, and your liability may be greater. (See Chapter 18 for information on insurance.)

VAT

VAT currently stands at 17.5%, but suppliers with an annual turnover of less than £50,000 are not usually VAT-registered, and not all goods are subject to VAT. However, most items associated with weddings attract VAT, with a few exceptions.

- **children's clothing** A child is defined as being under the age of 14, and the zero-rated clothes are only those that fit a child of 13 years or less (height 158cm, chest 84cm, waist 71cm, hips 86cm and shoe size 1½). However, if you have outfits specially made for your child attendants and you provide the dressmaker with the material you will have to pay VAT on the material. You will have to pay VAT on the dressmaker's time only if he or she is VAT-registered
- **wedding cakes** (if they are supplied independently of other catering)
- **food provided by the caterer that requires further preparation by the customer** (such as defrosting, cooking, re-heating or arranging or serving on plates) is not subject to VAT.

Look at estimates or quotations you receive to see if VAT is included or ask the supplier if there is VAT to pay. If there is, that particular supplier is VAT-registered, and you may be able to make savings by looking for one who is not.

Budget checklist

Item	Estimated cost	Actual cost	Who pays?	Deposit	Paid	Balance £
Press announcements						
Engagement						
Wedding						
Engagement party						
Wedding venue fees						
Bride						
Dress						
Veil or hat						
Shoes						
Lingerie/tights/stockings						
Jewellery						
Going-away outfit						
Beauty treatments						
Make-up						

Groom														
Wedding clothes														
Going-away outfit														
Barber														
Bridesmaids														
Adults' dresses														
Adults' headdresses														
Adults' shoes														
Children's dresses														
Children's headdresses														
Children's shoes														
Pages														
Outfits														
Shoes														
Ushers' outfits														

Item	Estimated cost	Actual cost	Who pays?	Deposit	Paid	Balance £
Best man's outfit						
Bride's father's outfit						
Rings						
Engagement ring						
Bride's wedding ring						
Groom's wedding ring						
Transport						
Bride and father to ceremony						
Bride's mother and attendants to ceremony						
Groom and best man to ceremony						
Bride and groom to reception						
Attendants and bride's parents to reception						
Bride and groom from reception						
Photographs						

video

Flowers

Bride's bouquet						
Bride's headdress						
Bridesmaids' bouquets						
Bridesmaids' headdresses						
Buttonholes and corsages						
Wedding venue decorations						
Car decorations						
Reception decorations						

Reception

Hire of venue						
Other hire costs (staff, furniture, crockery etc.)						
Food						
Drink						
Crèche service						
Entertainment						
Service charge/tips						
Other						

Item	Estimated cost	Actual cost	Who pays?	Deposit	Paid	Balance £
Honeymoon						
First night hotel						
Holiday						
Spending money						
Stationery						
Invitations						
Postage						
Order of service sheets						
Menus						
Place cards						
Other reception stationery						
Wedding insurance						
Hen and stag nights						
Any other costs						
Contingency of 5–10%						

Budget breakdown

The table below shows how the average total cost of £11,000 for a traditional white wedding is made up.

Item	£
Church fees	260
Bride's wedding clothes	800
Bride's going-away outfit	150
Bride's beauty treatments	75
Attendants' outfits	450
Groom's wedding outfit	250
Engagement ring	750
Bride's wedding ring	175
Groom's wedding ring	150
Transport	200
Photographs	400
Video	350
Flowers	300
Reception	
Hire of venue	700
Catering/food	2,000
Drink	800
Cake	200
Entertainment	650
Wedding stationery	160
Insurance	50
First night hotel	130
Honeymoon	2,000
Total	**11,000**

What is not included

These figures do not include the cost of any other celebration, such as an engagement party or stag and hen nights. Miscellaneous costs, such as cash spent on the day and so on are not included.

What it costs: the hard facts

The detailed budget breakdown shows how the average cost of £11,000 for a traditional white wedding is made up. Below are more details on these amounts, plus some cost-cutting suggestions.

In reality, many couples spend somewhere near the average for the majority of their costs, make savings where they can or where the item does not feature on their list of priorities, and spending more where something – the reception meal, say, or the honeymoon destination – is particularly important to them.

Church/register office fees

The fee for calling the banns and issuing the banns certificate is about £14. However, the usual church fees mount up to about £260, which includes the cost of the organist, church choir, bells and heating.

For a civil service, it costs £21 to give notice in your registration district. If you live in different districts from each other you will have to pay this fee twice. Other costs include the registrar's attendance fee of £36 and a copy of your marriage certificate (£3.50), making a total of £60.50 for the cheapest possible civil wedding.

Bride's clothes

The average cost of a traditional wedding dress with veil, headdress and shoes is £800. If you want to spend less than this, you could hire a dress for about £300. Another option would be to make your own (which can be cheaper as long as the pattern doesn't require a large amount of expensive material) – see pages 86–7. A secondhand dress could cost under £100, or you could borrow one from a friend or relative, which will cost nothing at all.

The average amount a bride spends on a going-away outfit is £150, but you could wear a dress or suit you already have if you prefer.

Bride's beauty treatments, make-up, hair

A budget of about £75 would cover some new cosmetics, a manicure and a session with the hairdresser on the day, although you could use your existing cosmetics and get friends to give you a manicure and do your hair.

Attendants' outfits

The average total cost is in the region of £450, but this clearly depends on the number of attendants you have. If you don't want to splash out and have the attendants' outfits specially made, you could look in high-street stores for inexpensive outfits. Other options are to make them yourself or look for secondhand ones.

Groom's wedding clothes

Hiring full morning dress costs about £60 and buying a suit off-the-peg costs between £150 and £300. Do not forget to allow for shirt, tie and shoes. Alternatively, you could wear an existing suit or borrow one from a friend.

Rings

The average cost of an engagement ring is £750, and £175 for the bride's wedding ring. The groom's wedding ring generally costs about £150. If you want to spend less than this on an engagement ring, shop around for less expensive designs and look for semiprecious stones or smaller diamonds. Alternatively, you could wear a family ring if you have one.

Transport

Expect to pay £200-plus for cars (two cars for about three hours), although if you want to save money, you could use cars belonging to family or friends.

Photographs/video

Using a professional photographer for the day will cost about £400. To bring this cost down to about £150, you could have a simple, civil ceremony and go for the minimum number of shots.

A professional video of the day, starting with the bride's departure from her house and ending after the speeches at the reception, will cost about £350. A shorter video, ending after the ceremony, costs £250 or less. Alternatively, you could get friends and relatives to take photographs/video for you, as long as you are confident of their abilities. Work out a list of important photographs and make one person responsible for taking them so that no vital moment or person is left out.

Flowers

On average, couples spend £250 to £300 on flowers for the day.

- A fairly simple, hand-tied bouquet costs £50-plus, while a wired shower style starts at about £95.
- Fresh flower headdresses cost from £35.
- Buttonholes are around £3 each (for a carnation), corsages £7.50 to £10.
- Floral arrangements for the church could cost from £100 and decorations for the reception range from £150, although costs vary quite dramatically depending on where in the UK you live.

However, flowers do not need to cost this much, and a skilled friend or relation could arrange the flowers for much less. If another couple is marrying on the same day you may be able to share the cost of flowers at the church, or you could choose to use the flowers that the church provides. Flowers in season and simple arrangements cost less than hot-house blooms lavishly displayed and can be just as effective.

The reception

The number of guests is the crucial factor here, with 100 being the average.

- The average cost of hiring a venue to accommodate this number is £700.
- Catering adds another £2,000 to the bill.
- Allow £800 for drinks.
- The wedding cake costs about £200.

- Entertainment: as a guide, a band playing for 3 hours costs from £500.
- A DJ playing recorded music for 3 hours would cost from £270.
- A string quartet playing background music for 3 hours would cost about £600.

Ways of cutting the cost for the reception include:

- holding the reception at home, or in a hall, which is cheaper than a hotel
- having a finger buffet instead of a sit-down meal
- offering sparkling wine rather than real champagne
- making the cake yourself, getting a friend to make it (this can cost nearly half the amount of having one professionally made) or buying one ready-made from a supermarket and having the icing done professionally
- having a short reception, which does not go on into the evening, saves on the cost of entertainment and refreshments
- having a paying bar instead of providing all the alcohol yourselves, or providing drinks for part of the evening, then having a paying bar.

Wedding stationery

The average total cost of stationery is about £160, including invitations, order of service sheets and reception items (place setting cards). It is cheaper to buy invitations ready-printed from stationers and fill in your own details or create your own on a computer. Also, you do not need to have service sheets (you can use the church's service and hymn books), menus etc.

Wedding insurance

Comprehensive cover should cost about £50 – see Chapter 18. However, you may decide to take the risk and save the money, particularly if you are having a small, simple wedding.

First night and honeymoon

The average cost of a hotel for the first night is £130. An increasing number of couples have a two-week honeymoon abroad, which costs on average £2,000. You can save money if you spend your first night at home or at a simple country inn or hotel. Choosing a shorter stay in the UK will keep the cost down. Renting a cottage is a cheaper option, particularly out of season, but make sure it is comfortable and well heated. Spending a few nights in France, Italy or Spain, for example, costs less than flying to a distant destination.

A couple who made money on their reception

Debbie and Adam were on a very tight budget. After a family register office ceremony, they asked 50 guests to a lunchtime buffet followed by square dancing. Both wore clothes they already owned for the ceremony, while Debbie found a wedding dress in a charity shop for £35 so she could look the part at the reception. As they had been living together for a couple of years they did not want household gifts, so instead asked everyone to contribute food or drink for the reception. They ended up with plenty of food. One aunt provided a whole dressed salmon, the groom's father gave a case of champagne, and puddings and salads were plentiful. What they had not expected was that some guests would give gifts of money instead of, or in addition to, food and drink. These more than covered the hire of the hall, band, photographer, glasses and crockery and other incidental expenses, and they finished with about £50 in hand.

Chapter 4

Getting organised

All weddings, no matter how small, require meticulous planning. You will need to make lots of lists and keep an assiduous check on what has been done and what remains to be done. Book your key venues and suppliers as early as you can – you can think about the details later. Do not feel that you have to take care of every last item yourself and delegate wherever you can. In this chapter is a detailed list of what you should be doing when.

Wedding organisers

If the idea of planning a wedding makes you want to tear your hair out, you could consider using a professional wedding organiser to take over as much or as little of the organisation as you wish. He or she will spend time talking to you to find out exactly what you have in mind and will liaise closely throughout the preparations. Experienced organisers are very knowledgeable about where to get the best deals for the services they need, and may be able to negotiate discounts which individuals could not achieve.

Look in the classified sections of wedding magazines for names of organisers. Before you sign any contract read the small print and make sure you know exactly what the company's terms are. Some charge a flat fee, while others take a percentage of the total cost, which could be far more expensive if you are having a large wedding. Before you book, follow up a couple of references from previous clients and get a detailed written quotation, outlining exactly what the organiser will and will not do.

Wedding on the Web

Lucy and Mark knew that most of their friends had access to the Internet so they decided to use it to help plan their wedding. When they sent out their formal invitations they included a note, giving the address of the web site and listing the sort of information their guests could find on it.

They put a photograph of themselves on the home page and included their wedding present list, directions to the church and reception venue, lists of train times, and telephone numbers and addresses of local B&Bs and hotels. They also displayed their chosen menu and asked their guests to email them if they wanted the vegetarian option.

After the event they put some of their photographs and the video of their wedding on their web site so that those who were unable to come on the day (including several of their friends who lived abroad) could see them.

Soon after your engagement

- Decide what type of wedding you are going to have: religious or civil, formal or informal.
- Draw up your preliminary budget (see Chapter 3).
- Decide who will pay for what.
- Work out how many guests you can afford/want to invite and draw up a guest list.
- Choose and book location for ceremony (you can book up to a year ahead for a civil ceremony, and may be able to make a provisional booking even further ahead).
- Cut out snippets from magazines and newspapers for ideas on flowers, dresses etc. (and keep a wedding file)
- Find out if you need to make any special arrangements regarding a wedding licence (see the Appendix), and if so start the necessary procedures.
- Choose and book venue for reception.
- Approach best man and attendants and make sure they keep the date free.

- Book the following:
    photographer
    video operator
    florist
    transport
    caterers
    toastmaster (if you are having one)
    entertainment for the reception.
- Order the wedding cake.
- Book the honeymoon.
- Book the wedding abroad (if having one).
- (Bride) shop for dresses and accessories for self and bridesmaids and place orders if these are being made for you.
- Start working out the details of the reception.

Setting the date and time

- For a formal wedding allow a bare minimum of three months for the organisation. Six is better, and a year is not too long if you want to marry at a popular venue on a Saturday. Some churches and reception venues are booked up for many months in advance, especially for summer weddings.
- Compare diaries early on to make sure you avoid other commitments and ensure all the key guests are free on the date you have chosen.
- Church weddings are not usually allowed on Sundays. Saturday is the most popular day, although there is nothing to stop you choosing a weekday if the minister agrees.
- By law, in England and Wales, a wedding must take place between 8am and 6pm, although Quaker and Jewish weddings, and marriages taking place under a registrar's special licence, are exceptions to this rule. In Scotland a religious wedding can take place at any time as long as the minister agrees. A civil wedding must take place during office hours.
- Register offices are open Monday to Friday, 9am to 4pm and Saturday mornings from 9am until 1pm.
- Some Christian ministers prefer not to conduct weddings during Lent (the period leading up to Easter). If you are permitted to

marry at this time, you may not be allowed to decorate the church with flowers.

- If you marry on a winter's afternoon, the light outdoors may not be very good for photographs. Winter weather may also be a limiting factor if guests have to travel far.

Four to six months to go

- Order the wedding invitations (printing takes two to four weeks).
- Draw up a wedding gift list (or organise one at a department store – see pages 78–9).
- If making your own fruit cake, bake it now.
- Contact the minister to confirm dates of the banns and details of the wedding.
- Book bellringers.
- Decide on the form of service and hymns you want for a church wedding.
- Arrange to meet organist and choir master to discuss choice of music, and book organist and choir or soloist.
- Book hotel for wedding night.
- Decide what the men in the wedding party will wear and buy any clothes needed.
- Consider arranging wedding insurance (see Chapter 18).

Two to three months to go

- Arrange a rehearsal for the ceremony.
- Check passports; apply for new ones if necessary, or apply for post-dated passport with name change (see pages 57–8).
- Apply for any visas needed for your honeymoon.
- Send out invitations (six to nine weeks before the wedding).
- Check off replies as they arrive.
- Book overnight accommodation for any guests who need it.
- Send gift list to those who request it.
- Make a list of the gifts (and who they are from) as they arrive and write thank-you letters immediately.
- Meet caterers to agree food and drink menus.

- Buy wedding ring(s).
- Buy wedding gifts for each other.
- Buy gifts for best man and attendants.
- Book groom's, best man's and ushers' morning suits if hiring (allow six weeks).
- Buy your wedding shoes and underwear before your first dress fitting so you can try on the whole ensemble together. Wear shoes around the house so they are comfortable on the day.
- Have first wedding dress fitting.
- Shop for going-away outfit.
- Shop for honeymoon clothes.
- Take your headdress along to the hairdresser to discuss a suitable style and have a trial run if necessary. Make an appointment for the day.
- Have a session with a beautician and try out any different make-up well in advance of the day. Make an appointment for the day.
- Book any beauty treatments you will want to have before the wedding.
- Have any vaccinations needed for honeymoon. Some can make you feel unwell, so choose a time when you can rest if necessary.
- Visit family planning clinic if necessary (see overleaf).
- Decide on bouquets, button holes, corsages and floral arrangements needed for church and reception and order them.
- Order other stationery such as order of service sheets and items for the reception.

Tip

Many brides lose weight in the weeks leading up to the wedding. Leave your final fitting as late as you comfortably can to keep adjustments to a minimum.

Your period needn't spoil your day

If your periods are very regular, either naturally or because you take the combined pill, five minutes spent with your diary will reveal whether a period is due on or around your wedding day or honeymoon. If this is likely to cause you a problem, talk to your GP or family planning clinic at least a month before the wedding day for advice on how you can use the combined pill to alter the dates on which your period will arrive. If you are not taking the pill, or use the progestogen-only pill, you could consider taking the combined pill for the short term in order to benefit in this way, but should take medical advice beforehand, as the combined pill is not suitable for all women.

If you have never taken the pill before, you should visit the clinic two to three months before your wedding, so that you have time to get over any of the minor side-effects which women often experience when they start the pill.

Alternatively, a doctor or nurse can prescribe other hormonal tablets which delay the onset of a period, without having any contraceptive effect. If you are going to a long-haul destination for your honeymoon be aware of the effect passing through different time zones will have on when you should take your pill. Again, see your GP or clinic in advance for advice. The Family Planning Association Helpline* can give advice on these and other matters.

One month to go

- Check that any guests who have failed to reply did receive their invitations.
- Draw up a draft seating plan if you are having a sit-down meal.
- Confirm date of wedding rehearsal.
- Hear banns read in church.
- Prepare a newspaper announcement.
- (Bride) book manicure for the day before.
- Check that everyone in the wedding party has their correct wedding attire.
- (Bride) have final fitting for wedding dress.

- Advise bank etc. of change of address and name (see overleaf).
- Arrange stag night and hen party.

Tip

Leave it as late as possible to finalise your seating plan and allow for some flexibility. People may cancel or decide that they can come after all just days before the event.

Two weeks to go

- Ice and decorate the cake if making it yourself.
- Order traveller's cheques or currency for honeymoon.
- Confirm all the arrangements: florist, photographer, video operator, cars, reception, cake, church details and honeymoon.
- Have stag night and hen party.

One week to go

- Wrap gifts for attendants, best man and each other.
- (Groom) place correct fees for minister, organist, choir, bell-ringers and church heating in cash in marked envelopes and give to best man, together with keys for going-away car on the day.
- Time the journey to the church so you know exactly what time you will need to leave home.
- Pack honeymoon luggage and check travel details and tickets. You can finish packing the night before the wedding if necessary.
- Have wedding rehearsal.
- Arrange for someone to take care of bride's dress and accessories after the wedding (usually her mother). The best man should take charge of the groom's clothes and, if they are hired, return them.
- Review the seating plan and prepare place cards.
- Confirm final number of guests to caterer.

The day before

- If using your own car to go on your honeymoon, check that it has petrol, oil and water and is in perfect running order.
- Pack going-away/honeymoon clothes and if possible have case(s) taken to reception venue.
- Give the best man and attendants their presents.
- (Bride) have manicure.
- Double-check all the arrangements.

Changing your surname

Every woman who marries has to decide whether or not to change her surname. You are not legally obliged to do so. The various options are listed below.

- **Changing to husband's surname** This is easy and makes any joint ventures straightforward. To make the change, send a copy of your marriage certificate to the relevant organisations (banks and building societies will want to see the original), so that they can change their records.
- Another common choice is to **keep your maiden name for work purposes**, using the title Miss or Ms as you prefer, and use your married name and the title Mrs elsewhere. Think this through before you make any changes, as confusion can easily set in if you are not consistent. If your job involves a lot of travel tell your employer if you change your passport and bank details.
- If a woman has children from a previous marriage who will be living with the newly married couple, she may wish to retain her previous married name or to change the children's surname to her new married name. This is a sensitive issue, which should be discussed with all parties involved, including the children and their father, if possible, before taking any action.
- You could use **both your surnames, hyphenated** if you wish. If both of you decide to adopt a new composite surname, you will need to change your names by deed poll or by statutory declaration after your marriage. A solicitor can advise on how to do this.

- Your **husband could change his surname to your maiden name**. However, unlike women, men do not have a legal right to change their name on marriage, so he would need to make the change by deed poll or statutory declaration.
- If you do choose to change your surname you should inform:
  your employer
  Inland Revenue★
  the Contributions Agency★ and the Benefits Agency★ (both part of the Department of Social Security – DSS)
  bank
  building society
  insurance companies
  credit-card and store-card companies
  passport office (see below)
  legal adviser
  financial adviser
  pension providers (if you have a personal pension or contribute to an FSAVC – free-standing additional voluntary contribution scheme)
  DVLA★ (the Driver and Vehicle Licensing Agency) to change driver's licence and vehicle registration documents
  Premium Bonds Office★
  any companies of which you are a shareholder
  motoring organisations
  any professional associations to which you belong
  any other clubs or societies
  GP
  dentist.

If you are on the Internet, you may wish to change your email address.

Travel documents for your honeymoon and changing your passport

- If you are going abroad on honeymoon and wish to **travel using your married name** you will need to obtain a post-dated passport. An amended or new passport can be issued up to three months before the wedding but cannot be used until the actual date of the marriage.

- The forms and leaflets you need are available from most post offices, regional passport offices and some travel agents. To **amend your existing passport** you need: leaflet PD1, form PD2 (to be completed by minister or registrar) and form C. This costs £11. To apply for a **new passport** you need: leaflet PD1, form PD2 and form A. The cost is £21 for a standard passport, or £31 for a 48-page passport.
- **Allow at least one month for the application to be processed** and up to three months if applying between February and June. If you leave it late, you can visit the London Passport Office★ in person and apply for a new passport or have one amended on the spot. Be prepared for a long wait if you visit at a busy time of year.
- **Check that the name on your passport and visa is the same as the name on your travel documents**. You can travel using your maiden name and change your passport on your return; or if the tickets are in your married name, take your marriage certificate with your existing passport. However, some countries will not grant a visa on post-dated or amended passports, nor on a passport in your maiden name accompanied by a marriage certificate. Check with the relevant consulate in advance. If you do change your name on your passport, remember to inform your tour operator as some assume you will be travelling under your maiden name. It is frustrating to go to the trouble of changing your passport only to find you have to take your marriage certificate after all because your tickets are in your maiden name.

On the day

In the hours before the ceremony:

- the bride has her hair done, does her make-up, dresses in her wedding clothes, and transfers engagement ring to her right hand
- flowers arrive at bride's home
- bridesmaids arrive and change
- chief bridesmaid or bride's mother helps bride arrange her veil
- best man and groom dress in their wedding clothes
- best man checks that he has the rings

- groom gives best man any cash or cheques he may need to pay for church facilities etc. plus any travel documents etc. for the honeymoon
- going-away clothes are taken to reception venue
- going-away/honeymoon luggage taken to reception venue
- groom's car left at reception venue if it is to be used to leave the reception
- best man collects buttonholes and order of service sheets to take to church.

Shortly before the ceremony:

- ushers arrive at church 45 minutes before ceremony begins
- couple and guests arrive at register office about 10 minutes before the service is due to begin
- photographer and video operator arrive at wedding venue
- organist arrives at church and begins to play quietly about half an hour before the ceremony is due to begin
- minister, choir and bellringers arrive about half an hour before the service begins
- guests begin to arrive at the church and are given order of service sheets by ushers, who also direct them to their places according to the plan (see page 134)
- best man and groom arrive at the church about 40 minutes before the ceremony begins and pose for photographs, then take their positions in the front pew on the right of the aisle. Best man may pay the minister now or after the service
- bridesmaids and bride's mother leave for church and pose for photographs on arrival, about 10 minutes before the ceremony
- bride's mother is escorted to her place in the front pew to the left of the aisle. She leaves a seat on her right for the bride's father
- bride and her father leave for church and are met in church porch by bridesmaids. They pose for photographs. Chief bridesmaid arranges bride's dress, train and veil. Ushers take their seats in church. The minister greets the bride at the church door and can then either precede her down the aisle or return to the chancel steps and wait for her there. The choir can either head the procession or be already seated in the choir stalls.

Chapter 5

Principal players

Your choice of best man and attendants can make a large difference to the smooth running of your wedding day. Think carefully before you decide who to ask and offer the roles to people who will enjoy performing them and whom you can trust to do a good job.

The best man

The groom usually chooses a relative or close friend for this job. Traditionally, the best man is single, but nowadays it is quite in order to choose someone who is married. The best man needs to be confident, dependable, a good organiser and someone who can be relied upon to stay sober throughout the proceedings. As well as giving practical help before, during and after the wedding, the best man is there to give moral support to the bridegroom both before the event and on the day. His responsibilities are listed below.

Before the wedding day he:

- helps the groom to choose the ushers
- organises the stag party and makes sure that the groom gets home safely after it
- arranges the hire of clothes for the groom, the ushers and himself
- attends the wedding rehearsal
- confirms all arrangements by liaising with the bride's family.

On the wedding day he:

- arranges for the honeymoon luggage to be taken to the reception venue

- briefs the ushers before going to the church
- organises the ushers at the church
- ensures buttonholes and order of service sheets are at the church
- organises parking arrangements at the church
- pays any church expenses on behalf of the groom
- drives the groom to the church, ensuring that they arrive about 40 minutes before the start of the ceremony
- takes care of the wedding ring(s) until they are needed during the ceremony
- signs the register as a witness (optional)
- accompanies the chief bridesmaid out of church
- assists the photographer in marshalling guests for photographs
- ensures that all guests have transport to the reception before leaving the church himself
- arranges his own transport to the reception
- possibly takes part in the receiving line
- generally looks after guests at reception
- keeps an eye on the clock so that proceedings don't overrun
- keeps an eye on any wedding presents brought to the reception and ensures that they are taken away safely afterwards
- introduces the speeches and toasts, reads messages from those who could not attend, announces the cutting of the cake
- delivers his own speech
- ensures the couple have transport from the reception and, if necessary, organises a non-drinker to drive them to their destination
- ensures that honeymoon luggage is in the going-away vehicle.

After the wedding he:

- takes charge of the groom's clothes and returns any hired items promptly.

Q *I can't decide whether to ask my brother or my best friend to be best man. Can I have them both?*

A Yes, as long as you can decide between you who is going to do what. Perhaps one could perform the best man's role during the ceremony, and the other could take over at the reception.

> **Q** *I have always been very close to my sister and would like her support at my wedding. Can I have a best woman?*
>
> **A** There is no reason why a best man has to be male, although she might prefer not to come on the stag night, depending on what sort of event it is going to be.

The ushers

The number of ushers you will need depends on how many guests you invite to the ceremony. A rough guide is three ushers per 100 guests. They help seat people in the church and hand out order of service sheets. Again, choose people whom you know to be reliable and able to deal with any problems that crop up on the day. The ushers have the following duties:

- arriving at the church early
- ensuring that order of service sheets are at the front of the church for the use of the wedding party and minister
- giving buttonholes to the principal male guests
- standing at the door and distributing order of service sheets or hymn and prayer books
- directing guests to their places in church. The bride's mother and other principal guests should be personally escorted to their seats
- helping any guests with small children or those who are elderly or disabled.

The chief bridesmaid and bridal attendants

Chosen by the bride, the bridesmaids are traditionally unmarried female members of her family or close friends. However, bridesmaids and pages may also be members of the groom's family. A married attendant is known as a matron of honour.

The very young attendants are not expected to do anything on the day except look decorative and behave themselves. Do remember, however, that although tiny bridesmaids and pages can look enchanting, they cannot be relied upon to keep still and quiet during the ceremony, so choose them with care and limit the number of those under five years old. The chief bridesmaid processes up the aisle behind the bride, followed by the other attendants. If you are planning to have a flower girl, whose job it is to strew the bride's path with petals as she leaves church, do check that the minister has no objections. The chief bridesmaid is usually expected to:

- help select the bridesmaids' outfits
- organise and attend the hen party
- possibly help the bride choose her wedding dress
- help the bride to dress on the day of the wedding
- be in charge of the younger attendants, making sure they have their posies etc. and know what to do in church
- ensure the younger attendants are well-behaved in church
- arrive at the church before the bride and help arrange her dress and veil before the procession goes in
- help the bride to lift back her veil at the top of the aisle
- hold the bride's bouquet during the ceremony
- perhaps witness the signing of the register
- leave the church with the best man
- at the reception help the best man make guests welcome
- keep a check on the younger attendants at the reception
- help the bride change out of her wedding dress before leaving. She may also take charge of the bride's wedding clothes if the bride's mother is not doing this.

If you have other adult bridesmaids, they could help the chief bridesmaid with some of these jobs.

The parents of the bride and groom

The bride's father has three important duties to perform on the wedding day:

- to escort his daughter down the aisle
- to give her away during the ceremony
- to make a speech at the reception.

The bride's mother has no formal duties, and most of her work goes on behind the scenes, ensuring that everything runs smoothly.

She may play a major role in the planning and organisation of the day. If the bride is getting married from her parents' home then her mother may help her to dress on the wedding day and make sure the flowers have arrived on time and that the best man has taken the buttonholes and order of service sheets to the church.

At the reception, the bride's parents act as hosts, greeting guests and seeing that their needs are met. The groom's parents traditionally have much less involvement with the proceedings, although they may well contribute both financially and with any practical help that they are able to give. The two families should liaise on the guest list, and at the reception both sets of parents take part in the receiving line (if there is one), greeting guests as they arrive and making introductions where necessary.

What happens when the bride's or groom's parents are divorced?

Where neither partner of the divorced couple has remarried, then ideally they should set their differences aside and sit together in church and at the reception and stand side by side in the receiving line. If animosity makes this difficult or impossible, then they should arrange unobtrusively to have the least possible contact during the day without making the rift too uncomfortably obvious to others.

Where divorced parents have remarried, the mother sits in the first pew with her husband, and the father and his wife sit behind in the second pew. In the receiving line divorced parents should stand together, while new partners should simply mingle with the other guests.

Q *My father wants to give me away, and so does my step-father. How can we resolve this?*

A In theory, you should choose which one you feel closest to, and the other should respect your decision, which should be relayed with great tact and sensitivity. If that seems too difficult, an unconventional solution would be to ask your mother to accompany you down the aisle.

Attendants at a civil ceremony

It is not usual to have bridesmaids and pages at a register office wedding, although it is not unheard of. However, you can have a best man, who can produce the rings at the appropriate moment, and the bride can ask a close relative or friend to give her special support on the day. If you marry at alternative licensed premises then you will be freer to make the occasion more like a traditional wedding and have as many attendants as you like.

Gifts from the bride and groom to the best man and their attendants

It is customary to give gifts to the best man and attendants as a way of expressing your appreciation and gratitude for their contribution to your wedding day. Jewellery is a popular choice, and you could give the best man and ushers cuff links, a tie pin or a watch, and the chief bridesmaid a necklace, ring or earrings. It is a good idea to give the same item to each of any younger bridesmaids to prevent comparisons, perhaps choosing something they can wear on the day. Watches are often popular with children and are a good choice for page boys. Ornamental keepsakes, such as a photograph frame or engraved mug might also be suitable. Alternatively, you could break with tradition and give cameras, computers, portable CD-players or any other gift you think would be welcomed.

Many couples give the two sets of parents a gift to thank them for everything they have done to help. If you want to stick with tradition, a decorative item for the home, perhaps engraved with details of the wedding, would be appropriate, but again the rules are there to be broken, so choose what you know would be most appreciated by the people concerned.

Chapter 6

Wedding guests

The task of deciding who to invite to your wedding will be a difficult one. If your parents are making a financial contribution to the day, they will almost certainly want to have a say in who should be on the list and may insist that you invite certain relatives and family friends. You, on the other hand, may want to ask all your friends and include only close family members. This task will require diplomacy, and you will have to work out a compromise that suits everyone.

Before you start writing your list you need to work out how many people you are able to invite. Your budget and the type of reception you would like are factors that will influence this, as will the size of the wedding venue. For example, most register offices cannot accommodate more than 30 guests, in which case you could choose to invite only the closest relatives and friends to the ceremony and extend the numbers for the reception. If you have a tight budget, you could have a small family gathering for the ceremony and reception and have an informal party for friends, either at home or elsewhere, at a future date.

Having decided how many people to ask, you should make a preliminary list, starting with the people you think should definitely be invited – your closest family and friends. Then write down the names of those who you will probably ask – more distant family members and friends. Finally, list those who you would like to ask if numbers allow, such as colleagues and acquaintances. The bride and groom should have equal numbers of guests, although this might not be possible if one partner's family is much larger than the other's, for example.

Whether or not you choose to invite a former spouse will depend on your circumstances and how appropriate you feel it would be for him or her to be present. Children of a former marriage are usually invited, however, and other members of your ex-husband's or ex-wife's family could be included if you think it is appropriate.

Inviting children

A question that inevitably arises when couples are compiling their guest list is whether or not to invite children. While some people are happy to involve them in the whole day, others are worried that they might disrupt the proceedings. The main reasons why people do not invite children are:

- they take up space on the guest list and thus limit the numbers of adults the couple can invite
- small children may get bored and may make noise during the ceremony
- their parents may find it hard work keeping them entertained during a long sit-down meal.

However, there are various solutions to these problems. You could:

- choose not to invite any children
- invite them only to the reception, in which case you should make this plain on the invitations
- provide entertainment and care for the children at the reception venue (see pages 180–1), and perhaps during the ceremony as well
- invite only children of very close friends and relatives, or those with whom you have a particularly close link – godchildren, for instance – and exclude others. You will need to make some tactful explanations to friends whose children are not included, but people are usually understanding of the problems.

We decided not to invite children

When Julia married Tom they were both in their forties, and almost all of their friends had children, ranging in age from 3 to 15. Julia explained why they decided not to ask any children.

'I am very close to many of the children, but we wanted to sit down in a lovely restaurant with all our best friends and have a really good meal. The food was expensive and not the sort children usually like to eat, but more importantly we knew kids would just get bored. Space was limited as well, so for each child we asked we would have had to leave out one of our friends.

'I was concerned that people would be upset or offended, or might even not come at all, so before sending any invitations I rang every friend with children and explained what we were doing and said I hoped they would understand and that it wouldn't be a problem. Most friends said they would actually prefer to come without children because then they would be able to relax and enjoy themselves more easily, and because I gave plenty of notice most people were able to make arrangements for the children to be looked after. One or two people tried to persuade us to make an exception but we had already decided not to do that. Unfortunately, my cousin and her husband decided not to come because they couldn't bring their children.

'I would advise anyone only to invite children if that's what they really want to do. If not, be sensitive to your friends' feelings, speak to them personally and explain, but be very firm and stick by your decision.'

The wedding invitations

The style of invitation you send out will set the tone for your wedding, so choose the most suitable type. A huge range of styles is available, and you can either buy them already printed (with space for you to fill in your details) from department stores and stationers or order your own from specialist printers or stationery design companies. Look in the *Yellow Pages* or at the small ads in wedding magazines then ring or visit one or two and ask to see samples of their work and a price list. Another option is to create them your-selves, either using specialist wedding software (see page 219) or a desk-top publishing system.

For a formal wedding, the invitations should be printed or engraved on good-quality white or cream card. The format is an upright, folded card measuring 14×18cm (5½×7in). Traditionally, invitations are engraved, which gives the lettering an embossed appearance, but this is expensive because a printing plate has to be made. Thermographic printing is cheaper and produces a similar result but does not look quite as smart. Flat printing is the least expensive option and produces lettering like that of a good com-puter printer. The print on invitations is usually black, but you could choose silver.

Quantity

You will need one invitation for each family or individual on your guest list. Etiquette demands that you also send one to the groom's parents, very close friends or relatives whom you already know will not be able to attend, the best man, attendants, and the minister and spouse (although they are unlikely to come to the reception unless they are also friends of the family). Add on another 20 or so to allow for any mistakes you may make while writing them and for any extra guests you may invite after the first replies have come in.

When to order

You will need to order your invitations about four months in advance. This is because they take about two to four weeks to be printed and you should send them out six to nine weeks before the wedding. You will also need to give yourself plenty of time to write them and you may have to rectify any mistakes the printer might make.

Wording

Work out what you want the invitations to say, then give the printer a typed sheet with the wording exactly as you want it to appear. Guests are expected to reply formally, but it can be helpful to enclose a pre-printed reply card for them to return.

Formal weddings

The traditional wording for a very formal wedding is as follows:

> *Mr and Mrs Mark Baxter*
> *request the pleasure of your company/*
> *request the honour of your presence*
> *at the marriage of their daughter*
> *Alice*
> *to Mr Edward Holland*
> *at St Mary's Church, Lymington*
> *on (day, date, month, year)*
> *at (time)*
> *and afterwards at*
> *(reception location)*

RSVP
(parents'/hosts' address)

Slightly less formal, but more commonly used is this wording:

> *Mr and Mrs Mark Baxter*
> *request the pleasure of the company of*
> *(Name of guest(s) filled in by hand)*
> ....
> *at the marriage of their daughter*
> *Alice*

If the bride's parents are divorced, if either is remarried or if one of them is deceased the same basic rule applies – the hosts send the invitation, and the announcement should make it clear how the hosts and bride are related to each other. In some situations, for instance where the bride's mother has remarried and changed her name, it is helpful to include the bride's surname as well. Some alternative wordings that follow the traditional style are given below:

The bride's mother as host, when the bride's father is deceased:

> *Mrs David Lloyd*
> *requests the pleasure of your company*
> *at the marriage of her daughter*

The bride's father as host, when the bride's mother is deceased:

Mr David Lloyd
requests the pleasure of your company
at the marriage of his daughter

If the bride's mother is divorced she uses her forename, Mrs Katherine Lloyd; if remarried she uses her new husband's name, Mrs James Wallace.

The bride's divorced parents as hosts, where neither has remarried:

Mr David Lloyd and Mrs Katherine Lloyd
request the pleasure of your company
at the marriage of their daughter

The bride's divorced parents as hosts, where the mother has remarried:

Mr David Lloyd and Mrs James Wallace
request the pleasure of your company
at the marriage of their daughter

The bride's mother and stepfather as hosts:

Mr and Mrs James Wallace
request the pleasure of your company
at the marriage of her daughter

The bride's father and stepmother as hosts:

Mr and Mrs David Lloyd
request the pleasure of your company
at the marriage of his daughter

The bride as host:

Miss Sally Lloyd
requests the pleasure of your company
at her marriage to

The bride and groom as hosts:

> *Mr Adam Jackson and Miss Sally Lloyd*
> *request the pleasure of your company*
> *at their marriage*

Continental Europeans and members of the practising Jewish community send cards with the names of both sets of parents:

> *Mr and Mrs John Collins*
> *request the pleasure of*
> *your company at the marriage*
> *of their daughter*
> *Anna*
> *to Matthew, son of Dr and Mrs Owen*

For a blessing service following a civil wedding, invitations should read as follows:

> *Mr and Mrs John Collins*
> *request the pleasure of your company*
> *at the Blessing of the Marriage*
> *of their daughter*
> *Anna*

For an invitation to the reception only, the wording is:

> *Mr and Mrs John Collins*
> *request the pleasure of your company*
> *at the Reception to celebrate the marriage*
> *of their daughter Anna*

You could include a note explaining that due to the size of the ceremony venue only a limited number of guests can be accommodated.

Informal weddings

Invitations still come from the hosts, whether the bride's family or the couple themselves, but you have a wider choice of what to say and how to say it. You can be freer with design as well and could include a sketch of the wedding venue, a photograph of yourselves, a poem or quotation or any other means you choose to personalise your invitations. Again, look at the small ads of wedding magazines for inspiration.

Typical wording, where the bride's parents are hosts, would read like this:

Mr and Mrs John Collins
invite you/have much pleasure in inviting you
to the marriage of their daughter
Anna
to Matthew Owen

If the bride and groom are hosts:

Anna Collins and Matthew Owen
(or Anna and Matthew)
invite you to their wedding

Using a computer

If you have access to a computer with a good-quality word processing or desktop publishing package and have the necessary skills and design expertise or know someone who has, you can produce your own invitations and other wedding stationery. You could also use one of the wedding software packages; these enable you to create your own invitations and monitor the replies as well as keeping track of your wedding plans – see page 219 for details.

Invitation checklist

Before having your invitations printed, check whether the cost includes the envelopes. When you receive the proof, check that:

- the invitation is worded correctly
- the lines break in the right places
- the day of the week and the date match

- all the names, including those of people and venues, are spelled correctly
- the address is complete and correct
- the punctuation is correct
- the style of lettering and the type of paper are the same as those you chose.

Overnight guests

Some guests may have travelled a long way and need to stay overnight. If you are holding your reception at a hotel you may be able to arrange a deal and book several rooms at a reduced cost for these guests. Otherwise, seek out reasonable accommodation within easy reach of the venues and either offer to book for your guests or send them details so that they can make their own arrangements. *The Which? Hotel Guide, The Which? Guide to Country Pubs* and *The Good Bed and Breakfast Guide* all provide information about accomodation in your area.

Sending the invitations

Include clear directions and/or a map showing how to get to the wedding venue and from there to the reception. If necessary these should be tailor-made for guests travelling from different directions. Do not enclose a wedding gift list but wait for people to ask for one to be sent. Send one invitation per family (unless the children are living away from home, say at university, in which case they should have one each) and write the names of those invited on the top left-hand corner of the invitation or fill in the space provided. Parents should assume that the invitation is for them alone if the children's names are not included.

Q *Can I use labels printed by my computer to send the invitations?*
A Not if the wedding is formal or you are concerned about using standard etiquette, which demands that envelopes be hand-written, with the correct full name and rank or title of the guest.

Tip

You might like to have a 'wedding book' at the reception, which all your guests are asked to sign and which will make a good souvenir of the day. Let people know in advance that the book will be provided so that they can think of an appropriate message. At the end of his speech the best man could remind the guests to sign the book and tell them exactly where they can find it.

Books specifically designed for this purpose are sold in department stores but you could use any book with blank pages. One option would be to buy a leather-bound book with blank pages and have your names and the date of your wedding embossed on the front.

Postponing the wedding

Occasionally circumstances demand that the wedding be delayed. You do not need to return wedding gifts if the wedding is postponed to a future date. Cards should be sent to guests telling them of the postponement and giving details of the new date if it is known. For details of what to do if the engagement is broken and the wedding cancelled, see pages 18–19.

Suitable wording for a printed notification of postponement would read as follows:

Owing to the recent illness/death
of Mrs Collins' father
the wedding of her daughter
Anna
to Matthew Owen
at (venue, time)
on (date)
has been postponed
until (time)
on (date)

Guest and gift checklist

Name	Address	Tel.	No. in party	Invitation sent	Accepted	Refused

Chapter 7

Wedding gifts

As soon as you have sent out your invitations people will start to ask you what you would like as a wedding gift. Although your guests are not obliged to give you anything (which is why it is impolite to enclose the list with the invitation), almost all of them will want to buy you something they know you will be pleased to receive. One way of ensuring you are given the things you need and avoid duplication is to organise a list, either your own or at a store. However, you are not forced to have a list and can leave the choice up to your guests. For a small wedding or where the partners have been living together for some time, this may be a straightforward solution.

Making your own list

One way to draw up a list is to browse round a number of different shops, picking out items you would like to receive. Type up a detailed list, including details of size, colour, manufacturer, model number and price. Either the bride's mother, the couple or even the groom's mother could take charge of the list. When guests ask to see it you can send the master copy with a stamped addressed envelope and ask them to cross off the item they choose and return the list or send it on. This method is cumbersome but does avoid duplication. A quicker method is to have several copies of the list and send one to any guest who asks. You may end up with some duplication but the whole process is speeded up and there is no danger of the list getting stuck with one person who then holds everyone else up. Finally, you could give the list-holder's phone number to any guests who ask so that they can ring up and find out what is on the list. The guests can then ask the holder to cross off a particular gift before buying it.

Putting your list with a store

Many couples prefer to place their list with one or perhaps two department stores. If most of your guests are local you could choose one in the nearest town. However, if they live in different parts of the UK you could choose a chain that has branches nationwide.

How you go about setting up your list depends on which store you place it at. Usually, you visit the store and either look through the catalogue or walk round the shop, noting which items you would like (writing down the description, size, colour, price and code). Some stores will produce as many copies of the list as you need to send to guests, while others prefer to keep the master list so that the guests have to ring up or visit to find out what is available. Whichever method the store uses, the guests then tell the store which gift they have bought or want to buy, and the store then crosses it off the list. The stores, which are computer linked if part of a chain, keep the list up to date and note who has bought what. They then inform you of what has been bought so that you can start writing thank-you letters.

You could put a list at more than one store, choosing one for household, practical gifts and another for more decorative or specialised items. Some stores offer incentives, such as gift vouchers or discounts, if you place your list with them, so it can often be worth shopping around before choosing one.

Gift list considerations

- List more items than there are guests, otherwise the last people to see the list will not have a choice.
- Choose items across the price range so that every guest can buy something within his or her means.
- Don't worry if some of the items you have chosen are very expensive as some people like to join up with friends and buy something more expensive than they could afford as an individual.

Delivery

Before you set up your list, ask how the gifts will be delivered to you. In some stores guests simply buy their gift and take it home ready to send to you or bring on the day. Other stores will deliver the gifts to you as they are purchased or will keep them all and deliver them after the wedding, notifying you of who has bought what in the meantime.

Q *Can I exchange a gift that I don't like?*
A If the same item is accidentally purchased twice or if you change your mind after receiving the gift, most stores will exchange it for something of the same value provided the item has not been used.

Compiling a wedding list

Couples who are setting up home for the first time will not need any help in drawing up a long list of things they need. However, for those who do need some help, wedding magazines provide lists of suggestions. Leave yourselves plenty of time as choosing the right items for every part of the house requires a great deal of thought, and the list needs to be ready about seven to ten weeks before the wedding.

The question of gifts is more difficult for the high percentage of couples who have lived together before marriage or who have been married before as they will have most household items already. So, if you are past the stage of needing saucepans and cutlery, here are a few suggestions:

- decorative items: pictures, plants, hand-embroidered cushions, antiques
- vintage wines
- luxury food items
- CDs or videos
- sports equipment
- plants for your garden
- tickets to a show or for travel.

> **Q** *Can we ask for money or gift vouchers as wedding gifts, and buy the things we want when we get back from honeymoon?*
>
> **A** It is considered bad manners to ask for money, since you place the guests in the awkward position of deciding what amount to give. This also applies to vouchers. However, these taboos are gradually breaking down, and a lot depends on the attitude of your guests. Some might be perfectly happy to give you a cheque or voucher, while others would prefer not to.

Thank-you letters

Write a letter of thanks for each gift as it arrives; if you let them accumulate the task will seem much more daunting. Keep an up-to-date list (see page 81) and make a note when the thank-you letter has been sent. You should send a hand-written letter for every gift you receive, even if you have already thanked the giver in person. Some gifts will be received on, or after, the day, and you should send thank-you letters for these as soon as you return from honeymoon.

The letter need not be long but should be specific about the gift so that if, for instance, the store has delivered the wrong number of bowls the person concerned can put things right. If you receive money or vouchers, tell the giver how you plan to use them.

For gifts given jointly by two or three people, write to each one separately. A present given by a large group of people such as work colleagues needs only one letter, addressed to the group as a whole.

Displaying the gifts

The custom of displaying the wedding gifts is becoming less common. However, if you do decide on a display, make sure the reception venue has somewhere secure, preferably out of sight of public areas, where the gifts can be shown. Group similar items such as glasses, linen etc. together, although if two items are nearly identical it is more tactful to place them apart. Cheques should be acknowledged by placing cards on the display table saying 'Cheque from Mr and Mrs John Smith'. You should not state the amount.

You will probably receive a number of gifts on the wedding day. Make sure that you have a safe place to put these and detail one of the bridesmaids to be responsible for keeping labels and cards with the gifts to which they belong. See Chapter 18 for details of how to make sure your wedding gifts are protected wherever they are.

Name of guest	Gift list sent	Gift received	Thank-you letter sent

Chapter 8

Wedding outfits

What you, the best man, ushers and attendants wear will depend on the wedding venue and how formal/informal your ceremony is going to be.

The bride

Choosing an outfit in which you will look and feel right on the day is one of the most important, enjoyable decisions you will make in the run-up to the ceremony. If you are lucky enough to know what you are looking for, the only issue is finding it or having it made for you. Otherwise, start your search by taking a careful look at every wedding picture you see – in magazines, local newspapers, photographers' windows and advertisements.

Traditional wedding dresses

Buying

You can buy your wedding dress off-the-peg at any number of specialist bridal shops or department stores. Give yourself plenty of time to find a dress – try on lots of different styles, including those that do not particularly appeal when on the hanger (often they look much better when you try them on). Wear make-up and arrange your hair in a similar style to the one you would like to have on the day so you can get a good idea of how the dress will really look. Ask someone whose opinions you trust to go with you.

> **Tip**
>
> If you can shop well in advance of your wedding day you might be able to pick up an end-of-season bargain, for example you could buy an end-of-season summer dress in the autumn to wear the following summer. Most shops bring in new ranges once or twice a year and sell off the remains of previous ranges. These sales are often advertised in local newspapers.

Buying secondhand

Look in the *Yellow Pages* or in the small ads in wedding magazines for shops that specialise in secondhand gowns. Many dresses are sold privately through advertisements in local newspapers or specialist advertisements-only magazines such as *Loot*. Expect to pay about half of what the dress originally cost. Some dresses are sold unworn, and the rest have been worn only once.

Having a dress made

Having a dress made will not necessarily be cheaper than buying a ready-made one – unless you can persuade a dressmaking friend or relative to make it for you – but you are more likely to get exactly what you want, and the dress will be made to fit you rather than being a 'standard' dress size (an important consideration if you fall between sizes or you are particularly short or tall, for example).

Finding a dressmaker

If you know someone who wore a made-to-measure dress that you admired, finding out who their dressmaker was is probably the best starting point – not least because if that dressmaker is already fully booked, she (or he) should know of other dressmakers for you to contact. If you do not have any personal recommendations, try the *Yellow Pages* (under 'Dressmakers' and possibly 'Wedding services'). Alternatively, look in the small ads section at the back of wedding magazines and also the bridal magazines published by pattern companies such as Vogue, Butterick, Simplicity and so on. For a small fee, the Butterick Company (of which Vogue Patterns is a subsidiary) can supply a list of dressmakers in your area. Other pattern companies may offer a similar service.

Getting the best from your dressmaker

When you find a dressmaker who seems suitable, ask to see examples of her (or his) work. If you are happy with what you see and the dressmaker is willing to take you on, you should arrange a meeting to talk about what you want. Take along pictures of the kind of dresses and accessories that you particularly like. These will give the dressmaker an idea of your likes and dislikes, which will, in turn, help her (or him) to come up with suitable designs for you. Before the first meeting it is also well worth your while visiting the off-the-peg wedding dress shops to try on dresses, veils and headdresses so that you get a good feel for what suits you (and what does not).

The next step will be for your dressmaker to show you a selection of sketches based on the ideas you discussed at the first consultation. If you like them and you feel comfortable about working with the dressmaker in what are going to be quite intimate situations, the next thing you need to know is how much it is going to cost. If, on the other hand, the sketches bear no relation to your dream dress and you feel that the dressmaker has not listened to any of your ideas, this may be the time to look for someone else: you will not feel your best on your wedding day if you have been bullied into wearing something that doesn't really suit you.

Tip

Long trains can be cumbersome at the reception, so if you are having a train, make sure it is detachable so it can be removed after the ceremony. Some dresses have a loop fixed on to the train so that the bride can hook it over her wrist and prevent it from trailing on the ground.

What will it cost?

The two main influences on the final cost of your dress are the fabric and your dressmaker's time. Clearly, the more fabric involved and the more expensive it is, the costlier the final dress will be. How much your dressmaker's time will cost depends on how elaborate the design is, whether it involves a lot of intricate hand sewing and how many fittings are necessary. The final cost will also be influenced by the number of times you change your mind about what you want, which is why many dressmakers can be reticent about putting a price on their work until it is completed – although most will be able to give you a rough guide.

If the estimated price sounds reasonable, you will need to agree (preferably in writing):

- exactly what the dressmaker is supplying – just the dress, for example, or the dress and other accessories
- the delivery date
- dates for fittings
- a schedule for payments – whether you will pay a deposit and make a final payment, for example, or whether you will need to make interim payments as well (which may be the case if some special detail, such as hand embroidery or covered buttons will be sub-contracted)
- who will pay for the fabric – this is usually the customer, although the dressmaker will usually supply routine haberdashery such as thread, binding, zips and so on.
- whether VAT is payable and, if it is, whether it is included in the quoted price.

Choosing the fabric

Be guided by your dressmaker's specialist knowledge when it comes to choosing the material for your dress: she (or he) will know which fabrics are best suited to achieving the look you want. She (or he) will also know the best sources of bridal fabrics at competitive prices – shops specialising in bridal fabric can be in the most unexpected places and are rarely to be found on the high street. If you have a particular fabric in mind, your dressmaker can also advise you on which styles will work best (make sure that you take a sample of it to your first meeting).

Making it fit

Before your first fitting, it is a good idea to buy your wedding underwear and, once you have the fabric to match them to, your shoes. Getting the right underwear is particularly important for very close-fitting styles and having the shoes is vital for getting the length right. A good dressmaker is unlikely to cut the fabric until she (or he) has fitted you for a 'toile' (a test garment usually made out of cotton). Depending on your chosen style, subsequent fittings may involve getting component parts right so don't expect to see the final product until quite late on in the process.

Having a dress altered to fit

A dressmaker can also alter an existing dress to fit you. You might need to have this done if you have bought a second-hand or off-the peg dress that doesn't fit you exactly or if you want to wear your mother's or grandmother's dress, for example.

Having a dress altered is also worth considering if you are on a tight budget, especially if you have an eye for a bargain and you manage to pick up a nearly-suitable dress in the sales or in a second-hand or charity shop.

Making your dress yourself

If you have little or no experience of dressmaking but are drawn to the idea of making the dress yourself because you are on a tight budget, you should consider the following practicalities before making up your mind:

- **have you got a sewing machine?** If not, don't assume that you will be able to borrow one unless you have a firm offer of a loan
- **have you worked out what the material will cost?** It may be that once you have added up the cost of the dress fabric, other material for linings, petticoats, stiffening and haberdashery, you will find that it is not quite as cheap as you thought it was going to be

- **where are you going to cut it out?** You need a large, level, scrupulously clean surface (not carpet) to cut out a long frock accurately
- **where are you going to sew it?** You need somewhere that is well-lit, clean and preferably away from anything that could get spilt on the dress – so the kitchen table is not ideal
- **how are you going to alter it to fit?** Unless you have the help of another person or a tailor's dummy, it will be very difficult to get a good fit on your own
- **do you have a full-length mirror?** Fitting will be nearly impossible if you have not
- **are you familiar with pattern instructions?** It might be an idea to look through the instruction sheets of a wedding dress pattern before you commit yourself. Even if you have to buy the pattern to do this, it will be cheaper than possibly ruining a lot of expensive material
- **do you have back up?** Unless you have a friend or relative who is willing to help out and/or advise you when you hit a tricky patch or make a mistake, it is probably not a good idea to tackle the job
- **could you make the bridesmaids dresses instead?** This could be a good compromise because the dresses will be less crucial and, especially if you are having young children as your bridesmaids, more manageable to make.

If you decide that your wedding dress is something you can tackle and you have someone who will help if the need arises, it would be a good idea to invest in one or more of the special bridal magazines published by pattern companies. Not only will they have suitable patterns but you will also find that they have addresses both of shops selling bridal fabrics and companies which sell fabric (often more cheaply) by mail order.

If, having considered the practicalities, you decide that it would not be a good idea to start practising your sewing skills on your wedding dress, there are still several options open to you – such as borrowing, hiring, having a dress altered or buying second hand.

> **Tip**
>
> After the wedding you can have your dress expertly cleaned and packed in acid-free tissue. Materials are also available to do the packing yourself. Some companies sell special boxes and tissue – complete with instructions on how to pack the dress away properly. Look in bridal magazines for addresses.

Hiring

Hiring is a less popular option than it used to be but it is still possible from some department stores or specialist shops. You will need to give about 12 weeks' notice and should be able to collect the dress a couple of days before the wedding for return two days after. Check:

- that the dress will be available on your wedding day (get this in writing)
- that minor alterations are possible
- that the fee includes insurance against damage and cost of cleaning
- how many days the hire cost covers
- what alternatives are on offer if the dress is unavailable for any reason.

Veils, headdresses and hats

Veils vary in price depending on the length, amount of decoration and type of fabric, which might be silk or nylon tulle, lace or organza. The general rule is that if your dress has a train you wear a full-length veil, which falls to the ground and is about a foot longer than your train. Otherwise, you can have a short, face-framing veil, one that skims your shoulders or reaches to your fingertips, and it can be worn piled high on a headdress or falling simply from a band or tiara. Try on a range of styles with your chosen dress and remember that how you wear your hair on the day can alter the look significantly.

A headdress can be worn with or without a veil. Once again, bridal magazines and shops will supply plenty of ideas, from simple circlets and Alice bands to tiaras. Floral headdresses are also popular (see page 97). You might prefer to wear a hat rather than a veil, in which case it is considered unnecessary to carry a bouquet.

Shoes

In winter white or pale-coloured shoes may be hard to come by outside specialist bridal shops, so buy them in spring or summer if you can. Shoes can be dyed or covered to get an exact match for your dress. Make sure the shoes are comfortable as well as stylish, since you will be on your feet for the greater part of the day. Very high heels can be hard to cope with under a full length dress, especially if you are not used to them. Wear the shoes round the house so that they ease to the shape of your foot, and rub the soles with sandpaper or a metal-bristled suede brush to make sure there is no danger of slipping.

Underwear

Choose a well-fitting bra in a flesh tone and try it on with your dress to ensure that neither the bra nor straps can be seen. Wear the bra for a few hours before the day to make sure it is really comfortable and does not ride up or slip down. Tights or stockings will fit better if they have been washed once. Buy two pairs just in case one is laddered as you put it on.

Other accessories

Make sure your car hire includes a white umbrella so that you can get into church without getting wet if it rains. Shawls, wraps, coats and cloaks can all be an integral part of your wedding outfit. Gloves may fit with your style of wedding dress but remember that your left hand will need to be uncovered during the ceremony. You do not have to carry flowers and could instead hold a prayer book or Bible, a fan or a small bag.

Tip

Ask the chief bridesmaid or your mother to carry an emergency repair kit containing tiny safety pins, needle and thread, spare tights, headache pills, tissues, comb and make-up.

Outfits for a civil wedding

A civil wedding allows you more freedom of choice, especially if you are marrying at alternative premises, such as a hotel or stately home. If you do decide to wear traditional bridal dress for a register office wedding, choose a fairly simple style without a train.

Alternatively, you can choose a smart dress or suit. You can opt for pastel colours, cream or ivory but there is no reason why you shouldn't wear a stronger colour if that's what suits you best. You could also wear a hat. If you have decided to have a themed wedding to suit the surroundings you could even wear medieval, Tudor or Victorian dress.

What to wear for a beach wedding

- Tight-fitting garments will feel uncomfortably hot. Choose light-weight cotton or crêpe de chine fabrics in a loose style
- Open sandals or bare feet are most comfortable. Enclosed shoes will make your feet hot and likely to swell, and heels will sink into the sand
- Pack your outfits carefully with plenty of tissue paper and hang them in a steamy bathroom for 15 minutes on arrival to let the creases drop out.

Going-away outfits

This is the outfit into which you will change before leaving the reception, although if you wear a very lavish wedding dress and have a long reception with dancing you may want to change earlier in the evening so that you can dance in comfort. Otherwise, the choice is yours and you can wear a dress, a suit or something more casual. What you wear can depend on where you are going after the reception. If you are flying off on honeymoon that day then comfortable clothes in uncrushable fabrics that will suit the climate of your destination are the obvious choice. If, however, you are spending a night at a hotel you can choose a dressy outfit that will look good in photographs as you leave but which can be worn again in future.

The groom

For a very formal church wedding the groom usually wears morning dress or a suit. The couple's fathers, the best man and the ushers should wear the same style of dress as the groom.

Traditional morning dress consists of a black or grey three-piece suit with tail coat, or black tail coat with grey pinstripe trousers and a grey waistcoat. The morning dress is worn with a wing-collared shirt and cravat, or an ordinary collar and tie. Make sure all the men in the wedding party know exactly what combination you have chosen so they can all wear the same.

You can choose a patterned or coloured cravat, waistcoat or cummerbund, which might pick up a colour from the bride's bouquet or the bridesmaids' dresses. Morning dress is extremely expensive to buy, and most men choose to hire it. Go to a reputable company well in advance for a fitting. Expect to pick it up a couple of days in advance and arrange for it to be returned within two days after the wedding.

Check whether cleaning is included in the price. All the accessories will also be available for hire. These include grey gloves, which traditionally are carried, not worn, and a silk top hat, which is worn only for some of the photographs. You can also hire tie-pins or cufflinks, but most men prefer to use their own. Wear a pair of comfortable and smart black shoes.

Two- or three-piece lounge suits are the usual alternative to morning dress for less formal church or civil weddings. Colour and style are entirely your choice. If you are wearing a dark suit, you could wear a colourful tie, shirt or waistcoat. The best man should also wear a lounge suit, which should complement the groom's outfit but need not be an exact match.

If you are getting married on a beach abroad, you need not wear jacket or tie. Trousers or shorts in cotton or linen, worn with a cool shirt would be fine.

The bridegroom can leave the reception wearing the same lounge suit he wore for the wedding or if he wore morning dress he can change into a jacket and tie with smart trousers or perhaps just a shirt and casual trousers.

Bridesmaids and page boys

The first decision you need to make is whether to buy, make or hire the outfits. They could come from the same source as the bride's dress, or the adult bridesmaids may be happy to make their own dresses or buy them off-the-peg from a department store or bridal shop. Decide on your budget and who will pay. Traditionally, the bride's family pay for the attendants' clothes, but bridesmaids or, if they are children, their parents, may be happy to contribute or bear the whole cost, particularly if you choose styles which can be worn again for parties. Make it clear when you ask them to be bridesmaids who is going to pay for their outfits.

Choosing a style

The bridesmaids' dresses could be similar to your wedding dress but not identical, for example if yours has a full skirt their dresses could be straight but with the same neck line or sleeves as yours. Alternatively, they could be almost identical in style but in a different colour and without beading or other detail that yours might have.

The adult and young bridesmaids do not have to wear the same styles as each other, for example the older girls could wear straight dresses while the younger ones wear dresses that are fuller in style. Another option could be to dress the children in a paler shade of the colour the adult bridesmaids are wearing or make the older bridesmaids' dresses one solid colour and the smaller girls' dresses cream or ivory with trimmings in your chosen colour.

Page boys could wear velvet suits or lounge-style suits with waistcoat, sailor suits or Scottish outfits with kilt and sporran. Miniature morning suits for children are available to hire.

The bride's mother

At a formal wedding the bride's mother has an important and prominent role to play as hostess. Her outfit should be chosen so that it does not clash with the bride's colour scheme, and although her clothes should be attractive and eye-catching they should not draw attention away from the bride. It is advisable for her to confer with the groom's mother before shopping so that they avoid wearing outfits that are too similar or that will not look good together in photographs. Large-brimmed hats can overshadow the face in pictures and cast unflattering shadows, so the style should be chosen with care.

Chapter 9

Flowers

To find a suitable florist, ask for recommendations or look in the *Yellow Pages* or local newspapers. Quite often photographers, hairdressers etc. have free leaflets listing local companies that offer wedding services so you might find one that way. You should then visit a few of them to see if you like their work. Ring in advance and ask when they will be working on wedding flowers, so that you get a chance to see some bouquets and arrangements, rather than just photographs.

As florists are always very busy during the summer months, you should book well in advance, although you do not need to think in detail about your flowers until you have chosen your outfit and colour scheme. Arrange to meet the florist a couple of months before the wedding to go through the arrangements in detail and make some firm decisions.

The initial meeting

- Take with you any **inspirational pictures** you have collected. Even if the flowers in a bouquet you admire are difficult to get hold of at the time of year you are getting married, the florist should be able to achieve a similar effect using different flowers.
- Take **swatches of fabric from your dress** and the bridesmaids' outfits if possible, plus sketches or photographs of the styles. These will help the florist to choose a style of bouquet to suit your dress.
- Any **colour or combination of colours is acceptable**, but if you choose white flowers be careful, as it can be hard to match

the shade with that of your dress. For example, a bluish-white dress would make creamy flowers look drab and discoloured.

- Work out **how much you want to spend on your flowers** so you can give the florist an idea of the size of your order. You should also have given some thought to how many buttonholes and corsages you need and where you would like to place flowers in the wedding venue and at the reception.
- Ask the florist to show you some **samples of the flowers** you have chosen a week or two before the wedding. Then, if they are not quite what you were hoping for, there will still be time to choose some others.

Which flowers?

Although most flowers are now available all year round (thanks to hothouse production) they are always more expensive out of season. Many flowers have traditional meanings, which you might like to take into account when making up your bouquet. Several of the flowers listed overleaf, such as chrysanthemums and roses, are available across several seasons.

The bouquets

Hand-tied bouquets are currently very popular and can vary in style a great deal, depending on the shape and size and choice of flowers and foliage. They are cheaper than the more formal wired bouquets, which, although very striking, can be heavy and cumbersome. Other options are a single flower or a tight ball (pomander).

Keep the style of your dress in mind when choosing your bouquet. Bodice detail may be hidden if it is behind a large bouquet, and you might prefer an arrangement that can be held in the crook of your arm. Shorter, simpler dresses call for smaller bouquets, while a tailored gown with a train can be just as beautifully offset by half a dozen lilies as by a more complex and sophisticated arrangement.

The bridesmaids' flowers should complement the bride's bouquet and are usually smaller posies using the same flowers. Very young bridesmaids may tire of holding a bouquet, so you could give them a pomander or flowers in small baskets to carry; these can both be looped over the arm.

Seasonal flowers and their meanings

Spring

apple blossom	good luck in future
camellia	perfect loveliness
carnation	deep love
daffodil	regard
daisy	innocence
honeysuckle	devotion
iris	burning love
jasmine	grace
lily	purity
mimosa	sensitivity
tulip	love
white lilac	youthful innocence

Summer

cornflower	hope
lily of the valley	renewed happiness
rose	love, happiness
red rose	I love you
white rose	I am worthy of you
sweetpea	delicate pleasures

Autumn

red chrysanthemum	I love you
white chrysanthemum	truth
gypsophila	fertility
orchid	beauty

Winter

snowdrop	hope
ivy	fidelity

Preserving your bouquet

If you want to toss your bouquet into the crowd as you leave, you might want to extract one or two flowers first and ask someone to press them for you as a souvenir. You can also arrange to have the whole bouquet preserved. The bouquet is photographed and the flowers dismantled petal by petal. These are then pressed and mounted on silk. Prices depend on the size of the finished picture. The cost of pressing the flowers (and picking them up by courier) is £55, and the picture costs between £30 and £200. A company called Pressed for Time* offers a nationwide service. Alternatively, a florist may be able to make a replica of your bouquet using silk flowers.

Floral headdresses

Floral headdresses – in the form of a circlet or coronet – are an imaginative alternative to tiaras, circlets or Alice bands. Flowers can also be attached to a hair band, wired or even woven into your hair. Ask your florist's advice on which varieties to use as some wilt far more readily than others. All fresh flowers are susceptible to heat, however, and may lose their freshness as the day wears on. Try to handle them as little as possible while your hair is being arranged.

Buttonholes and corsages

Buttonholes are worn by all the men in the wedding party – groom, best man, the ushers and the couple's fathers. Traditionally, the men wear a white or cream carnation or rose. However, you do not need to feel restricted to these flowers and you can choose any colour or flower you like to match those in your bouquet or pick up a shade from your colour scheme.

Corsages are worn by the mothers of the bride and groom and consist of two or three flowers and some foliage. Consult the wearers about their preferred colours and weight, because it may not be possible to attach a heavy corsage to a light silk outfit, for example, without damaging the fabric.

Flowers for a religious ceremony

You should discuss the church flowers with the minister when you first meet. Most will be happy for you to provide your own flowers (you can either ask your florist to arrange them, or the regular church arranger might do them for you, in return for a contribution to the church funds), while others have a policy of supplying all the floral arrangements. Alternatively, you could make use of the flowers that have been arranged for the Sunday service or choose not to have any at all.

Where to put flowers for the ceremony

In church, with the minister's permission, you can place flowers in some or all of the following sites:

- altar (some ministers prefer to leave this bare so that the cross remains the focal point)
- pulpit
- lectern
- windowsills
- font (may not be allowed, particularly if there is a christening the following day)
- columns
- church entrance
- chancel steps
- pew ends
- lych gate.

In a synagogue, flowers may be used on the *chuppah*.

Often more than one wedding is held on the same day, making it impossible to change the flowers. If this is the case, the cost of the flowers is usually divided between couples, and you should all meet with the church helpers to discuss what type of flowers would best suit you all.

Flowers for a civil ceremony

Most register offices keep an arrangement of fresh flowers permanently on display. Ask at your first visit whether you can bring in flowers of your own, as policies vary. On a busy day, when one wedding follows quite rapidly after another, there may not be time to set up new flowers. If you are marrying at a newly licensed venue, such as a hotel or stately home, then you should be able to use as many flowers as you wish.

Flowers for the reception

Some reception venues include a number of floral arrangements as part of the overall cost. Check this when you are making your booking. Most will be happy for you to provide your own flowers.

Where to put flowers at the reception

- At the entrance to the room.
- Elsewhere in the main room – on sills or side tables.
- On the buffet table.
- On each dining table, with a more elaborate arrangement for the top table. The main table could also be dressed with swags or garlands of flowers.
- On top of the cake and on the cake table.
- On pedestals around the room or marquee.
- In hanging baskets if you are having a marquee.

You could either continue the floral theme from your bouquet and wedding venue or choose a totally different style, using other colours and flowers. If your florist is arranging the flowers at the reception, he or she will want to know:

- when the flower arrangers can have access to the reception venue
- if there is another booking immediately before or after yours and, if there is, when the flowers must be removed. One option could be for the people using the room after you to use your flowers and contribute to the cost
- (if you are using a marquee) the colour of the lining, whether or not it has poles or a covered walkway that need decorating and, if so, how many there are
- (if you are using a marquee) whether you want to use pedestals or have hanging baskets and how many of them you need. (The marquee company will need to provide rope to attach the hanging baskets.) The benefit of having hanging baskets is that although pedestals look beautiful to the first few guests who enter the room, if it is a stand-up reception, they will not be seen by many people once the room is full. Hanging baskets will be visible to everyone throughout the proceedings.

Flowers checklist

Name of florist
Address
Telephone/fax
Contact
Date booking made
Confirmed in writing

	Colour	Type of flowers	No.	Delivery details	Who pays?	Cost £
Bride's bouquet						
Bridesmaid's bouquets						
Adults						
Children						
Headdresses						
Bride						

Adult bridesmaids

Child bridesmaids

Buttonholes

Groom

Best man

Ushers

Couple's fathers

Others

Corsages

Bride's mother

Groom's mother

Flowers in wedding venue

Altar

Pulpit

Lectern

Windowsills

Font

Columns						
Entrance						
Chancel steps						
Pew ends						
Lych gate						
Chuppa						
Reception flowers						
Entrance						
Hanging baskets						
Pedestals						
Covered walkway						
Cake table						
Head table						
Buffet table						
Any other flowers						
VAT						
Total cost						

Chapter 10

Transport

Most people who have a formal white wedding in a church or synagogue hire at least one chauffeur-driven car and, more usually, two. Hired wedding cars are comfortable and roomy, allowing the bride to travel to the ceremony in style and with her dress uncrushed. The bride's mother and attendants, who travel together, leave the house first and wait for the bride in the church porch. The second car takes the bride and her father (or person giving her away) from the house to the church. It is up to the best man to arrange for the groom to arrive at the church in plenty of time (usually about 40 minutes before the ceremony).

After the ceremony, the bride and groom leave for the reception in one car, followed by the bride's parents and possibly the attendants in the second. You need to think through the transport arrangements well in advance to make sure that suitable transport is available for everyone. On the day it is the best man's job to make sure that everyone can get to the reception without difficulty.

For a register office wedding the arrangements are usually less formal, and bride and groom can arrive together if they wish. You can use hire cars, private family cars or taxis.

Wedding cars

Hired cars are the most popular choice, and a wide variety are on offer, ranging from vintage Rolls-Royces and Daimlers, through American Cadillacs and stretch limousines, to open-topped E-type Jaguars. Personal recommendation is the best way to find a reliable hire company, otherwise you should try the *Yellow Pages* or a wedding magazine.

Transport arrangements checklist

People to be taken to the ceremony	Transport
Bride and bride's father	
Attendants and bride's mother	
Groom and best man	
Groom's parents	
Ushers	
To the reception	
Bride and groom	
Attendants and bride's parents	
Groom's parents	
Best man	
Ushers	
Guests	
From reception	
Bride and groom	

Book your transport well in advance and expect to pay at least £150, possibly substantially more for something unusual. Cars are usually decorated with white or cream ribbons, but if you want flowers or other decorations you may have to arrange these yourselves. When choosing the cars bear in mind that a white dress can look dull in front of a white car, and it may look better if you choose one in a darker colour such as maroon, navy blue or black. Many companies offer a complete package tailored to your requirements for the day.

Remember:

- visit the company and see the cars for yourself
- ensure that the car you see is the one you will get, not a similar one or a different model. Confirm this in writing
- ask whether the car is a genuine vintage, i.e. made between 1917 and 1930, or veteran, which can either be pre-1916 or pre-1905.

Cars made 'in the style of' older cars can look effective and should be cheaper to hire than an original

- inspect the general condition of the car: tyres, seating, wood-work, paintwork etc.
- ask if ribbons or flowers are included in the price
- check that a large umbrella in cream or white comes with the car
- the law requires you to wear a seatbelt in the front and back of a modern car, but vintage and veteran cars and some classic models have them in the front only or not at all. If the car was made before the seatbelt laws were enforced you are exempt from wearing them. This could be an important factor to consider if your dress is likely to be creased by a belt.
- ask for written confirmation of the cars to be provided, date and times, whether a chauffeur is provided (and if so, what uniform he or she will wear), insurance cover and any extra charges
- the confirmation should include an assurance that the cars will be used only for your wedding on that date and not for any others on the same day. This is because you do not want to find that your car is late picking you up because it was delayed at a previous wedding.

Borrowing cars

If you do not want to spend so much on your transport, you could ask whether family and friends have any suitable cars that you could borrow for the day. Give the cars a thorough clean and polish and decorate them with ribbons and flowers. Do make sure that there is room for you to get in and out comfortably in your wedding dress. Although open-topped cars sound attractive, the wind can wreak havoc with your hair and veil unless you travel exceptionally slowly.

Parking arrangements

Find out in advance what the parking regulations are at both the ceremony and reception venues, particularly if either is in a busy town. If no large car parks are available at the venue itself, check out other nearby car parks and include their details and perhaps a map with your invitations.

Other forms of transport

Horse-drawn carriages, with optional liveried coachmen and foot-men or pageboys, or closed carriages, with heated interiors for winter, are also available. Book well in advance for these, as popular summer dates can be booked up as much as two years in advance. This mode of transport, although romantic, is feasible only if the journey is fairly short and does not include any steep hills. In an open carriage you will be at the mercy of the weather, so you need to be reasonably confident of a fine day. Most companies offer a choice of colour of the horses. Expect to pay between £400 and £800, depending on the distance, number of horses and the type of carriage.

Leaving the reception

Traditionally, it is up to the best man to ensure that the newly-weds have the means of transport to leave the reception. This may be the groom's own car, left at the reception venue earlier. If fun-loving guests or ushers decide to 'decorate' the car it is up to the best man to make sure that it is not damaged and any embellishments can be easily removed. You can use one of your hire cars again, particularly if the reception has been a short one, but a private car or taxi is probably more suitable, especially as the cost per hour of a hired car is high.

Those wanting to leave in style could consider:

- a hot-air balloon (only possible when the weather is calm, and exactly where you will land cannot be guaranteed)
- motorbike with side car
- tandem bicycle
- rickshaw
- boat, from a waterside reception
- black taxi cab.

Transport hire checklist

Name of hire company	
Address	
Telephone/fax	
Contact	
Date booking made	
Number of cars booked	
Other modes of transport booked (horse and carriage etc.)	
Confirmed in writing	
Cost £	
Deposit £	
Balance due £	

Chapter 11

Music and readings for the ceremony

Adding carefully chosen music and readings is a way of making your ceremony more personal.

Religious ceremony

Music creates a memorable atmosphere for your wedding ceremony and is used:

- before the bride arrives (the prelude)
- as she walks down the aisle (the processional)
- while the register is being signed
- as the married couple leave the church (the recessional).

Two or three hymns and perhaps a psalm are also usually sung during the service.

Discuss the music the first time you meet the minister. Most churches are equipped with an organ, and the organist will be able to suggest suitable pieces if you need some ideas. Bear in mind the organist's abilities and the quality of the organ when making a selection. You will usually have to pay between £50 and £80 if the church organist plays for you. If a family member or friend is an accomplished organist, it should be possible to arrange for him or her to play at the ceremony instead.

You might like to have a choir to lead the singing during your service and perhaps sing a piece of your choice while you are signing the register. Some churches have their own choir, which you can hire for a small fee (probably no more than £100 and possibly less), but you could hire a professional choir or one from a local school instead.

The selection of pieces suitable for weddings is wide, and your local record library or shop should be able to provide some compilation recordings to help you choose. You do not have to restrict yourselves to religious pieces – but do check that your minister has no objections before settling on something secular.

The prelude

The organist plays softly for about twenty minutes before the ceremony is due to start. The pieces should be calm and peaceful, setting the mood for the event and leading up to the exciting moment when the bride arrives. Most organists will be able to suggest a repertoire, but suitable pieces include:

- 'Sheep may safely graze' by J.S. Bach
- Moonlight Sonata (slow movement); Pathétique Sonata (slow movement) by Beethoven
- Symphony no. 6 (slow movement) 'From the New World' by Dvořák
- 'Nimrod' from *Enigma Variations* by Elgar
- *Water Music*; Pastoral Symphony from *Messiah* by Handel
- 'Gymnopédie no. 1' by Satie.

The processional

Joyful and stately music is played as the bridal party enter the church and continues as they process down the aisle. The pace should be steady, making it easy to walk slowly without feeling rushed. You might like to choose one of the following:

- 'Trumpet Voluntary' by Boyce
- 'Theme from the St Anthony Chorale' by Brahms
- 'Trumpet Voluntary' ('Prince of Denmark's March') by Clarke
- 'Arrival of the Queen of Sheba'; 'Minuet' from *Music for the Royal Fireworks* by Handel
- 'Bridal March' by Parry
- 'Bridal March' from *Lohengrin* by Wagner.

Hymns and psalms

It is usual to have three hymns or psalms during the ceremony, the first at the beginning of the service, the second after the marriage and the third after you have signed the register. You can have just two hymns or only one if you prefer. It is advisable to choose hymns that are well known, especially if the congregation is small or you are not using a choir. Below is a selection of well-known popular hymns often used at weddings:

- 'Come down, O Love divine'
- 'Glorious things of thee are spoken'
- 'Jerusalem'
- 'Love divine, all loves excelling'
- 'Praise my soul the King of heaven'
- 'The Lord's my shepherd' (to the tune Crimond)
- 'Lord of all hopefulness'
- 'I vow to thee my country'
- 'Dear Lord and Father of mankind'

Suitable psalms, which may be said or sung, include:

- Psalm 37 ('Put thou thy trust in the Lord . . .')
- Psalm 67 ('God be merciful unto us and bless us . . .')
- Psalm 83 ('How lovely is Thy dwelling place, O Lord of Hosts! . . .')
- Psalm 128 ('Blessed are all they that fear the Lord . . .')

Signing the register

At this point in the proceedings you might like a friend or relative to play a solo on a musical instrument or sing. Alternatively, the church choir could sing a psalm or anthem. Another option would be to book professional instrumentalists or singers to perform your favourite pieces or arrange for a recorded piece to be played. Whatever you would like to do, tell the minister which pieces you have chosen to be performed to ensure there is no objection. If you want to use recorded music, you need to obtain permission to set up a sound system; make sure you leave enough time to test it properly and enlist a competent operator. The same applies if you want to make a recording of the ceremony. You can choose from a wide range of classical, modern and popular instrumental arrangements and songs. Some of the most popular pieces include:

- 'Adagio in G Minor' (orchestral recording or organ) by Albinoni
- 'Jesu, joy of man's desiring' (organ with or without choir or soloist) by J.S. Bach
- 'Flower Duet' from *Lakmé* (soloists) by Delibes
- 'Ave Maria' (choir or soloist) by Gounod
- 'Ave Maria' (organ or strings, with or without choir or soloist) by Schubert
- 'Exultate Jubilate'; 'Laudate Dominum' (soloist) by Mozart.

The recessional

This is the moment for a really joyful explosion of sound, as the newly married couple and their attendants leave the church. Traditional choices include:

- Toccata in G by Dubois
- March no. 4 from *Pomp and Circumstance* by Elgar
- 'Wedding March' from *A Midsummer Night's Dream* by Mendelssohn
- Postlude in D by Smart
- Fanfare by Whitlock
- Toccata from *Symphony No. 5* by Widor.

Tip

Performances that take place at wedding ceremonies and receptions – whether live or of recorded music – are deemed 'private' so you do not need to pay any copyright fees or obtain a public broadcast licence.

Order of service sheets

When you have made a final decision on the music and readings for your ceremony you can have order of service sheets printed. Order one for each guest, plus a dozen extra. These should be placed at the church before the service, and it is the ushers' job to give one to each guest and to ensure that one each are placed at the front of the church for the minister, bride and groom to use.

On the front of the service sheet the name of the church and the date and time of the ceremony appear in the centre of the page. The bride's name is printed in the bottom right-hand corner and the groom's in the bottom left-hand corner. Inside are printed all the verses of hymns, all the words of the prayers and responses, along with details of the music to be played. A printer will have a sample sheet on which you can base your layout, but you will need to provide a typed copy of the wording you want to use. Check this with the minister before going ahead with printing to ensure that all details are correct.

It is possible, though unlikely, that your chosen hymns will still be protected by copyright, in which case you will need to seek permission from the copyright holder to reprint the words in your order of service sheets. Details of this will be found in the hymn book, either in the acknowledgements at the front or under the paragraph on copyright. If permission is required, the relevant address will be shown in the hymn book. A few copyright holders ask for a reproduction fee, but most are happy with a brief printed acknowledgement.

Remember that you do not have to have printed order of service sheets. If you want to keep costs down you can use the service as laid out in a prayer book, and the congregation can sing from hymn books. Make sure that enough of these books are available for the ushers to distribute.

Bells

A glorious peal of bells enhances any traditional church ceremony. However, an increasing number of churches have only one bell, although they may be able to use a recorded peal. The bells can be rung before and after the ceremony, and the bellringers are paid in cash by the best man on the day. A peal of bells costs between £30 and £60.

Alice and Henry

Alice and Henry initially booked their wedding for 2.30pm, then changed the time to 2pm to fit in with their reception arrangements. Unfortunately the minister had made the change in his desk diary but had forgotten to make the change in the bellringers' book and the ringers turned up after the ceremony had started. Always double-check arrangements, especially if you make any changes.

Readings

Many people like to include one or two readings in their service, although this is not compulsory. Suitable Biblical readings include:

- I Corinthians, Chapter 13 ('Love is patient and kind')
- Ecclesiastes 4, 9–12 ('Two are better than one')
- I John, Chapter 4, 7–12 ('Beloved, let us love one another')
- Ruth 1, 16–17 ('Whither thou goest, I will go')
- Song of Solomon 8, 6–7: ('Set me as a seal upon thine heart').

If you want a reading taken from any source other than the Bible, get your minister's agreement beforehand. There are many suitable poems that could be read, and more details are given on pages 114–15.

Civil ceremony

The key point to remember is that any music or reading included in a civil ceremony must be non-religious. Many register offices will allow you to use your own music at the discretion of the superintendent registrar. Restrictions on space and the amount of time allowed for each wedding mean that you will almost certainly not be able to have live music, although you will probably be allowed to use your choice of recorded music for a few minutes before and after the ceremony.

Approved premises, such as castles and stately homes, will generally be more flexible, but do check before booking if music is very important to you, as some hotels and country houses have fairly strict policies about the use of music during the ceremony. At approved premises it is often possible to arrange the ceremony to include a prelude, processional and recessional (see pages 109–11) and you may be able to use live or recorded music.

As to your choice of music, any of the non-religious pieces listed on pages 109–11 would be suitable. You can get inspiration from the many compilations of romantic and mood music, both classical and modern, which are widely available on CD from record stores and libraries. Among the most popular modern pieces played at civil weddings are:

- 'Annie's Song' by John Denver
- 'The Miracle of Love' by the Eurythmics
- 'Your Song' by Elton John
- 'You've Got A Friend' by Carole King
- 'Love Me Tender' by Elvis Presley
- 'When A Man Loves A Woman' by Percy Sledge.

Readings

You may also be able to have one or more non-religious readings at a civil ceremony, again with the superintendent registrar's approval. These could be read by a family member or friend, or even by the bride or groom. Anthologies, such as *The Oxford Book of Marriage*, (Rubinstein, H (ed.), 1990, OUP), which is available from bookshops or libraries, are a useful source of suitable poems and prose. Suggestions include:

- 'If ever two were one, then surely we . . .' by Anne Bradstreet
- 'How do I love thee? Let me count the ways . . .' (from *Sonnets from the Portuguese*) by Elizabeth Barrett Browning
- 'Never marry but for love . . .' by William Penn
- 'My heart is like a singing bird . . .' (from *A Birthday*) by Christina Rossetti

- 'Shall I compare thee to a summer's day? . . .' ('Sonnet 18') by William Shakespeare
- 'My true love hath my heart and I have his. . .' (from *Arcadia*) by Sir Philip Sidney.

Alternative ceremonies

If you choose to have an alternative ceremony (i.e. one that carries no legal weight but which is a celebration of your marriage that takes place after a civil ceremony) you are free to choose any readings and music you wish, with or without religious content. See pages 28 and 146–8 for more information on the content of alternative ceremonies.

Music checklist

Name of musician(s)		
Address		
Telephone/fax		
Details of booking		
Cost		
Confirmed in writing		
	Name of piece of music	**Played by**
Prelude		
Processional		
Hymns		
Signing of the register		
Recessional		

Chapter 12

Wedding cake options

The traditional tiered wedding cake makes a grand centrepiece for the wedding feast and can take pride of place on a buffet table. At a sit-down meal the cake should be placed on a separate table where it can be seen by the guests but where it does not obscure their view of the bride and groom. Order the cake well in advance as traditional rich fruit cake improves with age and should be made at least two months before icing.

The first question to consider is how many people will the cake have to serve. Remember to allow for those absent on the day (either because they couldn't come or because you weren't able to invite them). You can send them a piece after the wedding in special little boxes (available in department stores); if you wish, these can be printed with details of your wedding.

No. portions needed	Shape	Size or tiers (allows for keeping top tier)
60	round, 2 tiers	25cm/10in, 15cm/6in
100	round, 3 tiers	28cm/11in, 18cm/7in, 12.5cm/5in
130–140	round 3 tiers	30cm/12in, 20cm/8in, 15cm/6in
	square 3 tiers	25cm/10in, 20cm/8in, 15cm/6in
160–180	round, 3 tiers	30cm/12in, 25cm/10in, 20cm/8in
	square, 3 tiers	28cm/11in, 23cm/9in, 18cm/7in
200–220	round, 4 tiers	30cm/12in, 25cm/10in, 20cm/8in, 15cm/6in
	square, 3 tiers	30cm/12in, 25cm/10in, 20cm/8in

Also decide whether you want to keep the top tier for a future celebration, such as your first wedding anniversary or the christening of your first child and remember to allow for this in your calculations. You will need about 2.25kg/5lb of fruit cake for every 45 to 50 guests. Another way to estimate the size needed is by diameter of the cakes (see opposite).

Fruit cake, being very rich, is economical to serve as only small slices need be given. If you choose sponge cake instead you will get approximately half the number of servings per tier.

Using sponge cakes instead of fruit cakes

More and more people steer away from heavy fruit cakes, opting instead for vanilla or chocolate sponge. These cakes can be iced to look like a conventional cake, and if tiered, can be stacked or arranged using special pillars with interior rods, which go through the cake and rest on the stand beneath. These bear the weight of the cakes on top. Alternatively, sponge cakes can be frosted, or covered with rich ganache icing. However, if the weather is hot these finishes are likely to melt, so the cake must be displayed somewhere cool.

Tip

One way to keep costs down but still provide a spectacular centre-piece to the wedding meal is to have a cake which can double as dessert. A pyramid of chocolate-iced profiteroles, decorated with spun caramelised sugar is ideal. Allow three buns per portion. You could also try a French croquembouche – a hillock of choux buns filled with flavoured creams, with caramel and spun sugar poured over – which is traditionally served at parties in France. A chocolate gateaux would be another good choice, or for a smaller gathering, a large Swiss roll, filled with cream and brandy-soaked glacé fruits would look sumptuous and taste delicious.

Shapes and decorations

Square and round are the most popular shapes and can be arranged either on pillars or stacked, with the tiers resting on top of each other. Flower shapes are another possibility, or you could choose rectangles, octagons or horseshoes. White royal icing is the traditional choice, but fondant icing – being much softer – is easier to eat and gives you more scope for imaginative decoration as it can be moulded and modelled. Although white is the most common choice, the cake could be iced in a colour to fit in with the scheme of the flowers or bridesmaids' dresses.

The cake can be iced with swags, flowers, latticework or many other decorations. Professional confectioners will have a book of photographs showing all the different designs they offer. On top you can have a bride and groom model or a small arrangement of fresh flowers, which should be ordered with your other flowers. Silk flowers are a good alternative to fresh, or a skilled confectioner can make sugar flowers which can be kept as a souvenir. These add considerably to the cost, however, as they are very time-consuming to make.

Who will make the cake?

Making the cake yourself, or asking a family member or friend to do it, is a good way to save money. Ingredients for a simple three-tiered wedding cake (feeding 80–100 people) cost about £45 from a super-market. Another way to keep costs down is to buy plain iced fruit cakes from a supermarket and construct your own tiered cake, which you can then have professionally decorated. Costs range from £6 to £26 per tier.

To make the cake yourself, start by baking it three months before the wedding. The tiers will probably have to be done in relays unless you have access to an extra-large oven. Once you have made the cakes, wrap them in greaseproof paper then in foil and store for at least two months in a cool, dry place until you are ready to ice them. Icing is a job best left to the professionals unless you are very experienced, and you should be able to take the cakes to a cake-decorator for icing and decoration four to six weeks before the wedding.

If you decide to have the cake made for you, consult the *Yellow Pages* for a suitable baker and confectioner. Shop around to compare prices and ask to taste a sample of a typical cake. Confirm all the details in writing when you order and remember to check:

- **when the cake will be delivered**
- **who will assemble it at the reception venue**. If you are using caterers they may do this or else the cake supplier will do it
- **how the cake will be packed**. Each tier should be boxed separately to avoid damage
- for a tiered cake, **whether the pillars and display tray are included in the price**
- **if the top decorations are provided**. Most confectioners will be able to offer you a wide choice
- **if the confectioner is insured against loss or damage of the cake prior to delivery or during transit**.

Tip

Storing the top layer is only possible if you choose a fruit cake, as sponge cakes do not keep for more than a few days. First you must strip off the icing, as this discolours if kept, and the marzipan, as this contains almond oil which turns rancid when stored. If it is likely that the cake will be used within the next year to 18 months, wrap it in plenty of acid-free tissue paper and store it in a cardboard box where the air can circulate round it. Do not keep it in an airtight tin or plastic box. Store in the coolest possible room, out of direct light. If it is likely that the cake is going to be kept for more than a year, wrap it in foil then put it into a double freezer bag and store it in the deep freeze, where it will keep well for up to two years.

Chapter 13

Photographs and video

As photographs and/or a video will be a lasting reminder of your wedding day, it is well worth hiring a professional for the occasion. In addition, you could ask one or two friends whom you know to be keen photographers to bring their cameras and take some extra shots – this way you will get some very personal and informal pictures as well.

Personal recommendation is the best way to find a reliable photographer/video operator, but the *Yellow Pages* will supply many names, and you will probably be able to find one or two in your local high street. Bridal magazines are another good source, both of names of photographers/video operators and of ideas for different photographic styles.

Visit more than one and ask to see photographs/videos from several previous weddings. Make sure you are shown photographs/videos taken by the person you are planning to book, and not a compilation taken by several people. You will need to book about six months ahead of the wedding, possibly longer for a popular photographer/video operator.

Photographs

Decide what style of photography you would like:

- do you want very formal pictures?
- are you interested in having some very informal, candid shots?

- would you like some photographs to be posed in a more original and artistic way, perhaps at a venue away from the church and reception such as a local park or riverside? Make sure your photographer is experienced at this type of work.

Your budget will dictate the number of photographs you ask for. A standard package usually contains 20 prints, starting with the groom's and best man's arrival at the church and ending at the reception when the cake is cut. You can add to this basic package as much as you like and can afford. The reportage style of wedding photography is very popular, and the finished album will tell the full story of the day, starting with the bride preparing to leave home and ending with the couple leaving the reception, with a mixture of traditional and informal photographs in between. However, you could pay up to £1,000 for this style of presentation, in a high-quality leather album.

Tip

Some couples use a professional photographer for the ceremony only and put a disposable flash camera on each table at the reception and ask the guests to take photographs. One of the bridesmaids could collect all the cameras at the end of the day.

Spend time talking to your photographer in advance of the day. You will need to consider the following points.

- **Does the photographer make you feel relaxed and do you think you can work happily with him or her on the day**? A good photographer must be helpful and unobtrusive but also needs to be able to manage people, persuade them to pose and make sure that the photography does not hold up the proceedings for too long.
- **How will the key shots be covered**? Are you in agreement with the photographer about the level of formality and the mixture of formal and informal photographs? Are there any special shots you want or any guest of whom you would like a close-up?

- **The photographer will need a timetable of the day and a list of the names of the most important guests who must be included**. You can also give a list of shots which you particularly want.
- Organising **group photographs** takes time, and your guests will not want to be kept waiting at the wedding venue for too long. One way of getting round this is to drop the traditional receiving line and have the group photographs taken at the reception venue while the guests are arriving and being given a drink. Tell the key people in advance that they will be wanted for group photographs at the start of the reception and make sure they know where to go when they arrive.
- **Check with your minister where and when photography is allowed in church**. Policies vary, and while some ministers are happy to have a few discreet photographs taken during the service – although not always of the marriage itself – others ask for no flash or stipulate a number of pictures allowed, and some will permit no photography in the church at all.

The photographer broke the rules

Marianna's vicar specified that only one picture could be taken during the signing of the register. However, her photographer chose to ignore this and slipped in several extra photographs, thus annoying the vicar and causing everyone to feel uncomfortable – a fact that inevitably showed up in the photographs. Tell your photographer what is allowed and make sure he or she knows that you are happy to go along with any rules laid down by the vicar.

Negotiating a package

Most estimates include an album containing a specified number of photographs. Some packages also include two smaller versions of the main album to be given to each of the sets of parents, and you can also select some photographs to be printed in a larger size for framing; these are charged for in addition to the basic package.

Some photographers quote for the amount of time they spend at your wedding on the day and charge extra for prints; others charge for prints but not for their time, while some base the cost on their time and offer unlimited prints.

Check for hidden extras such as development, VAT and delivery of proofs. If you want any special effects such as hand-tinting, sepia or black-and-white photographs, specify these when you make your booking and get confirmation of the cost. The photographer should send you a proof set of all the photographs taken about a week after the wedding, and you can choose the ones you would like included in your album. You can also circulate the proofs round any others who might like to buy prints.

Popular wedding-day photographs

The list below covers most of the usual wedding photographs, but you will probably not want to have all of them.

Before the ceremony

- Bride and bridesmaids at home, preparing for the ceremony
- Close-up of bride before wedding
- Bride and father before leaving home
- Guests arriving at wedding venue
- Groom and best man at wedding venue before the ceremony
- Ushers at the wedding venue
- Bridesmaids and bride's mother arriving at wedding venue
- Bride and father arriving at wedding venue

In the church (if permitted)

- Bride's procession down the aisle
- The marriage ceremony (if permitted)
- Exchange of rings
- Signing of the register
- Musicians performing
- Bride and groom walking back down the aisle
- Bride and groom emerging from church

After the ceremony

- Bride and groom together
- Couple with bridesmaids and/or pages
- Couple with best man, bridesmaids and/or pages
- Bridesmaids and pages
- Couple with bride's parents
- Couple with groom's parents
- Couple with both sets of parents
- Couple with all family members of both sides
- Couple with all friends
- Entire wedding party
- Guests throwing confetti
- Couple leaving for reception

At a register office/approved venue

Check whether there are any restrictions on where you can have photographs taken inside the venue.

At the reception

- Receiving line
- Informal photographs during reception
- Top table
- Each side table
- Speeches: bride's father, groom, best man
- Cutting the cake
- First dance (bride and groom)
- Bride throwing bouquet
- Couple leaving reception

Other shots

- Portrait of bride
- Portrait of groom
- Close-up of ring/s on finger
- Other special requests

Insurance

Ensure that your photographer is covered by a professional indemnity, which covers camera problems and lost or damaged film. Insurance cannot cover points of style, so if the photographs are not what you wanted or hoped for you will have to seek compensation from the photographer direct. If you take out wedding insurance (see Chapter 18), most policies cover you for the cost of a retake if the photographer does not show up on the day or the films or negatives are lost or damaged.

Digital photography

A new option, which is likely to become increasingly popular, is the use of digital cameras, which do not use conventional film. Instead, the images are stored digitally and are downloaded on to a computer, from which they can be transferred on to floppy disk or CD-Rom. This is a very quick process, which does not involve any developing costs, although the basic equipment is currently expensive. You can view each image on the computer screen and print out those you choose, using high-quality glossy paper and a good colour printer. The pictures can be cropped, enhanced and sized as you wish, and it is possible to send the images via email to any other computer. You could even create a web site of your own pictures.

If you are an Internet user, it is likely that you will have received some free web space when you signed up with you Internet service provider. You can use this space to design your own web page, which your friends can visit to view your wedding photographs on the Internet, see page 50. The pictures must be taken with a digital camera. You can download trial versions of web design programs from the Internet. Samples of this type of program are also often included on the free CDs given with computer magazines.

Photography checklist

Name of photographer	
Address	
Telephone/fax	
Contact	
Date booked	
Confirmed in writing	
Agreed fee	
What is included in the package?	
Time of photographer's arrival at bride's home/wedding venue	
Time of photographer's departure from the reception	
Date proofs will be supplied	
Special effects requested	

Video

More and more people are having professional videos made of their wedding day. It is tempting to ask a friend who owns a camcorder or is willing to hire one to do this for you, and you will certainly make a big saving. However, producing a well-shot, watchable video takes some skill, and you need to be certain that your friend is up to the task and is happy to concentrate on filming rather than entering into the fun of the occasion. Of course, if you are not worried about the occasional wobble or muffled sound, then an amateur video is worth considering.

If you decide to hire a professional, you should follow the same selection procedure as for a photographer. Styles of video vary, so look at a few samples to find the type that best suits you. Any reputable video service will provide insurance, and some also offer a customer dissatisfaction clause. With this, financial compensation may be available if an independent arbitration panel judges the final product to be of an inferior standard to that agreed in your contract.

As with photography, you should be able to agree on a package deal, which will include a specified number of copies of the video and will stipulate at what stage the filming will start and finish. Check with your minister that he or she does not object to a video being made of the ceremony. (You will probably have to pay the church a small fee for having a video of the ceremony.) Remember that to achieve the best effects the video company may have to set up microphones and extra lighting.

Tips for making an amateur video

- Well in advance, draw up a list of shots that should definitely be included. You can shadow the official photographer and take some film from the sidelines as the main shots are set up – but do not get in the way.
- Remember to take a spare battery and plenty of video tape.
- Visit the church and reception venue ahead of the day if possible and work out the best positions for your shots. Check the position of useful power sockets.
- If you use a separate microphone, which will give good sound quality during the ceremony and speeches, position it where guests are unlikely to brush against it or knock it over.
- Use a hand-held microphone and ask guests to speak directly to the camera.
- Take as many shots as you can of people smiling and laughing.
- You will get a much better finished result if you can get access to editing equipment, so that shots can be shortened or intercut.
- Use shots of the church/wedding venue interior, or close-ups of floral arrangements or the bridal bouquet, to intersperse with the action shots.
- Be on the lookout for unusual or amusing shots.
- Keep the camera steady, using a tripod when necessary.
- Each sequence should be fairly short, otherwise the finished film will run for hours.
- Be sparing with your use of the zoom lens.
- Bookshops and libraries have a wide stock of books with detailed information on making a successful amateur video.

Video checklist

Name of video company	
Address	
Telephone/fax	
Contact	
Date booked	
Confirmed in writing	
Agreed fee	
What is included in the package?	
Time of video operator's arrival at bride's home/wedding venue	
Time of video operator's departure from the reception	
When will the video be delivered?	

Chapter 14

Religious ceremonies

Most religious ceremonies follow a set traditional procedure, which you can discuss with the minister when you make the initial arrangements. You will have to satisfy various legal criteria before you will be permitted to have any sort of religious ceremony (see the Appendix).

Church of England marriage ceremony

When you first visit the minister who will conduct your marriage he or she will tell you about the procedure for arranging the wedding, publishing the banns and organising the ceremony itself. Details of the documents you need to produce at this meeting are given on page 204. At this first meeting you can set the date and time of the wedding and discuss details such as who will play the organ, whether you want to use the church choir, your choice of music and where you can put flowers. You can also book a date and time for a rehearsal if your wedding is not too far in the future.

The minister will want to discuss the religious significance of the marriage service with you, so you may be asked to attend a series of marriage preparation sessions, during which the ceremony will be explained in detail and you will have the opportunity to think through the implications of marriage. The ceremonies of the Church of Scotland★, Church in Wales and Church of Ireland are very similar to that of the Church of England.

Catherine and Alistair

Catherine and Alistair got married by special licence (see page 206) because neither of them lived in the parish of the church in which they were planning to marry. 'The vicar gave us the impression that he would arrange the licence but he went on holiday without having done so, and the deaconess who took over assumed that we had made the arrangements ourselves. Five days before the wedding we realised that we didn't have the licence, and my fiancé had to visit Lambeth Palace to sort it out. It was a close-run thing, and a better discussion, with proper clarification over who was responsible for what, would have avoided it.'

Order of service

You will need to discuss the order of the service and which version of the ceremony you would like to use (see below). The service usually begins with a few words of introduction and a hymn, followed by the marriage itself. After the marriage has taken place there may be prayers, further hymns and possibly an address and some readings before the register is signed. For more information on choosing music and readings, see Chapter 11. Once you have worked out the exact order and decided on the music and readings, you can draw up an order of service for printing (see page 112).

Versions of the marriage service

There are three current versions of the marriage service to choose from:

- The version from the **1662 Book of Common Prayer** – The language is old-fashioned, and the bride's promise to obey her husband is an obligatory part of the service. It is not used very frequently but it is sometimes chosen by couples who like the older, more formal language and want a very traditional ceremony.
- **The form of Solemnisation of Matrimony 1966** – Currently authorised for use until 31 December 2000, this version is popular and is likely to be re-authorised. The language is similar in

style to that of the 1662 version, but the bride's promise to obey and serve her husband is optional, and the language of the introduction is more moderate.

- The version from **The Alternative Service Book 1980** – This is also authorised until 31 December 2000, when it may be replaced by a new version. The language is modern and direct. Again, the bride can choose whether or not she wants to promise to obey. In the details of the ceremony given below, wordings are given from the 1966 and 1980 versions for comparison (as the 1662 language is very similar to 1966).

The ceremony

- Before the service starts the organist plays gentle music to create the right mood in the church. When the bride arrives the organist plays the music for the processional, and the groom and best man stand and move to the head of the aisle. The congregation then rises.
- The bride holds her father's right arm and, followed by the bridesmaids and pages, walks slowly down the aisle. The chief bridesmaid walks directly behind the bride, followed by the other attendants.
- The groom and best man may turn to greet the bride as she walks down the aisle or at the chancel steps.
- At the chancel steps the bride lifts back her veil if she is wearing one, perhaps helped by the chief bridesmaid. She hands her bouquet to the chief bridesmaid, who keeps it until the register has been signed.

The marriage

The minister greets the bridal party and congregation with a few introductory words and then begins the ceremony, which lasts about half an hour, depending on how many hymns and readings you are adding (with three hymns, two readings and an address, the service will take about 50 minutes). The congregation remain standing for the marriage itself and the hymns but may sit for the address and sit or kneel during the prayers. These moves can either be included in an order of service sheet, or the minister will tell the congregation what to do.

The service begins with a few words on the significance of marriage and its purposes:

1966: *'Dearly beloved, we are gathered here in the sight of God and in the face of this congregation, to join together this man and this woman in Holy Matrimony; which is an honourable estate, instituted of God himself, signifying unto us the mystical union that is betwixt Christ and his Church . . .'*

1980: *'We have come together in the presence of God, to witness the marriage of N. (groom) and N. (bride) to ask his blessing on them, and to share in their joy. Our Lord Jesus Christ was himself a guest at a wedding in Cana of Galilee, and through his Spirit he is with us now . . .'*

The minister then asks whether any member of the congregation knows of any reason why the couple should not be married:

1966: *'Therefore if any man can shew any just cause, why they may not lawfully be joined together, let him now speak, or else hereafter for ever hold his peace.'*

1980: *'But first I am required to ask anyone present who knows a reason why these persons may not lawfully marry, to declare it now.'*

He then asks the couple if either knows of any reason why they should not marry.

1996: *'I require and charge you both, as ye will answer at the dreadful day of judgement when the secrets of all hearts be disclosed, that if either of you know any impediment, why ye may not be lawfully joined together in Matrimony, ye do confess it. For be ye well assured, that so many as are coupled together otherwise than God's word doth allow are not joined together by God; neither is their Matrimony lawful.'*

1980: *'The vows you are about to take are to be made in the name of God, who is judge of all and who knows all the secrets of our hearts; therefore if either of you knows a reason why you may not lawfully marry, you must declare it now.'*

The couple are then asked in turn if each will marry the other:

1966: *'N. Wilt thou have this woman to thy wedded wife, to live together according to God's law in the holy estate of Matrimony? Wilt thou love her, comfort her, honour and keep her, in sickness and in health? and, forsaking all other, keep thee only unto her, so long as ye both shall live?'* (There is an option for the bride to obey at this point.)

1980: *'N, will you take N to be your husband? Will you love him, comfort him, honour and protect him, and, forsaking all others, be faithful to him as long as you both shall live?'*

The bride and groom respond *'I will'*. The minister asks who gives the woman to be married. The bride's father takes the bride's right hand and gives it to the minister who places it in the groom's right hand. This concludes the bride's father's role in the ceremony, and he steps back and joins the bride's mother in the front pew. Some couples prefer to omit this part of the ceremony.

Next the couple make their wedding vows, taking it in turn to repeat the words after the minister:

1966: *'I N. take thee N. to my wedded wife, to have and to hold from this day forward, for better, for worse; for richer, for poorer; in sickness and in health; to love and to cherish till death us do part, according to God's holy law; and thereto I give thee my troth.'* (Women have the option to obey in this service.)

1980: *'I, N., take you, N., to be my husband, to have and to hold from this day forward; for better, for worse, for richer, for poorer, in sickness and in health, to love and to cherish (or, to love, cherish, and obey), till death us do part, according to God's holy law; and this is my solemn vow.'*

Some couples choose to learn their vows off by heart so they can say them to each other without needing to be prompted by the minister.

The best man places the ring(s) on an open prayer book, which the minister offers him. The rings are blessed, then the minister gives the bride's ring to the groom, who places it on her finger and repeats the words:

1966: *'With this ring I thee wed; with my body I thee honour; and all my worldly goods with thee I share: In the name of the Father, and of the Son, and of the Holy Ghost. Amen.'*

1980: *'I give you this ring as a sign of our marriage. With my body I honour you, all that I am I give to you, and all that I have I share with you, within the love of God, Father, Son, and Holy Spirit.'*

If rings are exchanged these words are also repeated by the bride as she places a ring on the groom's finger. The minister then pronounces the couple man and wife:

1966: *'Those whom God hath joined together let no man put asunder . . . I pronounce that they be man and wife together, In the name of the Father, and of the Son, and of the Holy Ghost. Amen.'*

1980: *'I therefore proclaim that they are husband and wife. That which God has joined together, let not man divide.'*

The ceremony continues with prayers, hymns, readings and/or an address. If the service includes communion or mass it will take place at this point. The service ends with the signing of the register.

Seating plan during the marriage

ALTAR

Minister

Bride's father　　BRIDE　　GROOM　　Best Man

Chief Bridesmaid

Attendants

Bride's mother

Groom's parents

Bride's close family

Groom's close family

Other members of
bride's family

Other members of
groom's family

Friends

Friends

Signing the register

The bride and groom, chief bridesmaid and best man, other attendants, bride's and groom's parents and minister are all present at the signing of the register. This can either take place in the vestry (in which case the bridal party gain a few minutes of privacy in which they can relax a little before leaving church) or at a side table, in view of the congregation. Music is usually played or sung while the congregation wait for the register to be signed.

The marriage register is signed by the minister, the bride, using her maiden name, the groom and two adult witnesses – perhaps the two fathers or the two mothers or the best man and chief bridesmaid. Decide before the ceremony who will sign. The marriage certificate, which is a copy of the register entry, is given to the couple by the minister (although the best man will usually take charge of it during the day).

After the register has been signed, the bridal party and congregation leave the church. The chief bridesmaid returns the bride's bouquet to her and arranges her train. The bride takes her husband's left arm, the organist begins the recessional music and the bridal party leaves the church in the following order: bride and groom, chief bridesmaid and best man, other attendants, bride's mother with groom's father, and groom's mother with bride's father. The congregation follow, with those seated at the front of the church leaving before those seated at the back.

Outside the church

Once outside the church photographs are taken.

- The congregation may shower the couple with confetti if allowed by the minister. Alternatives to confetti are rice, which can sting but may be cleared up for you by the birds, or flower petals which could be provided in baskets by bridesmaids.
- The best man helps the photographer to marshal the guests into groups for the photographs.
- The best man or ushers should check inside the church to make sure that nothing has been left behind, including top hats and gloves belonging to the bridal party, cameras and umbrellas.
- When the photographs have all been taken, the bride and groom leave the church for the reception. Next to leave are the couple's parents and the bridesmaids and pages. Guests follow on, and it is up to the best man to make sure that everyone has the means to get to the reception. He should be last to leave the church but must also try not to arrive too late at the reception, where he may be wanted to take part in the receiving line.

Roman Catholic ceremony

The Roman Catholic ceremony can be conducted with or without a nuptial mass (mass is not permitted if one partner is non-Christian). The ceremony is similar to that of the Church of England and begins with a welcome, an introduction, and Bible readings but has a responsorial psalm. After the priest's address comes the marriage rite:

The priest then says: *'You have come together in this church so that the Lord may seal and strengthen your love in the presence of the Church's minister and this community. Christ abundantly blesses this love. He has already consecrated you in baptism and now he enriches and strengthens you by a special sacrament so that you may assume the duties of marriage in mutual and lasting fidelity. And so, in the presence of this Church, I ask you to state your intentions.*

'I shall now ask you if you freely undertake the obligations of marriage, and to state that there is no legal impediment to your marriage.'

He then asks the couple three questions to which they respond in turn after each question *'I am'*:

'Are you ready freely and without reservation to give yourselves to each other in marriage?'

'Are you ready to love and honour each other as man and wife for the rest of your lives?'

'Are you ready to accept children lovingly from God, and bring them up according to the law of Christ and his Church?'

Finally, the couple take their vows with words similar to those in the Church of England ceremony. The bride does not promise to obey.

Priest: *'You have declared your consent before the Church. May the Lord in his goodness strengthen your consent and fill you both with his blessings. What God has joined together, let no man put asunder.'*

The rings are then blessed and given with the words:

'May the Lord bless this ring (these rings) which you give (to each other) as the sign of your love and fidelity.'

The couple in turn then say:

'N. (Christian name only) take this ring as a sign of my love and fidelity. In the name of the Father, and of the Son, and of the Holy Spirit.'

If the marriage ceremony is taking place within a mass, the mass continues after the nuptial blessing. The signing of the register follows the final prayers and hymn, and the couple then leave church together.

Non-conformist or free church ceremonies

Marriages which take place in churches such as Methodist, Baptist and United Reformed Church use a ceremony very similar to that of the Church of England. The order of service may be slightly altered.

Quaker ceremony

Marriages take place with almost no ceremony, within a usual meeting for worship. An explanation of the procedure is given and the couple then stand and make their declaration of marriage using these words: *'Friends, I take this my friend, (full name), to be my husband/wife, promising, through Divine assistance (or, with God's help), to be unto him/her a loving and faithful husband/wife, so long as we both on earth shall live.'*

Wedding rings are not formally exchanged during a Quaker wedding, but the couple may like to give each other a ring after making their declarations. They sign the Quaker marriage certificate in front of two witnesses, and the certificate is read aloud by the registering officer, either immediately or towards the end of the meeting.

A period of silence then follows during which anyone present may speak. Friends can bless the couple and offer their support. At the end of the meeting the couple and the registering officer sign the civil register; and all those present can sign the Quaker marriage certificate.

Jewish ceremony

The wedding usually takes place in a synagogue, but other venues such as halls or hotel suites are also acceptable. A *quorum* of at least ten adult males should be present. Prior to the ceremony, the groom approaches the bride and lowers her veil over her face. The groom is taken to the wedding canopy or *chuppah* by his father and the bride's father. The bride is then escorted by her mother and the groom's mother to stand beside him. In an Orthodox ceremony, she walks round the groom a number of times, depending on custom, before standing on his right. While this is happening the rabbi or cantor chants a welcome blessing.

The ceremony itself begins with the rabbi reciting a blessing over a goblet of wine from which the bride and groom then drink. The groom places the wedding ring on the forefinger of the bride's right hand, saying '*Behold you are wedded to me with this ring according to the Law of Moses and Israel*'. (The bride may transfer the ring to her left hand after the ceremony.) The *ketubah* or marriage contract, which is written in Hebrew, has already been signed by the witnesses prior to the ceremony. The bride and groom do not have to sign the *ketubah* to make it valid in Jewish law, but may, if they wish, sign the abstract printed on the reverse side. The *ketubah* is read aloud, and the seven benedictions are recited over a goblet of wine. Sometimes this is done by various guests. The bride and groom drink again from the goblet, and the groom then crushes a glass with his right foot.

The rabbi invokes the priestly blessing. The newly married couple then sign the civil contract of marriage (if they have not already had a civil wedding) and are then taken to a private room where they spend a short time together and break their fast, which commenced at dawn, before going on to the reception venue.

Hindu ceremony

The ceremony can last for a good part of the day. The arrival of the groom and his party is traditionally heralded by special music played on the *shenai* (Indian flute). However, it is now more common to find bands playing or drums beating and leading the party. The groom and his family are formally welcomed outside the wedding venue by the bride's family and relatives. Other guests sometimes gather round to watch. The groom is treated to a ritual by the bride's mother, before being led into the *mandap* (canopy), where the ceremony will take place. The groom is accompanied by his siblings and their husbands/wives, who sit with him throughout the ceremony.

The bride, traditionally wearing red and white, is then led into the *mandap* by her maternal uncle (*mama*) or closest male relative, while the Brahman priest chants holy verses and *mantras* from the Hindu scriptures for good luck. During this time a shawl is held between the bride and groom, and the bride's right hand is placed over the groom's right hand. When the chanting is finished, the shawl is withdrawn. A loop of white cotton, entwined 24 times to symbolise different characteristics and virtues of human life, is put around the shoulders of the couple, binding them together for life. The bride and groom garland each other with fresh flowers.

The priest then lights the sacred fire (*agni*). This represents the mouth of Vishnu, a Hindu god, and symbolises illumination of mind, knowledge and happiness. Prayers are addressed to Lord Yama, the God of Death, that he grant the couple happiness and a long life. The couple take holy vows by walking clockwise around the fire four times, completing each circle in eight steps. Each circuit signifies the couple's promise to each other, with the priest, the sacred fire and God as witness to fulfil the following: *dharma* (duty), *artha* (wealth), *karma* (satisfaction), *muksha* (salvation). The eight steps signify food, strength, family, progeny, prosperity, happiness, religious practice and friendship. The couple are then declared husband and wife. The groom blesses the bride by putting *sindoor* (vermilion powder) in the parting of her hair to indicate that she is married.

Various other rituals are carried out. Some of these are significant while others bring a sense of fun and laughter to the ceremony. Food is eaten and photographs are taken. Nowadays, a reception is held, with cake-cutting, music and dancing. At the end of the day, the *vidai* (departure) takes place. This is a very emotional custom, as the bride's parents, close relatives and friends bid her farewell. Both bride and groom touch the feet of the elders as a mark of respect and to gain blessings for their new life.

Sikh ceremony

The Sikh culture has embraced some Hindu traditions and there are similarities between the wedding ceremonies of the two cultures. Like the Hindu ceremony, the Sikh ceremony takes place in the morning, and celebrations can last the whole day. The groom and his party arrive at the wedding venue, usually led by a band playing, or drum-beating. The bride's parents and relatives greet them, and other guests may observe. The priest says a welcome prayer, and the bride's male relatives present garlands and gifts to the male relatives of the groom. Sometimes the bride's mother presents a gift of jewellery to the groom's mother. The groom and his party are led into breakfast. During these proceedings, the bride stays out of sight.

The wedding ceremony is a formal event, usually held in the temple (*gudwara*). Inside the temple, guests must remove their shoes, wash their hands and cover their heads. In the prayer hall, the congregation sits on the floor facing the altar, where the holy book (*Guru Granth Sahab*) rests under a canopy. Men sit on the right side of the altar, women on the left. As guests arrive, special wedding hymns are sung accompanied by musicians playing *tablas* (two small drums) and the *baja* (Indian accordion). Guests and the groom kneel in front of the altar to pay their respects to the holy book before taking their places.

The priest calls for the groom to be seated in front of the altar. He then calls for the bride to be brought in and seated. The bride is led in by her brother(s) or closest male relatives and is seated on the left-hand side of the groom. She must keep her eyes lowered throughout the ceremony. More hymns are sung. While the priest recites a special prayer to start the ceremony the bride and groom and their parents stand. When the prayer ends, they sit down.

The priest reads from whatever page of the holy book he happens to open. Then he requests the bride's father to take one end of the brightly decorated long scarf (*laar*), which is draped round the groom's shoulders, and place it in the bride's hand. The other end is held by the groom. This signifies that the father is now giving his daughter away and that the couple are now partners who share one life. This is an emotional moment for the bride and her family. The couple hold the ends of the scarf throughout the ceremony.

The central part of the ceremony – *laama* – follows, when the groom leads the bride around the altar four times. The bride's male relatives may gather around the altar and help her one by one. The priest recites a prayer about the cycle of life and the seasons. This is said in four parts, interspersed with four short hymns sung to music. The couple remain seated during the recitals, but during the singing they rise and go slowly round the altar, the hymn being sung continuously until they have returned to the front and sat down. After the fourth cycle they remain sitting.

Finally, a hymn is sung to indicate that the couple are now married and the ceremony is over. Everyone stands up to recite the holy prayer, and people then begin to greet and congratulate each other. The bride's mother blesses the couple with sweetmeats, and close relatives then take turns to bless the couple with garlands, sweetmeats and money. All the other guests then come up to the couple and offer gifts of money.

The departure (*dhol*) takes place at the end of the day and is a very emotional time for the bride's family and relatives. Each member wishes the bride good luck and bids her farewell as she leaves for her new home with the groom and his family. Today, especially in the West, the bride and groom may have already set up their own home, but it is still customary for them to spend the first few days after the wedding in the groom's family home so that the bride can get used to her new family. After that the couple may go on honeymoon.

Muslim ceremony

The wedding ceremony need not take place in a mosque, and any respected male may officiate. The bride is asked if she consents to the marriage. She may convey her consent through her guardian, usually her father, or she may answer herself. The groom is then asked if he accepts the marriage, with the agreed dowry that he will give to the bride.

These are the elements of the ceremony which are needed to meet Islamic requirements, but different cultures include extra traditions. After the wedding a celebration for the couple's families, friends and neighbours may be held days, or even weeks, later.

Wedding rehearsals

Many ministers encourage couples to have a wedding rehearsal about a week before the actual day. This is so everyone in the wedding party knows exactly what to do and when on the day. It is attended by the bride and groom, best man, chief bridesmaid and bride's father. Other, younger attendants may be included if you wish.

Church of England service of blessing for second marriages

This service takes place in church after the couple have had a civil marriage. Since it is not a marriage service there is no need for banns to be called or for the register to be signed.

At the beginning of the service the couple to be blessed come into the church together without ceremony and sit at the front of the church. The minister leads some prayers and there may be readings, hymns or psalms and a sermon. The couple then stand and the minister says to them both:

'N. and N., you have committed yourselves to each other in marriage and your marriage is recognised by law. The Church of Christ understands marriage to be, in the will of God, the union of a man and a woman, for better, for worse, for richer, for poorer, in sickness and in health, to love and to cherish, till parted by death. Is this your understanding of the covenant and promise that you have made?' The couple respond: *'It is.'*

The minister then asks the couple in turn: *'N., have you resolved to be faithful to your wife/husband, forsaking all others, so long as you both shall live?'* The man and then the woman respond in turn: *'That is my resolve, with the help of God.'*

Rings are not exchanged during the service, but rings which were given during the civil ceremony may be blessed. The hand(s) wearing the ring(s) should be extended towards the minister, who says:
'Heavenly Father, by your blessing let this ring/these rings be to N. and N. a symbol of unending love and faithfulness and of the promises they have made to each other; through Jesus Christ our Lord. Amen.'

The minister then turns to the congregation and says to them:
'N. and N. have here affirmed their Christian understanding and resolve in the marriage which they have begun. Will you their relatives and friends do all in your power to uphold them in their marriage?' The congregation respond: *'We will.'*

More prayers and hymns follow before the end of the service, which may also include holy communion.

Chapter 15

Civil ceremonies

For many years the proportion of civil and religious marriages was roughly equal, but since the introduction of the Marriage Act 1994 permitting non-religious weddings to take place at premises other than register offices, the number of civil marriages has been steadily increasing, until currently 58 per cent of all weddings are civil. Although most of these still take place at register offices, an increasing number of couples each year choose to marry in alternative premises, licensed for marriage, and this number looks likely to increase as more and more venues apply for licences, thus widening the choice. The people most likely to choose approved premises rather than a register office are older couples who already live together, and where at least one of the two had been married previously. For more information about approved premises, see pages 23–4.

Whether you choose to hold your civil ceremony in a register office or elsewhere, you will have to satisfy various legal criteria before you can marry, see the Appendix.

The wedding day

You can either arrive at the wedding venue together or separately. Remember that register offices allow a fairly short time for each wedding, so time your arrival for about ten minutes before the ceremony is due to begin. You can have a best man and bridesmaids if you wish, but the law requires just two witnesses, who can be family members or friends.

Before the register office ceremony, you and your guests will gather in an ante-room. Wherever the marriage takes place, the couple will have a brief private interview with the superintendent registrar, in which all details are checked for accuracy and the attendance fee is collected. The couple and the guests then assemble in the room where the marriage is to be held.

The ceremony

Certain parts of the ceremony are obligatory, but for other parts you can choose from a variety of wordings in any combination you like. These are given below. At some register offices the superintendent registrar offers additional wordings to embellish the ceremony, which you can incorporate if you wish.

The ceremony begins with the superintendent registrar saying: *'This place in which you are now met has been duly sanctioned according to the law for the celebration of marriages. You are here to witness the joining in matrimony of (man's full name) and (woman's full name). If any person present knows of any lawful impediment to this marriage, he should declare it now.'*

The superintendent registrar asks the couple to stand. The guests remain seated. The superintendent registrar confirms the couple's full names and then says to them: *'Before you are joined in matrimony I have to remind you of the solemn and binding character of the ceremony of marriage. Marriage according to the law of this country is the union of one man with one woman, voluntarily entered into for life, to the exclusion of all others. Now I am going to ask each of you in turn to declare that you do not know of any lawful reason why you should not be married to each other.'*

The couple in turn then repeat, either: *'I do solemnly declare that I know not of any lawful impediment why I, (full name), may not be joined in matrimony to (full name).'*

or

'I declare that I know of no legal reason why I, (full name), should not be joined in marriage to (full name).'

or

In response to the question: *'Are you (full name) free lawfully to marry (full name)?'* respond *'I am.'*

The superintendent registrar then says to all those present: *'Now the solemn moment has come for these two persons to contract the marriage before you, their witnesses. Will you all please stand.'*

In turn, the man and then the woman take their partner by the hand, and if giving a ring place it on the other's ring finger and hold it there, whilst repeating either:

'I call upon these persons here present to witness that I, (full name), do take thee, (full name) to be my lawful wedded wife/husband.'
or
'I (full name) take you (or thee) (full name) to be my wedded wife/husband.'

Then the superintendent registrar says: *'(Full name) and (full name), you have both made the declarations prescribed by law, and have made a solemn and binding contract with each other, in the presence of the witnesses here assembled. You are now man and wife together.'*

After a pause, where the couple may kiss each other and be congratulated by the guests, the superintendent registrar says: *'Will you now all please be seated while the register is signed.'*

The register is signed by the couple, two witnesses, the registrar and the superintendent registrar. A copy is written on to a marriage certificate which is given to the couple.

Personalising a civil ceremony

In addition to the words printed above – which must be included by law – you may be able to add personal touches to a civil ceremony in the form of non-religious music, poetry, readings or vows (see Chapter 11). However, you must discuss any additions with the superintendent registrar when booking the wedding. Some will allow only minor inclusions, regardless of whether you are marrying in a register office or approved premises, while others are happy to allow you more freedom. Whatever you want to add, the content must be strictly non-religious, and you should check first with the superintendent registrar that any material you want to use is permissible.

At approved premises (stately homes, castles, hotels etc.), which are often booked for both the ceremony and reception, thereby saving you time as you do not have to travel from one to the other, you may be able to organise a longer, more formal ceremony. You could include a processional and recessional and perhaps some music during the signing of the register (see page 110–11). Do not take this for granted, however, and check before making any arrangements, as some approved premises prefer to keep the ceremony brief and simple.

Leaving the register office

You should be able to spend some time outside the register office posing for photographs, although depending on where the office is sited you may prefer to have photographs taken elsewhere. On a busy day the next wedding party will be arriving soon after your ceremony is over, so bear this in mind when briefing a photographer, if you use one. Find out what the register office's policy is on confetti.

Involving your children in your wedding

Some couples have children from a previous marriage whom they would like to give a special role on the day. You could ask them to witness your marriage if they are old enough (they do not have to be 18 years old but they do need to be old enough to understand what being a witness means). They could also be entrusted with your ring(s) and produce it/them for you at the appropriate part of the ceremony, while small children could act as attendants and wear traditional bridesmaid's or page's clothes and carry flowers, or be dressed in their party outfits if you prefer to be less formal. They can be seated directly behind you during the ceremony, if space permits, or in the front row of guests. After the ceremony, children can be given their own boxes of confetti to scatter.

Alternative ceremonies

Although not legally binding, an alternative ceremony can make an excellent follow-on from a civil marriage and enables you to have exactly the sort of ceremony you would like. You could create your own ceremony and write your own vows, which need not follow a particular set of beliefs but which can, if you wish, include religious elements.

A humanist ceremony

Humanists do not believe in any god, an afterlife or the supernatural. Their beliefs are founded on the idea that people should try to live full and happy lives and in doing this, make it easier for other people to do the same. A humanist wedding ceremony embodies these ideas and can be tailored to fit your wishes and personalities.

Suresh and Ruth

Suresh, who is Indian, and Ruth, who is English, had differing views from their parents regarding their wedding ceremony. Their parents felt that the religious element was important, although this would create difficulties because of the difference in cultures and expectations. Suresh and Ruth wanted a non-religious event. So they chose to have a humanist ceremony, which they wrote themselves, straight after their civil marriage. They wanted a ceremony where they could have control over the words they used and the content. The humanist ceremony accorded with their belief that people should have freedom of choice in the main decisions of life, and should be able to celebrate one of the principal milestones of their lives in a non-religious way. The ceremony gave them the opportunity to make a serious public commitment to share their lives, despite the cultural and racial differences in their backgrounds, in a setting that both found poignant, moving and very pertinent to each of them as individuals and as a couple.

A humanist celebrant, with whom they had met beforehand to discuss the content of the ceremony, conducted it for them. In his introduction, the celebrant said: '*Ruth and Suresh recognise the uniqueness of their marriage, which crosses cultural and racial boundaries. It is very important to them that everyone, whatever his or her beliefs, feels comfortable about the proceedings and respects the decisions they have made. Above all they want friends and relatives to be a part of their day and witness their commitment to each other.*'

Brothers of the bride and groom each gave a reading, then the couple repeated marriage vows similar to those used in a church service but without any mention of God. They exchanged rings, and music was played while they signed a register. The proceedings concluded with the bride's sister reading from an American Indian ceremony: '*Now you will feel no rain, for each of you will be shelter for the other. Now you will feel no cold, for each of you will be warmth to the other. Now there is no more loneliness. Now you are two persons, but there is only one life before you. Go now to your dwelling to enter into the days of your life together. And may your days be good and long upon the earth.*'

You can choose from a wide selection of poetry and readings, and whichever type of music you like to enhance the proceedings. Contact the British Humanist Association★ for more details.

If you are considering having a humanist ceremony it is a good idea to explain in advance to your guests, perhaps in an explanatory note sent out with the invitations, exactly who humanists are and what they believe. You should also remember that such a ceremony may not be entirely acceptable to others, such as your parents, particularly if they would prefer you to have a ceremony that meets their own religious beliefs.

Chapter 16

Organising the reception

The reception accounts for a large percentage of the cost of the wedding. The exact amount depends on how long the reception lasts, the number of guests, the venue and the type of meal and entertainment. To determine what sort of reception you would like ask yourselves:

- **how formal should the reception be**? This will affect your choice of venue, food and drink
- **how long will it last**? Shorter receptions are just as enjoyable as those that continue into the early hours of the morning and leave both you and your guests less tired. This can be an important factor if you are setting off on a long journey to your honeymoon destination that day
- **what time of day will the reception begin**? The meal served will depend on the time of day you get married. Many people marry in the mid-afternoon so that they can serve an early evening meal followed by entertainment. However, you could have a late-morning ceremony followed by a lunch and leave during the afternoon
- **how many guests will be at the reception**? Some people have a fairly brief reception immediately after the wedding for a small number of close family and friends, then throw a big party for everyone else on their return from honeymoon, while others have a quiet ceremony but invite more people to come along to all, or part, of the reception

Juliet and Peter

Juliet and Peter had intended to fly off to the USA on the evening of their wedding day. In the end we had to change our plans because we couldn t get on the flight we wanted. I was very glad about this when it came to the day because although our reception, a sit-down lunch in a restaurant, ended at 5pm, I was feeling exhausted by then. Neither of us had slept well for the previous couple of nights with pre-wedding nerves, we d both been up since 7am rushing around getting ready, and I d hardly sat down during the reception because I was busy going round the tables talking to friends. We took a taxi from the reception to a good hotel, where we unwound over a light supper and spent the evening lazing about and talking over the day.

Choosing a venue

Popular venues include hotels, restaurants, function rooms in pubs and sports clubs, village halls, marquees, your own or your parents' home. When you book a venue, confirm all the details in writing and leave nothing to chance. You can copy and complete the venue checklists given on pages 156 and 157. The hotel checklist includes space for details of food, wine and entertainment, as these would be part of the total package. If you are using another type of venue, you will find separate checklists for food, drink and entertainment on pages 165, 168 and 181.

Before you settle on any restaurant or hotel, have a meal there so that you can judge whether the food is good, the facilities adequate and the atmosphere right.

Wherever you hold your reception, check the following:

- is the room you would use large enough? Allow at least one square metre per person
- are there enough toilets and sufficient cloakroom space?
- are there plenty of parking spaces?
- are there facilities for disabled guests or people who are elderly and frail? Some seating should be available even if the guests are to remain standing at the reception

- is a separate room available where children could be entertained?
- how far is the reception venue from the place where the ceremony will be held? Try to keep the distance reasonably short.

Hotels

Most hotels can comfortably accommodate wedding parties of 50 to 100 guests, and some can cater for substantially more. At places where wedding receptions are held frequently, you should be able to arrange a package that includes all the catering, catering staff, wine and other drinks; the fee may also cover flowers, entertainment and a toastmaster. Check whether the venue can supply a cake stand and knife, a room where you can change into your going-away clothes, overnight accommodation for guests who need it and a safe place for displaying your wedding gifts.

The benefit of having your reception in a hotel is that you do not have to organise so much yourselves as the hotel will arrange the food, drink, entertainment and so on. Also, if you have chosen to have your civil wedding ceremony at a hotel, you will not have to travel anywhere to get to the reception. However, hotels can be an expensive option; they can be rather impersonal, especially if a large number of receptions are held there; you may have to share some facilities if another reception is taking place on the same day; hotels often need to be booked many months in advance; and there may be restrictions on the amount of time you can spend there.

Hotel checklist

Name of hotel	
Address	
Telephone/fax	
Contact	
Date booking made	
Confirmed in writing	
Number of guests	
Time of arrival at venue	

Time of departure from venue	
Which rooms have been booked?	
Bar facilities	
Cloakroom/toilet facilities	
Any shared facilities?	
Heating requested	
Toastmaster booked	
Who will provide flowers?	
Where will flowers be put?	
Other decorations	
Where will gifts be displayed?	
Are they insured at the hotel?	
Where will bride and groom change?	
Is a room available for children?	

Food

Type of seating plan agreed on	
Which dishes will be served?	
Any special dietary requirements?	
Number of children's portions	
How many serving staff will be available?	
What time will the meal be served?	
Cost per head of food	

Drinks

	Type of drink	Quantity	Cost per bottle
On arrival			
With the meal			
After the meal			

Evening bar			
Arrangements			
Total cost of drink			£

Entertainment

Background music provided by			
From (time)	To (time)		Breaks
Cost	£		
Dance music provided by			
From (time)	To (time)		Breaks
Cost	£		
Children's entertainment provided by			
From (time)	To (time)		Breaks
Cost	£		

Summary of Costs

Total cost of food	£
Total cost of drink	£
Total cost of entertainment	£
Cost of hiring the venue	£
Other items (make a detailed list)	£
	£
	£
	£
	£
	£
Service charge	£
Tips	£
VAT	£
TOTAL COST	£
Deposit paid	£
Balance due	£

Halls

If you have a smaller number of guests and a tight budget, consider hiring a hall or function room. Although rooms like these can be very well decorated and equipped, this is not always the case, so do pay a visit and check the facilities before making a booking. You will pay a fee for hiring the hall but will have to arrange catering and entertainment etc. yourself. Check:

- if there are any rules about the consumption of alcohol and smoking on the premises
- that the hall can be heated adequately
- whether you need to hire crockery, glasses etc.
- what facilities exist for preparing and serving food: for example, how much refrigerator and worktop space is available; whether the facilities for clearing away and washing up are good; and if you want hot food whether there are enough ovens
- that the seating is comfortable and there is enough of it
- whether there is a separate room where you can change
- that the venue's insurance covers loss of or damage to gifts
- how far ahead you need to book
- that someone can show you where everything is and how it works in advance
- how long before the event you can get access for decorating the hall and for caterers to set up.

Other hired venues

These include restaurants, or rooms in stately homes, castles, river boats, and so on. The number of possible venues to choose from is enormous, especially if you want to hold your reception somewhere a bit different.

Points to remember are:

- your favourite restaurant may be able to offer superb food, but you need to check that it also has facilities for changing, parking and so on. You also need to make sure that the tables can be arranged so that, ideally, everyone can see the bride and groom. There may not be space for dancing or any sort of live entertainment

- if you book a sumptuous room in a historical building you may have to hire many extra items, such as food and drink, tables, chairs, cutlery and crockery, glasses, serving staff, ovens and refrigerators. Even if the fee for the room itself is reasonable, these extras can add dramatically to the overall cost, so work out your budget carefully before committing yourself
- you need to check any time restrictions. Restaurants, for instance, often ask wedding parties to leave by about 5pm so that they can clear the room and lay the tables for the evening.

Venue checklist

Name of venue	
Address	
Telephone/fax	
Contact	
Date booking made	
Confirmed in writing	
Number of guests	
Time of arrival at venue	
Time of departure from venue	
When is access available before the reception?	
What are the arrangements for clearing away/locking up?	
Is smoking allowed?	
Is there a licence to serve alcohol?	
Parking facilities	
Cloakroom/toilet facilities	
Bar facilities	
Kitchen facilities	
Tables/chairs available?	
What do we need to hire separately?	

Heating requested	
Where will flowers be put?	
Who will supply them?	
Other decorations	
Who will arrange the flowers and decorations?	
Where will gifts be displayed?	
Where will bride and groom change?	
Is a room available for children?	
What does the cost include?	
VAT	£
TOTAL COST	£
Deposit paid	£
Balance due	£

Hiring a marquee

Those who wish to hold their reception at home but who do not have enough space inside the house can hire a marquee. However, you do need a large open space to accommodate it and it can be as expensive as holding the reception at a hotel (depending on the size and quality of the marquee). Marquees are ideal in late spring, summer and early autumn but you can have one in winter as long as you have adequate heating. If you choose this option you have to arrange catering, drinks, decorations etc. yourself.

Marquee checklist

Name of supplier	
Address	
Telephone/fax	
Contact	
Date booking made	
Confirmed in writing	
Size	
Number of guests	
When will the marquee be erected?	
Electricity Supply	
Flowers and decorations	
When will the marquee be removed?	
Cost of marquee	£
Extras booked	
Lining	£
Coconut matting	£
Dance floor	£
Spotlights	£
Chandeliers	£
Heating	£
Tables and chairs (no.)	£
Portable toilets	£
Other	£
VAT	£
TOTAL COST	£
Deposit paid	£
Balance due	£

The caterers will work in an adjoining tent (so allow for this when working out how much space you need for the marquee) and may need access to the kitchen in the house. You will also have to make sure that the marquee supplier provides enough electricity for them to cook and run a fridge. Once you have decided on your menu, the caterers will be able to tell you what equipment they will be using; you can then pass this information to the marquee supplier, who can then arrange the correct electricity supply. The marquee is usually put up three or four days before the event.

Checkpoints for hiring a marquee:

- if you are having the marquee in your garden, warn neighbours in advance about the influx of guests, noise levels and increase in demand for parking
- it is useful, particularly in cold or wet weather, to be able to walk straight out of your house into the marquee. It is ideal if you have French windows that can open directly into the marquee, but if you don't the marquee provider can construct a covered walkway from one of the doors of the house
- extras, which add to the cost of the marquee, include: lining, coconut matting, dance floor, chandelier lighting, heating, tables and chairs, portable toilets
- you will have to pay VAT but may be able to save on the overall cost by booking well in advance
- if you would like to have hanging baskets, the marquee provider can put in place ropes from which to hang them
- a 25 per cent deposit is usually requested on booking and is non-returnable.

Holding the reception in your house/flat

Home-based receptions involve a lot of work for the organisers but can have a very relaxed and informal atmosphere. The cost is relatively low, especially if you produce the food yourself. However, if you do not want to take on the job of feeding everyone, you can hire a caterer.

Checkpoints for having the reception at home:

- be realistic about the number of people you can accommodate in comfort

- check whether you have enough crockery, tables etc. If not you may be able to borrow or hire them
- if you are going to hire caterers, make sure you have adequate facilities for them
- enlist lots of help from family and friends and delegate as much as you can
- tell neighbours well in advance about the increase in noise levels and demand for parking.

Home checklist

Number of guests	
Parking arrangements	
Which rooms will be used?	
Cloakroom/toilet facilities	
What arrangements have been made for flowers and other decorations?	
What items do we need to hire? (list them)	
Who will help?	

The food

Having decided on the venue, the next decisions you need to make are what sort of food to serve and who will prepare it. If you are using a hotel or restaurant, the food will be prepared as part of the overall package, and you will be offered a choice of menus for different types of meal, each priced per head. For other venues you will probably want to use an outside caterer.

Choosing a caterer

Book early, but not until you have compared various services and received several estimates. Personal recommendation is always preferable, otherwise you should follow up references from any caterers you are considering. Once you have chosen a caterer, you will need to supply the following information:

- the date and time of your reception
- the facilities available at the location
- the budget per head and estimated number of guests
- the kind of meal you would like
- whether any guests have special dietary requirements (although this information may not be available until you have had replies from all your guests)
- whether you would like them to supply champagne and wine (see page 166–7).

Most caterers will supply you with a number of sample menus to choose from and should be able to add any other dishes that you particularly want. Check whether the price includes:

- tables and chairs
- table linen
- crockery, cutlery and glasses
- flowers
- serving staff
- cloakroom attendants
- clearing up after the event.

Also check whether:

- for a buffet, you are being charged per person or per plate. Some caterers charge extra for second helpings
- bread, for example, is charged as an extra
- you are expected to pay for the catering staff to have a meal during the reception
- VAT is included
- tips are expected or if a service charge is added to the fee.

Sort out all these points before you confirm the price, both verbally and then in writing. Tell the caterers of any last-minute additions or deletions to the guest list. You will be expected to pay for the number of meals ordered, even if on the day some guests do not attend.

What sort of food?

When choosing the food for your reception, remember that, particularly with large numbers of people, you are catering for a wide range of tastes. If you want to choose some adventurous options, make sure you also include some dishes that appeal across the board. It is wise to include a vegetarian option as well, and some plainer food for children.

Sit-down meal

This is the most formal, and most expensive, option. Although it provides a welcome opportunity for guests to sit down, it also limits their chances to mingle, due to the constraints of a seating plan (see pages 171–2). For a reception that continues for several hours, however, a sit-down meal provides a good opportunity for guests to relax for a couple of hours before the entertainment begins.

Buffet meal

A buffet meal can be cheaper than a sit-down meal as you need only one or two people to serve the food from the main table (unlike a sit-down meal, where you need a number of people to serve at each table). If you prefer, guests could help themselves. Buffet food can be just as substantial as a sit-down meal, but it is perhaps easier to provide a wider choice, such as a vegetarian option, a fish dish and a meat dish, with a variety of vegetables and salads. Guests can then choose exactly what they like. You could arrange a seating plan or let guests find their own seats once they have selected their food.

CanapØs and finger buffets

Trays of canapés and cocktail snacks can be taken round by catering staff and offered to guests. Choose foods that are easily managed with fingers if the food is to be eaten standing and serve everything in bite-sized portions, avoiding foods that crumble or drip.

For a finger buffet choose eight to ten different canapés and budget for 12 or more pieces per head. Cold foods are the easiest option, but a few hot items are always welcome. Hot canapés can be greasy, so serve them on sticks or mini forks and provide napkins. If serving them straight from trays, ensure that hot items are offered at a temperature suitable for eating immediately.

Tip

Double-check the portion sizes with caterers and err on the side of generosity. There is nothing worse than a buffet table that runs dry before everyone has been served.

Hiring a caterer checklist

Name of caterer	
Address	
Telephone/fax	
Contact	
Date booking made	
Confirmed in writing	
Number of guests to be served	
Number of children's portions	
What dishes are being served?	
Any special dietary requirements?	
Number of serving staff	
Does the cost include:	
Tables and chairs	

Table linen	
Crockery, cutlery and glasses	
Flowers	
Ovens	
Refrigerators	
Serving staff	
Cloakroom attendants	
Clearing up	
Are the caterers providing drinks? If so, what types and amounts are agreed?	
Corkage charge	£
How and when will caterers get access?	
Electricity supply needed	
Cost per head of food	£
Cost of drink	£
Extra costs (itemise)	
Service charge	£
Tips	£
VAT	£
TOTAL COST	£

Catering at home

Tackle this only if you are sure that you – or your friends and family – are happy to take on this extra task at an already busy time. If you feel you can cope, this is a good way to save money. Start the preparations well in advance and ask your neighbours and friends if they have any spare capacity in their freezers. Unless you are an accomplished caterer, go for simplicity.

You will also need to be able to make tea or coffee for your guests, so make sure you have the means to do this and hire anything you are lacking, for example a large urn for heating water, extra crockery or perhaps a large coffee filter machine. Remember to enlist people to help with setting up as well as clearing up, both during and after the reception. Keep a list of who is doing what, who has loaned what and what has been hired.

You will need a large table to lay out the buffet. Arrange the food in a logical order, either starting at one end and working down to the other, or starting at both ends and working towards the centre. Place plates, cutlery and napkins at the starting points.

One month or more before the wedding

- Finalise menu and start making any dishes that can be frozen.
- Make notes while you are making the food of anything needed for serving, such as garnishes or cream.
- Arrange to borrow or hire any equipment you need.

A week before the wedding

- Double-check that you have everything you need and confirm orders for hired items and drinks.
- Order bread for delivery/collection on the day.
- Make any dishes that can be refrigerated until needed.
- Two days before, buy perishables such as cheese, salads, fruit and cream.

The day before

- Take frozen dishes out of the freezer.
- Lay the buffet table and put out glasses, crockery and cutlery.

On the day

- Ask someone who is not going to the wedding to garnish the food and set it out on the table no more than two hours before it is to be eaten. Leave chilled dishes in refrigerator until shortly before serving.
- Prepare the salads
- Chill wines.
- Arrange hot dishes ready for reheating.
- Dress salads just before serving.

Catering at home checklist

Number of adult guests
Number of children

Food
Dishes chosen

Any special dietary needs

Dish	No. of portions	Who will prepare it?	Where will it be stored?	What is needed to serve it?

Other foods needed (bread, dressings etc.)

Crockery, cutlery etc.	How many are needed?	Borrow/ hire	Who from?

Setting out, serving, clearing away		
Task	When should it be done?	Who will do it?

The drink

If you have decided to hold your reception at a hotel or restaurant the drinks will almost certainly be provided as part of the overall package, and you will need to discuss which wines to serve when you make the catering arrangements.

If you are using caterers at home or at another venue they may also provide the wine, but it could be worth your while doing some cost comparisons, as you might be able to save money by providing the wine yourself. Caterers usually charge a corkage fee for handling and serving the drinks if you do this but they may provide glasses and ice. For a hired venue such as a hall or stately home, check that it has a licence to consume alcohol; if not, you can apply for a temporary (occasional) licence from the magistrate's court.

On arrival

It is usual to serve guests with a drink as soon as they arrive at the reception or have been greeted by the receiving line. Champagne, buck's fizz, sparkling wine or a choice of medium or dry sherry are all traditional, but a glass of red or white wine – or, in winter, mulled wine – would also be acceptable. Non-alcoholic drinks should be available throughout the reception for drivers, non-drinkers and children; these could include fruit juices, mineral water, soft drinks both fizzy and still, and, if you like, non-alcoholic wines and beers.

With the meal

You can limit the choice by serving sparkling wine, or even champagne if your budget can stretch to it, throughout the proceedings. Alternatively, you can serve a choice of red or white wine throughout the meal.

For the toasts

Champagne is the traditional choice, but many excellent sparkling wines are much cheaper.

After the meal

Most guests appreciate tea or coffee at the end of the meal. If the reception is going on into the evening you can continue to serve wine and non-alcoholic drinks or let guests choose their own drinks from the bar, if there is one. You can either foot the bill throughout the evening or pay for drinks up to a pre-arranged limit, after which guests buy their own. During a reception that goes on for several hours in the evening, it is a good idea to offer tea or coffee again, mid-way through the proceedings.

Providing the drinks yourself

This is a money-saving option if you are holding the reception at a hired venue or at home. Shop around local off-licences. Most will offer champagne and wine on a sale-or-return basis. If you live near a Channel port and have the time, it could be worthwhile buying your wine and champagne in France. Do some research before you go, and take a detailed shopping list with you – it is easy to get carried away, and the object is to end up making a saving. However, remember that you will have to provide proof at customs that the alcohol you are bringing back to the UK is for your wedding and not for re-sale.

Off-licences will often deliver the wine and supply glasses free if you order all your drink from them. You may even be able to return the glasses unwashed – it is certainly worth asking, as this can be a big chore. Hire enough glasses for one-and-a-half times the number of guests. For a reception held at home, put one or two people in charge of serving the drinks. At a hired venue you could consider hiring the services of a bartender, but check his or her references before booking.

Your off-licence or local supermarket may sell ice, or you might find a supplier who can deliver ice on the day through the *Yellow Pages*. To chill white wine and champagne, float bottles in plastic rubbish bins filled with ice and water. One case of wine takes an hour to cool, and you can move chilled bottles to the top of the bins and put more in underneath as you start to use them. Still white wine can be opened ahead of time, and the corks pushed gently back in until the wine is needed.

Providing the drinks yourself checklist

	What will be served?	Quantity	Cost
On arrival			
With the meal			
For the toasts			
After the meal			
Total cost of drinks	£		
Cost of glass hire	£		
Corkage	£		
Ice	£		
Bar staff	£		
Other costs			
TOTAL COST	£		

Estimating quantities

One bottle of wine serves six glasses, or twelve if it is being mixed with orange juice for buck's fizz. During a reception lasting three hours each guest will, on average, consume half a bottle of wine. This allows for those who drink far less than this. If the reception is going on for longer you should increase this allowance accordingly. It is always better to over-estimate (if you buy on a sale-or-return basis, you can always get a refund if you have any drink left over).

Hiring a toastmaster

For a formal wedding with a large number of guests you could consider hiring a toastmaster. Hotels will be able to organise this for you, or you may find someone suitable through the *Yellow Pages* or the Guild of International Professional Toastmasters.* A toastmaster announces the guests as they arrive, makes an announcement when the meal is to be served, introduces the speech-makers, announces the cake-cutting ceremony and tells guests what the order of events will be afterwards. The best man or another male guest can be asked to perform these tasks instead if you prefer.

Reception stationery and decorations

You can personalise your reception with printed items, ranging from menus, place cards, napkins and coasters to matchbooks, napkin rings, small boxes of sweets and ribbons. You will find a wide range of designs at stationers or specialist printers, who advertise in bridal magazines. Order items about three months before the wedding day. You can save money by writing menus and place cards by hand on plain white or coloured card. For information on where to use flowers at the reception, see page 99. Other decorations, such as banners or balloons, can be printed with your names and the date of the wedding if you wish. A cracker at each place is also a fun extra. An evening could end with fireworks if the venue is suitable. Look for companies who can put on a display in the *Yellow Pages*.

Chapter 17

At the reception

When planning your reception, it is vital to work out a careful timetable. Allow enough time for all the guests to arrive, be greeted and mingle whilst having a drink but do not keep them waiting too long before the meal is served (if you are having one). Allow for the meal to be served and eaten unhurriedly, then add some time for the speeches, toasts and cutting the cake. If you are leaving the reception at this point, the guests can mingle again while you get changed, and can then say their goodbyes. Otherwise, give an interval for people to move around and stretch their legs before they are seated again for any entertainment and dancing that is to follow the meal. Remember that the reception might start late if the ceremony overruns (which could be a result of the bride arriving late, the service taking longer than you thought or the photographs taking a long time). So build some contingency time into your timetable, just in case.

The receiving line

At a formal wedding you can have a full receiving line to greet guests as they arrive. If you are using a toastmaster he can announce the name of each guest. The traditional order for the receiving line is:

- bride's mother
- bride's father
- groom's mother
- groom's father
- bride
- groom
- best man (if he arrives at the reception from the church in time)
- chief bridesmaid.

Time spent talking to each guest should be kept brief, otherwise guests will have to queue. To prevent delays, and to give a more informal start to the reception, the two of you could greet the guests on your own or you could circulate among them as they arrive, making sure you talk to everyone present. You could ask guests to sign a wedding book (see page 75) at this point, and this might also be an opportunity for some more photographs to be taken while your guests are chatting.

Q *My parents divorced acrimoniously years ago and refuse to speak to each other, never mind stand together in the receiving line. What shall I do?*

A For a formal receiving line, they could stand in the following order: bride's mother, groom's father, bride's father, groom's mother. However, it is probably best to dispense with a formal receiving line altogether and greet the guests without your parents, who can mingle separately.

Seating plans

If you are having a sit-down meal (or perhaps a buffet) you will need to give some thought to a seating plan. Traditionally, the newly-weds sit with their families at the top table, sitting in the following order, from left to right facing the table:

- chief bridesmaid
- groom's father
- bride's mother
- groom
- bride
- bride's father
- groom's mother
- best man.

Although this is the convention, you can alter it to suit your needs, perhaps including another family member to partner an unaccompanied parent, for instance, or changing the positions of the best man and chief bridesmaid.

Q *My parents are divorced and re-married. How do I organise the seating plan for the top table?*

A If the wedding is being hosted by your parents, you could stick with the convention and seat your parents at the top table and your step-parents among the other guests. However, this may not feel right and, if everyone gets along reasonably well there is no reason why both parents and step-parents should not be seated at the top table.

As far as the other tables are concerned, people closest to the bride and groom should sit nearest the top table. The rule is that married couples do not sit together at wedding receptions. However, rules are made to be broken and you should seat people where you think they will be happiest. It is a good idea to mix up groups of say, friends and work colleagues among relatives and other guests during the meal, especially if the reception is going on into the evening, so that guests can meet new people, and friends will have a chance to catch up with each other later on. If the meal is the only opportunity people will have to socialise, you could seat friends nearer to each other.

Be especially thoughtful when seating people who have come on their own or who know very few people at the reception and place them next to someone who can be relied on to include them in the conversation.

Tip

Do not write out the master seating plan, which will displayed on the day, too early as guests may drop out at the last minute or ask if they can bring someone extra along. If this happens you may have to swap a lot of people round to accommodate the changes and perhaps write out the seating plan a second time.

Tom and Mandy

The only hiccup on Tom and Mandy's wedding day was that the hotel laid out the tables to a completely different plan from that agreed.

'We'd been offered a choice of two table layouts to accommodate our 100 guests. We'd chosen one and then spent hours working out who was sitting next to whom. When we walked into the dining room after the wedding and all the guests had taken their places we found the tables were facing the wrong way, so we did not have the view of the sea we'd wanted from the top table, and guests who were supposed to be sitting right next to the top table were as far away as was possible. Not only did the hotel not apologise, but they said that they could not fit everyone in using the configuration we'd asked for – which was one that they had originally suggested. My advice would be to double-check that everyone can be seated as you would like before you spend any time on the detailed seating plan, and confirm the arrangements a couple of days before.'

Toasts and speeches

As guests reach the end of the meal, the toastmaster, or best man if he is acting as master of ceremonies, asks for silence so that the speeches may be made. Some couples like to cut the cake before the speeches so that it can be sliced into portions while the speeches are being made and served with coffee immediately afterwards. Otherwise, you can have the cake cutting ceremony afterwards.

The main purpose of the speeches is to thank publicly everyone who has contributed to the success of the day; to introduce the toasts to the bride and groom and bridesmaids; to entertain the guests briefly with thoughts on marriage, reminiscences about the bride and groom and so on. The best speeches are brief. None should last much more than five minutes, and three minutes would be plenty for the bride's father and groom.

If you are nervous at the prospect of making a speech, remember that the guests will be warmly disposed towards you, and the happy atmosphere on the day will help to carry you along. A sincere speech, even if it is quite brief, will be well received. That said, no one who feels that the prospect of making a speech would ruin their day should be made to do so. If this applies to you, you could decide to give the very briefest of thanks before proposing the toast or even ask someone else who enjoys public speaking to give the speech in your place.

The bride's father

He is the first to speak and should keep his speech fairly brief and to the point. If, for any reason, the bride's father is not present, the person who gave her away, or another close relative, can be asked to give the speech instead. In his speech the bride's father should:

- greet the guests and thank them for coming
- congratulate the groom and welcome him into the family, perhaps also mentioning the groom's parents
- end the speech by proposing a toast to the bride and groom. This can be made to 'the bride and groom', 'the happy couple' or he can use the couple's names.

During his speech, the bride's father can talk about the pleasure he has had from raising his daughter and include one or two anecdotes about her childhood or growing up. He can also offer the couple advice on marriage, speaking from his own experience, if he wishes.

The groom

The groom replies to the toast on behalf of the bride and himself. His speech may be a little longer than that of the bride's father. He should:

- thank the bride's father for the toast. He should also thank the bride's parents for allowing him to marry their daughter and, if applicable, for their generosity in hosting the wedding
- thank the guests for attending the wedding and for their gifts
- say something about his good fortune in meeting his bride and his confidence in their future happiness together. He can include one or two anecdotes about their courtship if he wishes
- mention his own parents and thank them for all they have done for him both in bringing him up and in helping with the wedding preparations
- give special thanks to everyone who has helped with the wedding day, mentioning in particular any friends or family members who have made a special contribution, and the best man

- finally, praise the bridesmaids for their role during the day and propose the toast saying either, 'to the bridesmaids' or using their names.

The best man

The best man makes the final speech. He can speak for a little longer than the other two and can include one or two jokes or amusing anecdotes, bearing in mind his audience, which is likely to range from children to elderly relatives. However, he can also take the opportunity to say something more serious about his relationship with the groom and what it means to him. He should:

- thank the groom for the toast on behalf of the bridesmaids
- congratulate the newly-wed couple
- thank anyone connected with the wedding who has given him particular help
- end his speech with a toast to the bride and groom
- finally, read out any telemessages or cards that have been received, first vetting them for unsuitable comments. If there are a great many he could read one or two messages and list the names of other senders

---

Q *Can the bride make a speech? I don't like the idea of sitting in silence and would love the opportunity to say thank you as well for all the help we have had in the run up to the wedding.*

A There is no reason why you shouldn't make a speech, and an increasing number of brides choose to do so. You can speak before the groom and ask your father to give you an introduction, or after the groom, before the toast to the bridesmaids, which means the groom will have to stand again to make the toast. Otherwise you could make your speech a little later in the proceedings, after the cake has been cut and before guests rise and move into a different room. Your speech can be similar in tone to the groom's, thanking your family and the guests, and saying something affectionate about your new husband.

Speeches at second marriages

The speeches at the reception of a second marriage are usually less formal, and the bride's father does not have to make a speech, as he will probably not have given his daughter away. He, or another friend or relative, may propose a toast to the bride and groom. Traditionally, this speech would be made by a man, but there is no reason why a woman could not make it if you prefer. The groom responds to the toast with thanks on behalf of himself and his new wife. It is inappropriate in either speech to mention previous marriages.

How to write and deliver a good speech

- The key to giving a good speech is to **plan it in advance**.
- **Don't write the speech out and read it word for word**, as this will make your delivery stilted. Instead, write key points with a few memory-jogging phrases for each on a series of numbered cards, which can be kept in your pocket until they are needed. Practise the speech beforehand so that it becomes very familiar, then use the cards as prompts to guide you through the speech. This method also allows you to improvise or add to the speech if something occurs to you on the day and will help to make the speech sound more spontaneous.
- **Organise your speech so that it gets off to a lively start and engages the audience's attention**. The middle section should be the longest, and you should conclude with a neat lead in to the toast at the end.
- **Make a special note of all the people you have to thank**, with links or brief anecdotes next to them.
- **Read the draft of your speech out and time it**. Then leave the draft for a day or two before looking at it again.
- **Keep the speech short and to the point** without being brusque. Don't tell long-winded jokes or anecdotes. Brief stories, which arrive quickly at their point, are the best.
- **Be careful about jokes**, especially if you are making them at someone else's expense. It is acceptable for the best man to raise

a laugh at the groom's expense if it is done affectionately, but you should steer clear of humorous references to the bride's mother or the bride. Jokes should be kept clean and mild. One-liners are often more effective than longer jokes.

- You can learn a lot about how to improve your delivery simply by **taping the speech and listening to it carefully**. You can also try it out on trusted friends and judge the effect of any jokes or anecdotes you plan to use.

- On the day, **do not have more than a couple of drinks before making your speech**. When the moment comes, try to relax, take a few steadying breaths before you rise, and smile at your audience as you begin to speak.

- **Stand naturally, with your hands at your sides, or in front of you holding your prompt cards**. Do not grasp your lapels or lean forward with your hands resting on the table.

- When delivering the speech **aim to sound neither pompous nor overly informal**. Even at a very relaxed reception a certain level of formality is appropriate for the speeches. Use everyday language rather than formal expressions but avoid slang and clichés.

- **Use your normal voice, not an assumed accent or 'stage' voice**. Keep your head up and speak clearly and not too fast.

- **Remember to breathe normally, and pause slightly between sentences to breathe**. People often 'forget' to breathe when they are nervous, and you can find yourself running out of breath towards the end of a sentence.

- **Keep your gaze just above the heads of your audience** and do not stare round at doors, windows or the ceiling. When mentioning anyone specifically or proposing a toast you should look towards the person concerned without staring or making them feel uncomfortable.

- You could look at one of the several **books of wedding speeches** – available from bookshops and libraries – for inspiration, although it is not a good idea to copy a speech verbatim. If you prefer to write a speech from scratch, books of suitable quotations, anecdotes and jokes both for weddings and for after-dinner speeches can provide material that you can weave in among stories of your own.

Cutting the cake

Once the speeches and toasts are over, the best man, or toastmaster, announces the cutting of the cake. The bride holds the cake knife and the groom puts his hands over hers to make the first cut. It is helpful if the cut has been discreetly started beforehand, so that you do not have to struggle to get the knife through hard icing. Photographs are usually taken at this point. One cut is all that is needed, then the cake is taken away and cut into small portions which are distributed by the bridesmaids and pages or by the waiters and waitresses.

Entertainment

You can arrange background music – either live or recorded – while the guests are arriving and eating. At a longer reception, you will also need music for dancing in the evening.

Ask for recommendations and look at advertisements in wedding magazines and the *Yellow Pages*. Try to attend a performance, or at least listen to a tape, by any musicians you are considering hiring before booking them and discuss the sort of music you have in mind to make sure it is within their range. The cost will depend on:

- how many players are involved
- how busy they are
- how long you want them to play for
- how far they have to travel
- whether you ask them to learn any new items specially for the occasion.

Confirm in writing details of the date, venue, amount payable, cancellation policy, length of time for playing and for breaks.

Orchestras, bands and groups

Hiring an orchestra or band is ideal if you have a large number of guests and want dancing to live music. Most musicians who play regularly at weddings have a suitable repertoire, which should be varied in order to appeal to the wide age range at the wedding. A barn dance or Ceilidh are other options, for which you can use recorded or live music, but you would need to hire a caller to direct the dances.

You should find out what the musicians' policy on taking breaks is. Do they provide recorded music to be played while they are having their breaks or do they let one person at a time rest while the others continue playing? You will probably want some form of music to fill in the gaps if the musicians do have their breaks at the same time so it is best to know in advance if you have to make your own arrangements for this.

Ensembles and soloists

These are good for background music at a smaller venue or in addition to dance music at a large reception. You could choose a pianist, flautist, harpist, string ensemble, jazz musicians, steel band, fiddlers, medieval minstrels or singers.

Recorded music, discos and DJs

Live entertainment is not cheap, and you can keep costs down by using recorded background music. A hotel may have a selection of suitable CDs which can be played over a sound system, or at other venues you can put together your own recorded music and ask a friend to play it over your own sound system or one which has been hired or borrowed. You can provide dance music in the same way.

Using a DJ who provides a sound system and selection of music is another good way to entertain your guests and is cheaper than using live musicians. Make sure the DJ knows the types of music you want and understands that the volume must not be too loud.

Dancing

Traditionally, the bride and groom dance alone together for a few minutes before other guests join in. During the evening the bride should dance with all the men in the family party, and the groom with the women. The best man should also dance with the women of the wedding party, including the bride. In the intervals between dances the couple should circulate together and separately and make sure they speak to everyone present, taking the opportunity to thank any who have been particularly helpful towards making the day a success.

Suitable music for the first dance

- 'Hawaiian Wedding Song' sung by Andy Williams
- 'When a Man Loves a Woman' sung by Percy Sledge
- 'The First Time Ever I Saw Your Face' sung by Roberta Flack
- 'My Love' sung by Paul McCartney
- 'We've Only Just Begun' sung by The Carpenters
- 'Wonderful World' sung by Louis Armstrong.

Entertainment for children

If you are having a large number of children at your wedding reception, remember that they might get bored so it could be worthwhile arranging entertainment specifically for them. If your budget allows, you could hire a professional entertainer, who could also look after them during the ceremony if you like (look in the *Yellow Pages*). Otherwise, you could arrange for a few helpers to keep an eye on the children while they are playing in a separate room. The parents of the children might be able to help on a rota basis, so that no one misses too much of the reception.

Entertainment possibilities include:

- **a professional children's entertainer** – perhaps a clown, magician, Punch and Judy or other puppet show. Some entertainers offer party packages which are intended for children's birthday parties but could be adapted for a wedding
- **a bouncy castle**
- **a children's disco**
- **a selection of videos** for the children to watch. Feature-length cartoons are popular
- some companies, such as the Wedding Crèche Service, offer an **'activity crèche'** service, where children are looked after for you and kept occupied with toys, games, storytelling, music, face painting, playdough and crayons or even gym equipment.

Entertainment checklist

Name of musicians for background music	
Address	
Telephone/fax	
Contact	
Date booked	
Confirmed in writing	
Arrival time	
Play from:	To:
Breaks agreed	
Where will the musicians perform?	
Particular items requested to be played	
COST	£
Deposit paid	£
Balance due	£
Name of musicians/DJ for dance music	
Address	
Telephone/fax	
Contact	
Date booked	
Confirmed in writing	
Arrival time	
Play from:	To:
Breaks agreed	
Where will the musicians perform?	
Particular items requested to be played	

COST	£
Deposit paid	£
Balance due	£

Name of children's entertainer	
Address	
Telephone/fax	
Contact	
Date booked	
Confirmed in writing	
Entertainment agreed	
Arrival time	
Entertain from:	To:
Breaks agreed	
Where will the entertainment take place?	
VAT	
COST	£
Deposit paid	£
Balance due	£

Leaving the reception

Towards the end of the festivities the best man should tell you when it is time to change. The chief bridesmaid can help the bride, and she or the bride's mother can take charge of the bride's dress. The best man takes care of the groom's clothes, returning any hired clothes by the agreed date.

The best man makes sure your transport is ready and announces that you are ready to leave. The guests gather at the door and may throw confetti or flower petals. The bride tosses her bouquet, or a posy of flowers removed from it, into the crowd, and everyone follows the couple outside to give them a final send-off as they drive or are driven away. The couple's departure is the signal for the guests to begin leaving, and indeed no one should have left before this (although this does not apply if the party goes on until the early hours of the morning and the couple plan to stay until the end. If this is the case, it would be a good idea for the best man to announce this during the speeches).

Now is the time to settle the bill and check that nothing has been left behind by guests. The bride's parents, best man or chief bridesmaid remove the remains of the cake, the couple's wedding clothes, telemessages and cards and any flowers which they would like to take home. They also arrange for the wedding gifts to be taken somewhere for safe keeping until the couple return from honeymoon. The hosts and best man are the last to leave the reception.

Chapter 18

Insurance

When you are planning your big day, insurance will probably not be at the top of your list of things to organise, but it is worth setting some time aside to check that you will not lose out financially if anything goes wrong.

Whether or not you choose to buy one of the specialist wedding policies depends on how much money you will be investing in your wedding and the kind of mishap you are worried about. You should also bear in mind that while wedding insurance covers you up to – and including – the day itself, it does not cover you afterwards. So since you may be making large purchases (such as engagement and wedding rings) several months before the wedding and you will have your rings and wedding presents for a long time afterwards, you should check that your existing house contents insurance covers you for these things.

Do you need wedding insurance?

The main reason for buying wedding insurance is to cover yourself against the cost of having to cancel or reschedule your wedding. So whether this sort of insurance is worthwhile depends to a large extent on the cancellation fees your suppliers will charge you and whether they will waive the fees if you subsequently reschedule the wedding.

A wedding insurance policy will not cover you if you have to cancel simply because either of you has had a change of heart, or reimburse you if you knew you were going to cancel before you took out the insurance. However, in the main you will find that you can buy cover against unforeseen disasters that cause you to cancel:

- the death, illness or injury of the bride, groom or a relative – but check the definition of 'relative' carefully because it varies from policy to policy
- the inability of one of the above to attend the wedding because of jury service, redundancy, cancelled leave (if in the Armed Forces) or, with some policies, extreme weather conditions (such as being snowed in and unable to get to the wedding as a result)
- failure of suppliers (e.g. florists, caterers, wedding cars, photographers and so on) because they have gone out of business – but note that you will not be covered if a supplier simply fails to meet the terms of your contract and is still in business. This is because you can sue instead (see 'When things go wrong' on page 190)
- the ceremony or reception venue no longer being available for you to use
- being unable to find replacements for lost or damaged wedding dress, hired suits and bridesmaids' dresses.

Tip

The best insurance against failure of suppliers to deliver, is to choose reputable firms, to ensure that you have a clear written agreement and – if possible – to avoid making full and final payment until after the delivery of goods and services.

You will also find that most policies will pay out:

- for the cost of arranging alternative transport because the wedding car did not turn up
- if you managed to avoid cancelling the wedding by getting a different supplier to do the job – the most you can claim is typically 25 per cent of the original supplier's invoice
- for loss of deposits you have paid to suppliers who fail to deliver goods or services (because they have gone out of business)
- for the loss of deposits paid for live entertainment if the entertainment does not arrive (for whatever reason)
- for replacing or repairing the wedding rings (but not the engagement ring), wedding clothes (of key people) and wedding presents

if they are lost, stolen or damaged (although you may already have this cover – see 'Cover outside the home' on page 188)

- if you need to re-stage the wedding to take photographs or record a video because the original film or negatives were lost or damaged (however, no policy will pay out to re-stage the photography just because you were disappointed with the results)
- for the legal expenses involved in defending your case if you are sued by a supplier for damage you or one of your guests caused or – less probably – if a guest sues you. (However, if you are holding your reception at home, your legal liability if people injure themselves when visiting you is already covered by your contents insurance – see page 188)
- if you hire a marquee and your supplier tells you that you are responsible for insuring against damage to it. Note that this cover may be offered as an add-on for which you will have to pay more.

Tip

If you know you would not want to re-stage your wedding just for the photographs but would be disappointed if you had no record of your big day, consider appointing a friend who is good at photography to step into the breach if the need arises. Alternatively, ask your wedding guests for copies of photos they may have taken.

Where to buy wedding insurance

If you are offered wedding insurance by one of your suppliers, do not take it until you have compared the policy cover with those offered elsewhere. Although only a handful of policies exist, they do vary. If, for example, your main worry is the cost of cancellation, it would be sensible to find a policy that gives a broad definition of 'relative'. You will also find that the limits for what will be paid out in the event of a claim are higher with some policies than with others or that you can select different levels of cover to suit your particular wedding arrangements.

To get an idea of what is on offer, consult *The Insurance Buyer's Guide to Schemes, Packages and Unusual Risks* – try your nearest large public library. This will also tell you whether you can buy direct from an insurer or whether you have to go through a broker or other insurance intermediary. Whichever policy you choose, expect to pay from about £50 for a standard policy to over £200 for deluxe cover.

Why you should check your existing insurance

There are two main reasons for looking at your existing insurance:

- to see whether you really need to buy special wedding insurance (see pages 184–6)
- to make sure that you have sufficient insurance for those things that a special wedding policy will not cover.

Cover for valuables

It is unlikely that you will find wedding insurance that will cover your engagement ring, and you will also find that the wedding rings are covered only if they are lost or damaged in the week leading up to the wedding. So as soon as the engagement and/or wedding rings have been bought, you should make sure that your existing contents insurance provides enough cover in case they are lost, damaged or stolen. Many contents policies have what are called 'single item' limits for valuable belongings – £1,000, for example – although it might be lower or higher. The limit represents the most that will be paid out in the event of a claim, even if the cost of replacing each ring is more than your insurer's single-item limit. You should also check the limit if your wedding dress is particularly costly.

Tip

Make sure that your fiancé(e) keeps the receipt for each ring since it may be needed as evidence if you do ever have to claim for its loss. If the ring is an antique (and so could not be replaced as new), get it professionally valued: the Incorporated Society of Valuers and Auctioneers* can provide you with a list of valuers who will undertake insurance valuations. Whether your ring is antique or new, it is a good idea to take a photograph of it (this will help to identify it if it is ever stolen).

Cover outside the home

Because you will be wearing your ring(s) when you are away from home, it is worth finding out whether you have 'all risks' cover (sometimes called 'cover away from the home'). If you do not already have this cover, expect to pay more for your insurance and note that there may be a different single-item limit so check that too. The advantage of buying an all-risks extension to your contents policy is that your belongings are usually covered when you are abroad, and some insurers will give you a discount on your travel insurance, which could be useful for the honeymoon.

It is also worthwhile checking your insurer's single-item limits and all-risks cover if you are expecting to receive particularly valuable engagement and wedding presents. This is especially important if you plan to put them on display at the reception: if you do not have all-risks cover, you may not be able to claim if something happens to them on the way to the reception venue – although this is less of a problem if your reception is held at home.

Tip

If you are getting married abroad, it is unlikely that standard travel insurance will provide the level of cover you will need to replace your rings, the wedding dress (and other wedding clothes) and any wedding presents that you may receive should they fail to arrive at your destination or get stolen. So in addition to travel insurance, you should make sure you arrange an all-risks extension to your contents policy (which will provide better cover for your belongings than travel insurance).

Checking your contents policy

You may also need to increase the total amount you have your contents insured for (to include your rings and presents). Some house contents policies automatically provide extra cover for weddings, but for a limited amount of time only – 30 days each side of the wedding day, for example, but check your policy to make sure. With other policies, you will need to increase your cover and possibly pay a higher premium. If you are getting married in your parents' home town and a large number of presents are being brought to your wedding, it is likely that you will need your parents to look after these presents until you get back from your honeymoon. If this is the case, you will need to check your parents' house contents policy as well as your own.

Tip

If your reception is to be held at home – and especially if you are hiring outside suppliers – it is worth informing your existing insurers that this will be the case. If anything is damaged or goes missing during the reception, your insurers could refuse to pay any claims you make on the grounds that you did not tell them that there were going to be a large number of people in the house.

Insurance for the honeymoon

If you are planning to go abroad for your honeymoon, you will need to organise travel insurance. The main reason for buying travel insurance is to cover yourself against the costs of emergency medical treatment while you are abroad and the potentially very expensive bill if you are legally required to pay damages to someone whose property you have damaged or whom you have injured while on your travels. You also need additional cover for cancellation, delayed or missed departure, legal expenses and personal accident. However, if you already have an all-risks extension to your house contents policy, you may not need a travel policy to cover your money and belongings and you may be able to get a discount on your travel insurance.

You also need to check that your policy covers you for taking part in any dangerous activities – scuba diving or white-water rafting, for example. However, what you consider dangerous and what your insurer considers dangerous may differ so to be on the safe side, ask whether your planned activity is covered. If it is not or if it is specifically excluded from the cover, find another insurer.

When things go wrong

If you buy wedding insurance, you have a measure of cover if your suppliers fail to deliver but only if it is because they have gone out of business. If they simply failed to deliver what you had ordered (and they are still in business) or failed to comply fully with the terms of your contract with them, insurance will not cover you because you can seek compensation directly from the supplier. The same is true if a wedding present you are given turns out to be faulty in some way.

The Sale of Goods Act 1979 (as amended) states that goods bought from a business must comply with their 'description' and 'be of satisfactory quality' so if you ask your florist to supply red roses, for example, you should not receive pink carnations; similarly, a spin drier you are given as a wedding present should spin. The Supply of Goods and Services Act 1982 (common law in Scotland) states that 'services' supplied by a business should be carried out with 'reasonable care and skill'. For example: hired cars should not break down, marquees should not collapse and the photographs should not be blurred. If you book your honeymoon through a tour operator, you have added protection against a substandard holiday or against the tour operator going bust in the form of the Package Travel Regulations 1992.

If you feel that your suppliers have let you down and it is not possible to get the problem sorted out before the wedding, you can ask your supplier not only to refund your money but also to compensate you for any additional expenditure you may have incurred as a result of their incompetence. You may also be able to claim for the loss of enjoyment you suffered. Where contractors know that they are providing services for a wedding, the loss-of-enjoyment factor will be greater than usual because of the one-off nature of the event. If you have a complaint, you should make your dissatisfaction known clearly and politely to the person in charge and you should follow this up in writing explaining what you want them to do to rectify the situation and the amount of financial compensation which you expect to receive. If your supplier ignores your complaint or fails to offer you satisfactory compensation, you can pursue the matter in the small claims court (sheriffs court in Scotland).

Chapter 19

Financing your future

In purely financial terms, wedded bliss is well worthwhile: as a married couple you are likely to pay less tax, your future pension will go up and, from the moment you sign your marriage certificate, you will automatically be entitled to at least some – if not all – of your spouse's wealth. How far your other finances are affected by marriage depends on more personal factors such as whether one or both of you decides to change your name, how joint you want your finances to be, how financially dependent one of you will be on the other and how keen you are to exploit the tax rules which favour the married state.

Some couples choose to draw up a pre-nuptial agreement, which covers how their assets would be divided in the event of a divorce. Although no one wants to consider divorce before they have even got married, some couples feel happier if they know where they stand financially. For more information on this, see pages 117–18.

Marriage and tax

Before April 1990, marriage meant that a man became responsible for his wife's tax affairs, and a woman's income from savings and investments was regarded as belonging to her husband so he had to pay the tax on it. Since then, however, husband and wife are treated as individuals, with each responsible for their own tax affairs. This means that you will still get your own slice of tax-free income (your personal allowance), pay your own tax bill and, if applicable, have to fill in your own tax return. Apart from having to tell your tax office if you change your name, in practical terms you will see very little difference in your dealings with the Inland Revenue. In financial terms, however, the tax system looks favourably on married couples:

- the amount of tax one (or both) of you pays will decrease because you will be able to claim a reduction in your tax bill in the form of the **married couple's allowance**
- you may be able to make extra **tax savings on your mortgage payments** in the first 12 months after you marry
- any **gifts** you make to each other will be free of tax
- you may be able to save tax by **rearranging the ownership of your savings and investments**.

The married couple's allowance

Despite its name, this extra personal allowance is automatically given to the husband unless you tell your tax office otherwise (see 'How to claim the allowance', opposite). How much tax you save in the year in which you marry depends on the date of your wedding: the earlier in the tax year you marry, the more tax you save (see 'How much is the married couple's allowance?', below). In the 1998–9 tax year, the basic married couple's allowance for a full tax year is £1,900, which represents a maximum tax saving of £285 (to make the allowance worth the same to all taxpayers, the most you can deduct from your overall tax bill is 15 per cent of the allowance – but this is due to go down to 10 per cent from 6 April 1999). In the tax years following the one in which you married, you get the whole of the allowance.

How much is the married couple's allowance?

If the date of your marriage is between:	You will get an allowance of:	Which represents a tax saving of:
6 April and 5 May	£1,900	£285
6 May and 5 June	£1,742	£261.30
6 June and 5 July	£1,584	£237.60
6 July and 5 August	£1,425	£213.75
6 August and 5 September	£1,267	£190.05
6 September and 5 October	£1,109	£166.35
6 October and 5 November	£950	£142.50
6 November and 5 December	£792	£118.80
6 December and 5 January	£634	£95.10
6 January and 5 February	£475	£71.25
6 February and 5 March	£317	£47.55
6 March and 5 April	£159	£23.85

The figures are for the 1998–9 tax year. Note that if you or your spouse is 65 or more at the start of the tax year in which you marry, you may be entitled to a higher married couple's allowance – check with your tax office.

How to claim the allowance

If you want to get the benefit of the married couple's allowance, you have to let your tax office know that you are married, which you can do either by phone or by letter. If you are an employee and therefore pay tax under the Pay As You Earn (PAYE) system, your tax office will change the code that tells your employer how much tax to deduct from your pay so you should see the effect of claiming the married couple's allowance quite quickly. If you are self-employed, the married couple's allowance will be taken into account when calculating your tax bill for the year, provided that you fill in the relevant boxes in the allowances section of your tax return.

Although the allowance is automatically given to the husband, you can choose either to split it equally between you (note that a wife can claim her half without her husband's consent) or to transfer the whole allowance to the wife. Electing for the wife to get the whole allowance is a good idea if the wife is an employee and the husband is self-employed because you get the tax saving more quickly. There is no advantage if you are both self-employed or if the wife does not pay tax.

If you want to change the way you share the allowance, you have until the end of the tax year in which you marry to notify your tax office. However, if you want to change the split in future tax years, you have to make the change before the start of the tax year to which you want the change to apply. Note that the deadlines are different if you want to transfer allowances because you have not made use of them – see 'Transferring surplus allowances', opposite.

When not to claim the married couple's allowance

Lone parents who have a child/children living with them whom they support financially can claim the additional personal allowance (worth the same as the full married couple's allowance but also due to be restricted to 10 per cent from 6 April 1999).

> **Tip**
>
> Do not put off contacting your tax office because you hate writing letters: claiming the married couple's allowance, changing the way it is shared between you or simply informing your tax office of the change in your marital state can all be done by phone. If you do not know the number, ask your employer or check any communications from the Inland Revenue.

If you are a man and you are getting married you can choose either to carry on claiming the additional personal allowance until the end of the tax year in which you marry or claim the married couple's allowance (you – as an individual – cannot claim both, although the exception to this is if you have children and your spouse is totally incapacitated). You will be better off continuing to claim the additional personal allowance if the wedding took place on or after 6 May (when the married couple's allowance starts to decrease – see 'How much is the married couple's allowance?', page 192). However, you cannot transfer the additional personal allowance to your wife.

If you are a woman, you can continue to claim the allowance for the rest of the tax year in which you married and you can also have half the married couple's allowance (which goes automatically to your husband) transferred to you.

> **Tip**
>
> If you have a child and you had not realised that you could have been claiming the additional personal allowance before your marriage, talk to your tax office. You can backdate claims for allowances for up to six tax years.

Transferring surplus allowances

If one of you does not have enough income to make full use of the tax savings that the married couple's allowance brings, you can transfer the unused part of the allowance to your spouse at any time during the tax year. It is also possible to transfer all – or any unused part – of the blind person's allowance (provided you qualify for it). If you get a tax return, you can transfer your allowances by completing the relevant boxes in the allowances section. If you do not get a tax return, contact your tax office so that it can make the necessary adjustments.

Extra tax savings on your mortgage

In the 1998–9 tax year the Inland Revenue will automatically pay 10 per cent of the interest payments on the first £30,000 of your mortgage (this may differ from year to year). Everyone, whether married or unmarried, will get this tax relief.

If you plan to sell your home either to buy a different joint home or because you are moving into your partner's home, you will carry on getting tax relief on your old home for 12 months after the wedding or until it is sold (whichever comes first). This is in addition to the tax relief you will jointly get on the new home. If you are both selling up, you each get tax relief on your old homes (for a maximum of 12 months or until you sell) as well as tax relief on the mortgage for your new home.

Warning

If you bought a property together (as single people) before 1 August 1988 you will find that you actually get less tax relief as a result of getting married. This is because before that date, while married couples had to share the £30,000 limit, single people had a limit of £30,000 each – so two single people buying a property together were able get tax relief on the first £60,000 of their mortgage.

Tax-free gifts

It may seem an odd concept that gifts attract tax at all but they do: in the form of inheritance tax for the recipient and capital gains tax for the person making certain sorts of gift (in general, things which can rise and fall in value such as antiques, property and shares). The tax rules for gifts largely exist to deter people from giving away their wealth before they die as a way of avoiding inheritance tax. So it is unlikely that you will have to tell your tax office about all your wedding presents – although it may be interested if they are very valuable. As soon as you are married, there is no need to worry about tax on anything you give to your spouse because gifts between husband and wife – whatever the gift is and whatever it is worth – are exempt from both inheritance tax and capital gains tax, which can work to your advantage (see below). The tax rules are also quite generous when it comes to wedding presents:

- before the wedding, the bride and groom can give each other gifts of up to £2,500
- each parent of the bride or groom can give one or other of them a gift up to the value of £5,000
- a grandparent (or great-grandparent) can give up to £2,500
- anyone else can give £1,000.

Note that if a gift exceeds the limits given above and the person making the gift dies within seven years of making it, there may be inheritance tax to pay but only if the donor's estate is worth more than a certain amount (£223,000 for deaths occurring in the 1998–9 tax year). If the gifts fall within the limits given above, there will be no inheritance tax to pay.

Tip

Strictly speaking, to qualify for their tax-free status, wedding gifts have to be made 'in consideration of the marriage' and 'conditionally on the marriage taking place', so encourage generous relatives to write you a letter which makes the reason for their gift clear.

Your savings and investments

Because husbands and wives are taxed independently of each other, you will see no change in the way your savings and investments are taxed. However, you may want to rearrange your joint finances to make the most of the tax concessions available to married couples.

- If you have **savings or investments in joint names** – a joint building society account, for example – the income is automatically treated as being paid to you in equal shares, with each of you being responsible for paying the tax on your own share. However, if you own the savings or investments in unequal shares, you can ask your tax office to tax the income on that basis – so if you paid in a third of the money held in a joint savings account and your spouse paid in two thirds, you can ask to be taxed only on one third of the income.

- Perhaps more worthwhile – **if you and your spouse pay different rates of tax or one of you pays no tax at all** – is to put the savings and/or investments solely into the name of the spouse paying less or no tax. However, you have to be prepared to relinquish control over the money you give to your spouse so think carefully if you are not happy to do this.

- If you make a lot of **capital gains** – you dabble in the Stock Market, for example – and you regularly make full use of your own capital gains tax exemption of £6,800 (in the 1998–9 tax year) consider giving your spouse any investment that you would want to sell to make use of the fact that you each get your own £6,800 exemption. However, this will not help if your spouse also makes substantial capital gains and/or refuses to sell.

Marriage and your pension

Although it is probably not at the forefront of your mind as you plan for your big day, your pension may receive a substantial boost as soon as you have tied the knot – particularly if you are a woman. If you belong to an employer's pension scheme, you are very likely to find that – without your having to increase your pension contributions – your spouse will automatically become entitled to receive a widow's or widower's pension and possibly a lump sum when you die. In its current form, the state pension scheme pays either a pension or an allowance and a small lump sum but only to widows (provided the husband has made sufficient National Insurance Contributions throughout his working life). This discriminatory – and somewhat anachronistic – practice is due to change in 2001 according to proposals announced by the government in

November 1998. Widowers will become entitled to state payments although most help will go to widowers with children.

If you have a personal pension, where your contributions build up a fund, this should be paid as a lump sum to your spouse in the event of your death. You can also arrange for your spouse to receive a pension if you die after retirement by buying what is called a 'joint life annuity'. The exception to this is where you have invested part of your National Insurance Contributions in a personal pension (these sorts of plans are variously called 'appropriate', 'rebate-only' or 'contracted-out' pension plans). These pension plans must make provision for a pension to be paid to your widow or widower (if 45 or over at the time of your death unless you have children).

Whichever sort of pension you have, make sure that the provider of it knows that you have married. You should tell the Contributions Agency★ (the government agency in charge of National Insurance Contributions) that you are now married as a matter of course.

Marriage, money and property: wills (England and Wales)

There is more to the toast 'health, wealth and happiness' than you may have imagined because (unless you live in Scotland, see opposite) as soon as you marry, your spouse automatically becomes entitled to at least £125,000 of all your worldly goods. This is because your marriage automatically declares any will you may have made as a single person null and void (in legal parlance, your marriage 'revokes' the earlier will). If you want to be confident that in the event of your death your spouse will get all your worldly goods, you will have to make another will in his or her favour. If you do not do this, the law decides how much he or she will get and shares out your estate – everything you own after subtracting debts and any jointly owned assets, such as your home – as follows (note that the amount of the limits given below may change from time to time):

- if your estate is worth less than £200,000 (less than £125,000 if you have children) your spouse gets everything
- if your estate is worth more than £200,000, your spouse gets £200,000 plus half the remaining estate. The rest passes to

whichever generation of relatives is still alive in this order: your parents, your siblings, your nephews and nieces. If there are no relatives to inherit the remainder of the estate, your spouse gets everything

- if your estate is worth more than £200,000 and you have children, your spouse gets £125,000 plus the right to the use of and/or income from (called a life interest) half the remaining estate. Your children get the rest.

As well as making sure that your wealth goes to those people you want to have it, making a will simplifies and shortens the process of sorting out your affairs. Making a new will after your marriage is particularly important if you have children from an earlier liaison and you want them to inherit part of your estate.

Making a new will is less urgent if your matrimonial home is your main asset and it is already in your joint names since half of it, if you are 'tenants in common', will pass to your spouse through the intestasy provisions; if you are 'joint tenants', the share will pass automatically to your spouse whether or not you make a will, i.e. by survivorship.

Tip

If you want to avoid the problem of being without a will from your wedding day until you have time to make a new one after your marriage, consult your legal adviser before your wedding. Your adviser should be able to draw up a specially worded will that will not be automatically revoked by your marriage. This should say that the will is made in contemplation of marriage to a named person and it should also specifically state that the person whose will it is (the testator) intends that the will shall not be revoked by his or her marriage to the named person.

Wills in Scotland

If your permanent home is in Scotland and you die without making a will, the rules are different from those in England, Wales and Northern Ireland. Your spouse gets the house or flat (up to £110,000 in value), furniture (up to a value of £20,000) and a cash sum of £50,000 provided that there are no children or other descendants. If there are, the cash sum is reduced to £30,000. Your spouse is also entitled to half (a third if there are children) the remaining 'movable' estate – which means anything that is not land or buildings. If there is anything left after that, the remainder goes to the nearest relatives of the person who died following this order: children, grandchildren, great-grandchildren then siblings and finally parents.

Tip

To find out more about tax and marriage, ask your tax office for leaflet IR80 *Income tax and married couples.*

Marriage and your joint finances

Although you have little say in the way marriage affects your tax, pension or right to inherit, it is entirely up to you whether or not marriage has an effect on your day-to-day finances. However, it is worth spending time talking about how you will organise your finances not least because it could spare you a few rows: according to a survey conducted early in 1998 for Relate★ (the relationship-counselling charity), money came top of the list of the reasons for marital strife, with nearly half the people in the survey saying that it was the most common cause of arguments.

If you were living together before you married, you will probably have come to some arrangement for sharing the household bills and other joint spending. However, if you are setting up home together for the first time, it would be worthwhile deciding:

- what you both agree is joint spending
- what you are each going to contribute to joint spending
- what you both agree is personal (and private) spending
- who is going to pay for what
- how you are going to share bills
- how you are going to share your assets – your home or shares, for example
- who is going to be in charge of the finances

- how you will agree spending priorities
- how you will make financial plans for the future – whether it is saving for a holiday or for when you have children.

Once you have decided all that, you will be in a position to see if you need to make any adjustments to your existing financial arrangements, such as making your bank account a joint one or arranging for your spouse to be the joint owner of your home.

Warning

According to Relate*, lack of openness in financial arrangements can be a major source of friction and can even point to an underlying lack of trust in other areas of your relationship. In the Relate survey, women were found to be particularly sensitive to trust and secrecy issues related to money.

Joint or separate bank accounts?

If you decide that you are going to pool your resources (whether in whole or in part) to pay for what you have decided is joint spending, you may find it useful to open a joint bank account. You can either run this along side your own personal current accounts – because you want to keep some of your finances separate and private, for example – or you can arrange for both your salaries (if applicable) to be paid into a joint account and close your sole accounts. An alternative, if you want to share everything with your spouse but you do not want to close your sole account – because it is convenient for work, for example – is to make both your sole accounts joint ones.

You will have to open the joint account together, but whether you both have to sign cheques is up to you. Once the account is open, you will each get your own cheque book, cheque guarantee card (provided the bank is happy to provide this straight away), payment and cash card (or 'multi-function' card which combines all three types of card). You will also become joint owners of the money in the account and jointly responsible for any debts (called 'joint and several liability'). This means that your current account provider can recover money to pay off debts from either account holder regardless of who actually spent the money.

The same is true if you arrange for your spouse to be an additional cardholder on your credit card. However, if you each have an existing credit card in your pre-marriage names, there is no particularly good reason for changing the arrangement – especially since having two different cards gives you more flexibility and possibly a higher joint credit limit. The only situation in which it could be worth making your spouse an extra cardholder on your credit card is if he or she has been refused a credit card of his or her own.

Warning

If you have a very different attitude towards money from that of your partner – one of you is a saver while the other is a spendthrift, for example – you may find it less stressful to keep your financial arrangements separate.

Medical insurance

If you have private medical insurance (which aims to pay for private health care) either through your job or that you have bought yourself, make sure that your employer or the insurer knows that you have married. If you want your spouse to benefit from the policy, you may find that it does not cost that much more to cover him or her under a joint policy.

Life insurance

If you want your spouse to benefit from any life insurance you have, you will need to tell your employers (if they provide death-in-service benefits) and also your insurers that you have married. It would also be a good idea to check that the policies are 'written in trust' to your spouse so that the proceeds will be paid directly to him or her. This has two advantages:

- the money can be paid more quickly
- the money does not count towards your estate for inheritance tax purposes.

Appendix:
Wedding law

Anyone getting married in the UK must meet the legal requirements, whether they are having a civil wedding or a religious wedding of any denomination.

The law in England and Wales

The basic rules that apply to all marriages in England and Wales are:

- the couple must be of different sexes
- you must be aged 16 or over but you need your parents' written consent if you are under the age of 18
- you must be free to marry, i.e. you must not be related to each other in any of the ways specified on pages 213–14. Also if either party has been married previously, the former marriage must have been ended by decree in the appropriate Court.
- you must have two witnesses
- the wedding must take place in a district register office, in any premises approved by the local authority for marriages (hotel, stately home etc.), in a church or chapel of the Church of England or Church in Wales, in a military chapel, a synagogue or in any other place of worship that has been registered by the Registrar General for England and Wales★ for the solemnisation of marriages.

The service may not be conducted privately – which means that the doors may not be locked during the ceremony, thereby preventing potential bona fide objectors being present. The marriage (both civil and religious) may take place on any day at any time between 8am and 6pm and need only be in front of two witnesses, who can be total strangers to each other and to you. (These restrictions do not apply to Jewish or Quaker weddings.)

The law in Scotland

Marriage law in Scotland differs in a few crucial ways. The minimum legal age is 16 whether you have parental consent or not.

There are no restrictions on the time or place at which a religious marriage can take place as long as the legal and civil requirements are met. In theory, you are free to marry outdoors at midnight if you can find an authorised minister to conduct the ceremony. If you want to get married on a boat it must be tethered, and if you are marrying in a hot-air balloon it must be anchored to the ground. However, civil weddings in Scotland must take place in a register office by arrangement with the registrar.

Documents required for marriage

For a civil wedding in the UK, when making a marriage application to the registrar you should take your birth certificate or passport. For a church wedding you will need to show your certificate of baptism to the minister (and confirmation certificate, in the case of the Roman Catholic Church). Most churches require at least one of you to be baptised. If you are marrying for the second time you will need to show your decree absolute or the death certificate of your former spouse. If you are under the age of 18 consent from your parents or guardians will normally be required.

Setting the date

Until very recently once you gave notice of your intention to marry to a registrar you would be issued with a certificate valid for only three months. But now, in the case of both civil and religious weddings in England or Wales, the date of the marriage can be set for up to a year in advance. In Scotland, however, setting the date has always been left to the discretion of the minister or registrar, providing the date meets with Scottish legal requirements.

Church of England weddings

If you are getting married in an Anglican church the form of service must be agreed with the minister. There are three permitted options: the traditional *Book of Common Prayer* service, the slightly revised (1966) form of that service or the modern language service from the *Alternative Service Book*.

Marriage by banns

You should agree the date of your wedding with the minister at the earliest opportunity. If either (or both) of you lives in the parish where you are to marry, the minister will arrange to have banns read in the church on three Sundays prior to the wedding. This is usually on consecutive Sundays and must be carried out within three months of the date of the wedding. It is customary for the couple to attend the service on those three Sundays to hear their banns read. The purpose of the banns is to make public your intention to marry and to invite any objections to the ceremony taking place. The fee for the calling of banns is £14 (in 1999). If one of you lives in another parish the banns must also be read in that church for which the same fee is charged, and in addition a banns certificate must be obtained from the minister of the second church, for which the fee is £8. In addition, you may choose to be married in the church where one (or both) of you worships and is on the church electoral role. In that event the banns must be called in that church and also in the parish or parishes where you both live.

Marriage by common licence

This is used where either (or both) of you is a national of a country outside the old Commonwealth, the European Community and the United States, or where there is insufficient time to call the banns. As with banns, one of you must be living in the parish where you are to marry, or be on the church electoral role, and the minister will be able to advise about applying for the licence. Where a licence has been obtained no banns are called, but an affidavit – verifying the details given and that there is nothing in law to prevent the marriage – has to be sworn. The affidavit must be sworn within the three-month period before the date of the wedding. You should note that common licences are not available if one of you has been divorced (and the former spouse is still living) and it is also a requirement that at least one of you must be baptised. The fee for a common licence is currently £53.

Marriage by special licence

This licence is issued on the authority of the Archbishop of Canterbury, and exceptional reasons why one of the other preliminaries on page 205 cannot be used must be given. It is generally used where neither of you is resident in the parish where you wish to marry or if the wedding is to take place in an unlicensed building, such as a private chapel. These licences are issued by the Faculty Office,★ which you should approach after consultation with the minister. Again, special licences are not available where one party is divorced, with a former spouse still living, or where neither party is baptised. The fee is currently £120.

Civil weddings in England and Wales

A civil wedding is one that takes place in a register office or other building approved for civil marriage.

Unless you are marrying in the Church of England or Church in Wales by banns or by common licence or special licence you or your partner must give notice to the superintendent registrar at the register office(s) for the district(s) where you live (not necessarily the register office where you are going to get married). This notice can be given either by certificate or by licence (see below).

You can give notice of your intention to marry a year in advance of the wedding day and can marry in any register office in England and Wales as long as you live in either country.

Marriage by certificate without licence

Both of you must have lived in a registration district in England and Wales for at least seven days immediately before giving notice at the register office (if you live in the same district you need only give notice once but if you live in different ones you must give notice in each).

When the superintendent registrar has accepted the notice, it is then entered into the marriage notice book and also displayed on a public notice board for 21 days. This provides the opportunity for anyone who has an objection to your proposed marriage to make a statement.

The fee for giving notice is £21 and this will have to be paid twice if you each live in separate districts. You will also have to pay a fee of £30 to the registrar for attending your marriage at a register office. After 21 days the superintendent registrar may issue a certificate of authority for the marriage to proceed. This is not the same thing as a marriage certificate, which you can request after your wedding, but a document that is held at the register office until the day of your wedding. If your notice of marriage is being displayed in two districts you must ensure both certificates of authority for the marriage are available prior to the wedding as you will be asked to produce them before the ceremony can go ahead.

The date of your marriage can then be set to take place at any time within a year of the date when notice was given. If you find that you wish to postpone the wedding beyond that time you will have to apply and pay for a notice (or notices) again.

Marriage by licence

If you cannot or do not want to wait for the 21 clear days to pass before marrying, you should apply for a superintendent registrar's certificate. If either one of you (it need not be both) has been a resident in a registration area for 15 days prior to giving notice and all your documentation is in order, a licence can be issued (the other party must be in England or Wales on the day notice is given). This means the marriage can take place after one clear working day following the day on which you gave notice of your intention to marry.

The notice of a marriage by certificate and licence is not posted publicly. There is an extra charge for the licence which means the marriage would cost £97.50.

Marriage in Scotland

For both civil and religious weddings in Scotland a minimum period of 15 days' notice must be given to the registrar in the district where the wedding is to be held, although four to six weeks' notice is preferred. Banns are no longer required for a religious ceremony. A schedule is then issued to the bride or groom up to seven days before the religious ceremony. It must be given to the minister before the service. For a civil wedding the schedule remains at the register office.

The order and content of the marriage service may be amended, and the minister or registrar may agree to the inclusion of non-scriptural readings of poems or prose. There is no residency requirement for marrying in Scotland.

Marriage in Northern Ireland

To be permitted to marry in a church, one of you must have been resident in a parish/district for seven days before giving notice of your intention to marry. To marry in a register office, one of you must have lived in a district for at least 15 days and the other for at least seven days.

Roman Catholic weddings

Anyone having a Roman Catholic wedding must give notice to the superintendent registrar (see pages 206–7), and in some cases the registrar must be present at the religious ceremony. Unlike Church of England or Church in Wales and Scottish ministers, Roman Catholic priests are not allowed to act on behalf of the State.

A Roman Catholic priest may insist on a lengthy period (usually at least six months) of notice of your intention to marry as it is regarded as essential for you to prepare properly for such a serious commitment. If the marriage is mixed (i.e. one of you is not Roman Catholic), the parish priest will have to apply for special permission on your behalf. Both ministers can attend the ceremony.

Jewish weddings

Jewish weddings can take place anywhere – in a synagogue, private house, hired hall or in the open air – as long as they are held under the *chuppah* or wedding canopy, which symbolises home, and the couple has the necessary legal documents (marriage licence or certificate for marriage, see pages 206–7). The ceremony can be celebrated at any time, except during the Jewish Sabbath (from sunset on Friday until sunset on Saturday) or on festival or fast days. It must also be performed in the presence of 10 men, and two witnesses who are not related to either bride or groom. Both the latter must be of the Jewish faith and free to marry. If either the bride or the groom is not Jewish, he or she must convert before getting married. The process is long and demanding, involving instruction and an examination. The Jewish wedding ceremony is recognised officially by the State. You can, however, if you wish, have a civil wedding and then have a religious ceremony at another time. Most couples, where both partners are Jewish, opt for a Jewish ceremony under Jewish auspices. The groom must be a member of the synagogue in which the couple is to marry.

Nonconformist or Free Church weddings

Nonconformist or Free Churches such as the Methodists, United Reformed Church, Baptists and Presbyterians and the Orthodox Church all require you to go to your local register office and apply to the superintendent registrar for either a licence or certificate (depending on the time you have available before you intend to marry). Whether you will need a registrar to attend the religious ceremony itself depends on whether there is a person in your place of worship licensed to act as a registrar (usually this is the minister) to witness your marriage. In addition to the 'authorised person' the marriage must be witnessed by at least two people.

Muslim, Hindu and Sikh weddings

See 'Nonconformist or Free Church weddings' for information.

Quaker weddings

The Religious Society of Friends has its own registering officer, who is allowed by law to witness the marriage and signing of the marriage certificate. Quakers wishing to get married must apply to the registering officer of the monthly meeting of the area in which they intend to get married. Ideally, they should do this at least three months before the planned date (and certainly no fewer than six weeks before). The couple must then complete a declaration of intention of marriage. All the legal requirements for a wedding in England and Wales or in Scotland must also be met. Notice of the intention to marry is then made public at the meetings.

If only one partner is a member of the Society of Friends the marriage is still usually permitted, providing two letters of recommendation can be produced from adult members of the society confirming their approval of the marriage.

Marriage certificates

On the day of your wedding at a register office or approved premises you can purchase a marriage certificate for £3.50. This is optional but a very useful document to have in your possession. You will both be asked to disclose your addresses at the time of your marriage and your ranks or professions. The certificate also includes your natural or adoptive fathers' names as well as their ranks or occupations. If for any reason either of you does not wish to reveal this information there is no legal obligation to do so.

Divorce and remarriage

Whether you are allowed, as a divorcee, to remarry depends on the type of ceremony you wish to have.

Church of England

According to the regulations of the Convocations of Canterbury and York, 'the Church of England should not allow the use of the marriage service in the case of anyone who has a former partner still living'.

These regulations do not carry the weight of law but the majority of ministers object to divorced people marrying in church on moral grounds, even if the divorced partner is the innocent party. It is still worth discussing your hopes of marrying in church with your minister as in certain cases a service of blessing might be appropriate. Make it clear beforehand if you hope to have hymns, bridesmaids, flowers and wear traditional wedding clothes to your service of blessing as some ministers do not approve of this.

Civil weddings

You will need to provide proof of how the previous marriage ended. This could be a divorce absolute document, with the original court seal, or a death certificate or a certified copy; photocopies of these documents are not acceptable. In Scotland there is no equivalent to the decree nisi so you can remarry directly after the divorce is announced.

After taking personal details, the registrar will ask you to sign a declaration that you are eligible to marry. A false declaration could invalidate the marriage and may render you liable to prosecution under the Perjury Act, with the further possible offence of bigamy being taken into account.

Roman Catholic church

If either the bride or groom is divorced the couple are not permitted to have a Roman Catholic wedding; only those whose former partner is deceased or whose marriage was annulled can have a Roman Catholic ceremony.

Jewish faith

If either the bride or groom or both is divorced they must produce the decree absolute and the Jewish bill of divorce.

Quakers

Whether or not divorcees can remarry is left to the discretion of the Friends of the monthly meetings. The general consensus is that re-marriage following divorce should be permitted.

Marrying abroad

Be sure to check all legal requirements for the wedding as they can differ from country to country. When looking through the brochure or making an initial enquiry check whether you need:

- a 10-year passport
- a visa
- your birth certificate
- return tickets to the UK
- your original decree absolute
- original marriage certificate or former partner's death certificate
- parental consent if you are under 18 (21 in some countries)
- legal proof if your name has been changed by deed poll
- proof of vaccinations, if required.

If you require documents you should take originals, or copies certified by a notary, although some countries require you to send them in advance.

If your wedding is not being arranged through a travel agent check the minimum length of time you have to be resident as this can vary from two days to several months. Prior to leaving the UK find out from the consulate, embassy or high commission of the country in which you wish to marry what the legal requirements are.

People you may not marry

It is forbidden in the United Kingdom for a man or a woman to marry certain blood relations. However, contrary to popular belief, first cousins are not prohibited from marrying. It is worth noting that some religions do not allow marriage between other relations.

Blood relatives

A man may not marry his: mother, sister, daughter, father's mother (paternal grandmother), mother's mother (maternal grandmother), son's daughter (granddaughter), daughter's daughter (granddaughter), father's sister (aunt), mother's sister (aunt), brother's daughter (niece), sister's daughter (niece).

A woman may not marry her: father, brother, son, father's father (paternal grandfather), mother's father (maternal grandfather), son's son (grandson), daughter's son (grandson), father's brother (uncle), mother's brother (uncle), brother's son (nephew), sister's son (nephew). These restrictions apply to half-blood relations and persons born out of wedlock.

Adopted relatives

If the adoption was authorised by an order of the court under the Adoption Act then the above restrictions apply. These are not removed even if another person has by a subsequent order been authorised to adopt the same person.

Step-relatives

Step-relatives aged 21 or more may marry provided that the younger member of the couple has at no time, before the age of 18, lived under the same roof as the older person. Neither must he or she have been treated as a child of the older person's family. Unless these conditions are met a man may not marry a: daughter of a former wife, former wife of his father, former wife of his father's father, former wife of his mother's father, daughter of a son of a former wife, daughter of a daughter of a former wife.

A woman may not marry a: son of a former husband, former husband of her mother, former husband of her father's mother, former husband of her mother's mother, son of a son of a former husband, son of a daughter of a former husband.

Relatives you may marry

The law was relaxed in 1960 to allow a man to marry his former wife's sister, aunt or niece and the former wife of his brother, uncle or nephew. Under previous legislation, these unions were prohibited unless the former spouse was deceased. The revisions in the law also apply to women.

The former spouses (in either or both cases) must be deceased if a man intends to marry the mother of a former wife or the former wife of a son, or if a woman intends to marry the father of a former husband or the former husband of a daughter.

Addresses

Association of Interchurch Families
35–41 Lower Marsh,
London SE1 7SA
Tel: 020-7523 2152
Fax: 020-7928 0010
Email: aife@msn.com
Web site: www.aifw.org

Baptist Union
Baptist House, 129 The Broadway,
Didcot, Oxfordshire OX11 8RT
Tel: (01235) 517700
Fax: (01235) 517715
Email:
baptistuniongb@baptist.org.uk
Web site: www.baptist.org.uk

Benefits Agency
Look in the phone book for your
local office

British Humanist Association
47 Theobalds Road,
London WC1X 8SP
Tel: 020-7430 0908
Fax: 020-7430 1271
Email: info@humanism.org.uk
Web site: www.humanism.org.uk
*Publishes a leaflet on humanist weddings
and a book,* Sharing the Future, *on
organising a humanist wedding (£5 inc
p&p)*

Catholic Enquiry Office
The Chase Centre, 114 West Heath
Road, London NW3 7TX
Tel: 020-8458 3316
Fax: 020-8905 5780
Email: cms@cms.org.uk

Church of Scotland
121 George Street,
Edinburgh EH2 4YN
Tel: 0131-225 5722
Fax: 0131-220 3113
Web site: www.cofs.org.uk

**Contraceptive Education Service
helpline**
Tel: 020-7837 4044
*Open 9am–7pm Monday–Friday for
advice and information on contraception,
sexual health and clinic details*

Contributions Agency
Look in the phone book for your
local office

Dhaktivedanta Mamor
Wedding Registration Department
Hilfield Lane, Aldenham,
Watford, Herts WD25 8EZ
Tel: (01923) 855350
*Will contact your local temple on your
behalf for a Hindu wedding ceremony*

**Division of Ministries (Methodist
Overseas Division)**
Church House, 25 Marylebone
Road, London NW1 5JR
Tel: 020-7486 5502
Fax: 020-7467 3761

DVLA
Swansea SA99 1DE
Tel: (01792) 772151

Faculty Office of the Archbishop of Canterbury
1 The Sanctuary, Westminster,
London SW1P 3JT
Tel: 020-7222 5381
Fax: 020-7222 7502

Federation of Synagogues
65 Watford Way, London NW4 3AQ
Tel: 020-8202 2263
Fax: 020-8203 0610
Email: info@kfkosher.org
Web site: www.kfkosher.org

General Register Office for Scotland
New Register House, 3 West
Register Street,
Edinburgh EH1 3YT
Tel: 0131-314 4447
Fax: 0131-314 4400
Email:
marriage@gros-scotland.gov.uk
Web site: www.gro-scotland.gov.uk
The web site gives you all the information you need for marrying in Scotland, including a downloadable list of all the register offices and the documents needed

General Register Office (Northern Ireland)
Oxford House, 49–55 Chichester
Street, Belfast BT1 4HL
Tel: 028-9025 2021
Fax: 028-9025 2120
Email: gro.nisra@dfpni.gov.uk
Web site: www.nisra.gov.uk

General Synod of the Church of England
Enquiry Centre, Church House,
Great Smith Street,
London SW1P 3NZ
Tel: 020-7898 1000
Fax: 020-7898 1461
Web site: www.cofe.anglican.org
The Enquiry Centre provides information about marriages in the Churches of England and Wales

Guild of International Professional Toastmasters
12 Little Bornes, London SE21 8SE
Tel: 020-8670 8424
Fax: 020-8670 0055
Email: ivor@ivorspencer.com
Web site: www.ivorspencer.com

Inland Revenue
Look in the phone book for your
local office

Jewish Marriage Council
23 Ravenshurst Avenue,
London NW4 4EE
Tel: 020-8203 6311
Fax: 020-8203 8727
Email:info@jmc-uk.org
Web site: www.jmc-uk.org

Lesbian and Gay Christian Movement
Oxford House, Derbyshire Street,
London E2 6HG
Tel/fax: 020-7739 1249
Email: lgcm@aol.com
Web site: www.lgcm.org.uk
Send written request for details of ministers who are willing to conduct blessings for lesbian and gay couples

London Beth Din (United Synagogue)
Adler House, 735 High Road,
London N12 0US
Tel: 020-8343 8989
Fax: 020-8343 6257

Marriage Care (formerly the Catholic Marriage Advisory Council)
1 Blythe Mews, Blythe Road,
London W14 0NW
Tel: 020-7371 1341
Fax: 020-7371 4921
Email: marriagecare@btinternet.com
Web site: www.marriagecare.org.uk

Methodist Central Hall Westminster
1 Forest Gate, Central Buildings,
Westminster, London SW1H 9NH
Tel: 020-7222 8010
Fax: 020-7222 6883
Email: events@wch.co.uk
Web site: www.wch.co.uk

Muslim Educational Trust
130 Stroud Green Road,
London N4 3RZ
Tel: 020-7272 8502
Fax: 020-7281 3457

Office for National Statistics
PO Box 56, Southport PR8 2GL
Tel: 0151-471 4817
Fax: 0151-471 4549
Web site: www.statistics.gov.uk
Send £5 and a letter to request an up-to-date list of alternative licensed venues (payment by cheque, postal order, debit or credit card)

Pink Triangle Trust
34 Spring Lane, Kenilworth,
Warwickshire CV8 2HB
Tel/fax: (01926) 858450
Email:
ceremonies@pinktriangle.org.uk
Web site: www.galha.org/ptt.htm

Premium Bonds Office
Blackpool, Lancashire FY3 9YP
Tel: (01253) 766151
Fax: (01253) 793666
Web site: www.nationalsavings.co.uk

Pressed for Time (UK) Ltd
37 Lower Swanwick Road, Lower
Swanwick, Southampton
SO31 7HG
Tel: (01489) 574668
Fax: (01489) 574157
Web site: www.pftuk.co.uk
Will collect a wedding bouquet from anywhere in the UK, photograph it, take it apart and create a picture of the bouquet using the petals and foliage

Reform Synagogues of Great Britain
The Sternberg Centre, 80 East End
Road, London N3 2SY
Tel: 020-8349 4731
Fax: 020-8349 5699
Email:
admin@reformjudaism.org.uk
Web site: www.refsyn.org.uk

Registrar General for England and Wales
Marriages Section, General Register
Office, Smedley Hydro, Trafalgar
Road, Southport PR8 2HH
Tel: 0151-471 4803
Fax: 0151-471 4523
Web site: www.statistics.gov.uk
Advice and information about civil marriages in England and Wales

Relate
Herbert Gray College,
Little Church Street, Rugby,
Warwickshire CV21 3AP
Tel: (01788) 573241
Fax: (01788) 535007
Email:
enquiries@national.relate.org.uk
Web site: www.relate.org.uk
Offers courses on marriage preparation at some centres. Contact headquarters, or your local branch (number in phone book), for details

Religious Society of Friends (Quakers)
Friends House,
173–177 Euston Road,
London NW1 2BJ
Tel: 020-7663 1000
Fax: 020-7663 1001
Web site: www.quaker.org.uk

Royal Institution of Chartered Surveyors (RICS)
Surveyor Court, Westwood Way,
Coventry CV4 8JE
Tel: 024–7669 4757
Fax: 020–7334 3800
Email: info@rics.org.uk
Web site: www.rics.org

Scottish Episcopal Church
21 Grosvenor Crescent,
Edinburgh EH12 5EE
Tel: 0131–225 6357
Fax: 0131–346 7247
Email: office@scotland.anglican.org

Under-Secretary of State
Foreign and Commonwealth Office,
Consular Division, 1 Palace Street,
London SW1E 5HE
Tel: 020–7238 4567
For information on marriages abroad, and marriages to foreigners

Union of Liberal & Progressive Synagogues
The Montagu Centre, 21 Maple
Street, London W1T 4BE
Tel: 020–7580 1663
Fax: 020–7436 4184
Email: montagu@ulps.org
Web site: www.ulps.org

Unitarian and Free Christian Churches
Central Administration Office, Essex
Hall, 1–6 Essex Street, London
WC2R 3HY
Tel: 020–7240 2384
Fax: 020–7240 3089
Email: ga@unitarian.org.uk
Web site: www.unitarian.org.uk
May be able to supply details of ministers willing to conduct blessings for same–sex couples

United Reformed Church
86 Tavistock Place,
London WC1H 9RT
Tel: 020–7916 2020
Fax: 020–7916 2021
Email: urc@urc.org.uk
Web site: www.urc.org.uk

Wedding Crèche Service
1 Netley Mill, Shere,
Surrey GU5 9JT
Tel: (01483) 202490
Email: weddingcreche@yahoo.com
Web site: www.weddingcreche.com
Uses qualified staff to provide childcare and entertainment with toys, crafts, music and games

Marriages abroad:tour operators

Kuoni Weddings
Tel: (01306) 747007

Malta Tourist Office
Tel: 020–7292 4900

Thomas Cook
Tel: (01733) 418450

Thomson Weddings in Paradise
Tel: (08706) 080169

Unijet
Tel: (0990) 114114

Virgin Weddings
Tel: (01293) 744265
Includes Disneyland, underwater and helicopter weddings, as well as more conventional destinations

Passport offices

The telephone number for all offices is (08705) 210410. Calls are routed to the passport office that covers the area from which you are calling.
Web site: www.ukpa.gov.uk
Has details of how to change your name on a passport and how to apply for a new passport

Belfast Passport Office
Hampton House, 47–53 High Street, Belfast BT1 2QS
Areas covered: all of Northern Ireland

Durham Passport Office
Milburngate House,
Durham DH97 1PA
Areas covered: not yet finalised

Glasgow Passport Office
3 Northgate, 96 Milton Street, Cowcaddens, Glasgow G4 OBT
Areas covered: all of Scotland and Greater London

Liverpool Passport Office
5th Floor, India Buildings, Water Street, Liverpool L2 0QZ
Areas covered: Cheshire, Cleveland, Cumbria, Derbyshire, Durham, Greater Manchester, Humberside, Lancashire, Merseyside, Northumberland, North Yorkshire, Shropshire, South Yorkshire, Staffordshire, Tyne and Wear, West Yorkshire

London Passport Office
Clive House, 70 Petty France, London SW1H 9HD
Deals with personal callers only from any part of the UK. Postal applications from residents of Greater London should be sent to the Glasgow office

Newport Passport Office
Olympia House, Upper Dock Street, Newport NP20 1XA
Areas covered: Avon, Berkshire, Clwyd, Cornwall, Devon, Dorset, Dyfed, East Sussex, Gloucestershire, Gwent, Gwynedd, Hampshire, Hereford, Isle of Wight, Mid Glamorgan, Oxfordshire, Powys, Somerset, South Glamorgan, Surrey (exc. London boroughs), West Glamorgan, West Sussex, Wiltshire

Peterborough Passport Office
Aragon Court, Northminster Road, Peterborough PE1 1QG
Areas covered: Bedfordshire, Buckinghamshire (exc. London boroughs), Cambridgeshire, Essex (exc. London boroughs), Hertfordshire (exc. London boroughs), Kent (exc. London boroughs), Leicestershire, Lincolnshire, Norfolk, Northamptonshire, Nottinghamshire, Suffolk, Warwickshire, West Midlands

Photographs and videos

Association of Professional Videomakers
Ambler House, Helpringham, Lincolnshire NG34 0RB
Tel: (01529) 421717
Fax: (01529) 421742
Email: jan@videomakers.com
Web site: www.apv.org.uk

Digital cameras: information
www.epi-centre.com/reports/reports.html
Reviews of digital cameras

Guild of Wedding Photographers UK
Carlton Place, 22 Greenwood Street, Altrincham, Cheshire WA14 1RZ
Tel/fax: 0161-926 9367
Email: info@gwp-uk.co.uk
Web site: www.gwp-uk.co.uk

Master Photographers Association Ltd
Hallmark House, 1 Chancery Lane,
Darlington, Co Durham DL1 5QP
Tel: (01325) 356555
Fax: (01325) 357813
Email: enquiries@mpauk.com
Web site: www.mpauk.com

Society of Wedding and Portrait Photographers
Colomendy House, 1 Vale Road,
Denbigh LL16 3DF
Tel/Fax: (01745) 815030
Email: enquiries@swpp.co.uk
Web site:
www.swppuk.freeserve.co.uk

Publications

Inclusion in this list in no way constitutes an endorsement by Consumers' Association or Which? Ltd, except in relation to its own publications.
Gordon, K., 1998, *Rites and Ceremonies: A Guide to Alternative Weddings* (Constable)
Ross-Macdonald, J., 1996, *Alternative Weddings: An Essential Guide* (Taylor)
Simpson, J., 2000, *Noble's Wedding Venues Guide* (Pavilion)

Wedding software

PC Wedding Kit
Includes database for keeping track of guests, gifts and invitations and to produce your own stationery. By MGI software, it is available from retailers

The Wedding Program
A cross between a personal organiser and a DTP package, this American web site allows you to download software to keep track of your guest and gift lists, sort out a seating plan and also create all your own stationery. Available from the web site: www.itheeweb.com/software.html

Wedding web sites

www.confetti.com
Comprehensive, popular and interesting site on wedding planning

www.coolwhite.com
Links to honeymoon, gift and wedding list companies, caterer and venue suggestions

www.places-to-marry.co.uk
Licensed venue listing covering England, Wales, Scotland, and destinations overseas

www.webwedding.co.uk
Includes a comprehensive directory of suppliers on a clickable map

www.weddingguideUK.com
Useful practical guide to all aspects of planning a wedding

www.weddinglink.co.uk
Comprehensive links listing for suppliers of wedding products from favours to tiaras

www.weddingsabroad.com
Guide to overseas venues and other aspects of planning a destination wedding

www.weddings-and-brides.co.uk
General wedding information on clothes, products and services

www.weddings.co.uk
General wedding guide including a bulletin board where brides-to-be can exchange ideas.

Index

abroad, marrying 7, 25–7
  insurance 188
  legal requirements 26, 212
  wedding packages 25, 26
alternative ceremonies 7–8, 23, 28, 115, 146–8

banks
  joint/separate bank accounts 201–2
  personal loans 31–2
  wedding bank account 36
banns 44, 52, 54, 205
Baptists 21, 137, 209
beach weddings 90, 91
beauty treatments 45, 53, 54
bells 52, 59, 112–13
best man 50, 60–2
  best woman 62
  duties 55, 58, 59, 60–1, 103, 183
  gifts to 53, 55, 65
  more than one 61–2
  toasts and speech 175
blood relations 212–13
bridal attendants 50, 62–3
  chief bridesmaid 63, 131
  child attendants 37, 62–3, 92
  civil ceremonies 65
  flower girls 63
  flowers 95
  gifts to 53, 55, 65
  matron of honour 62
  outfits 45, 87, 92
  page boys 92
budget 30–48
  average cost of a wedding 44
  breakdown 43, 44–8
  checklist 38–42
  discounts, negotiating 36
  financing the wedding 30–3
  preliminary and final budgets 34–6
  sharing the costs 34–5
  written quotations 35
buttonholes and corsages 46, 61, 97

cake 37, 46, 47, 116–19
  as dessert 117
  cake cutting ceremony 173, 178
  making it yourself 52, 55, 118
  quantities 116, 117
  shapes and decorations 118
  sponge cakes 117, 119
  storing the top layer 119
cancellation 37
cars see transport
catering 159–69
  at home 164–6
  average cost 46
  buffet meal 161
  canapés and finger buffets 161–2
  cancellation 37
  caterers 51, 52, 160–3, 166
  checklists 162–3, 165–6, 168
  drinks 166–9
  sit-down meal 161
  VAT 37
ceremony see alternative ceremonies; civil
  ceremonies; religious ceremonies
checklists
  budget 38–42
  catering 162–3, 165–6, 168
  entertainment 181–2
  flowers 100–2
  gifts 81
  guests 76
  music 115
  photographs and video 126, 128
  reception venues 151–3, 155–6, 157, 159
  transport 104, 107
children
  as witnesses 146
  bridal attendants 62–3, 92
  special roles 146
  wedding guests 67–8, 180
Church of England 20–1, 24, 129–35, 142,
  203, 205–6, 210–11
Church of Ireland 129
Church of Scotland 21, 129
Church in Wales 21, 129, 203
civil ceremonies 7, 8, 20, 22–4, 143–8
  approved licensed premises 7, 23–4, 143,
    145
  bridal attendants 65
  ceremony 144–5
  fees 44
  flowers 98–9

legal requirements 206–7
marriage by certificate without licence
    206–7
marriage by licence 207
music and readings 113–15
outfits 90
clothes *see* outfits
complaints and compensation 190
confetti 135, 146
contraceptive pill 54

date and time, setting 51–2, 204
divorce 8–9, 17–18
remarriage 24–5, 210–11
dressmakers 83–4
drinks 46, 47, 166–9

engagements 11–19
breaking off 18–19
formal announcements 11–12
parties 13
rings 13–14, 16
telling parents and friends 11
entertainment 178–82
average cost 47
checklist 181–2
for children 180
dancing 179–80
ensembles and soloists 47, 179
orchestras, bands and groups 47, 178–9
recorded music, discos and DJs 47, 179
etiquette 10

finances, joint 200–2
financing the wedding 30–3
credit card payment 33
loans 30–2
flower girls 63
flowers 51, 53, 94–102
average costs 46
bridal attendants 95
bridal bouquet 46, 95
buttonholes and corsages 46, 61, 97
checklist 100–2
church flowers 46, 98
civil ceremonies 98–9
floral headdresses 46, 97
florist 94–5
preserving the bouquet 97
reception 99
seasonal flowers and their meanings 96
foreigner, marrying a 27–8
in a foreign country 28
in the UK 27
gay and lesbian relationships 29
gifts 61, 77–81
checklist 81
delivery 79
displaying 80–1
exchanging 79

insurance 185–6, 188, 189
lists 52, 77–8, 79
money and vouchers 80
tax-free gifts 195–6
thank-you letters 52, 80
to bridal party 53, 55, 65
to parents 65
guests 66–76
checklist 76
children 67–8
former spouses 66–7
invitations 68–74
list-making 50, 66
overnight accommodation 52, 74

Hindus 22, 138–9, 209
honeymoon
average cost 47–8
insurance 189
passports and visas 52, 57–8
paying for 33
traveller's cheques and currency 55
humanist ceremonies 146–8

insurance 47, 52, 184–90
existing cover 187–9
honeymoon 189
life insurance 202
medical insurance 202
photographs and video 125
specialist policies 184–7
Internet 50, 125
invitations 47, 52, 68–74
checking and sending 73–4
engraved 69
flat printing 69
formal weddings 69, 70–2
informal weddings 72–3
ordering time 69
quantity 69
thermographic printing 69
to reception only 72
wedding software packages 69, 73
wording 69–72

Jewish faith 21–2, 51, 72, 98, 137–8, 208–9,
211

legal requirements 203–13
Church of England weddings 205–6
civil weddings 206–7
documents 204
England and Wales 203–4
Jewish weddings 208–9
licences 50, 205–6, 207
marriage certificates 135, 210
marrying abroad 26, 212
Muslim, Hindu and Sikh weddings 209
Nonconformist or Free Church weddings
    209

legal requirements *continued*
  Northern Ireland 208
  parental consent 203
  prohibited marriages 212–13
  Quaker weddings 210
  remarriage 210–11
  Roman Catholic weddings 204, 208
  Scotland 204, 207–8
  setting the date 204
Lent 51–2
licences 50, 205–6, 207
  common licence 205–6
  special licence 51, 130, 206
life insurance 202

marquees 99, 156–8, 186
Marriage Act 1994 7, 20, 143
marriage certificate 135, 210
marriage preparation courses 9
marriage statistics 8
matrimonial home 198, 199
matron of honour 62
medical insurance 202
Methodists 21, 137, 209
morning dress 53, 91
music and readings 108–15
  alternative ceremonies 115
  bells 52, 59, 112–13
  checklist 115
  civil ceremonies 113–15
  hymns and psalms 52, 108, 110, 112
  non-religious 114–15
  organ and choir 52, 59, 108–9
  readings 113, 114–15
  recorded music 110–11
  while signing the register 110–11
Muslims 141, 209

Nonconformist (Free Church) 21, 137, 209
Northern Ireland 208

order of service sheets 47, 59, 61, 62, 112
organisation 49–59
  setting date and time 51–2, 204
  timetable 50–6, 58–9
  on the web 50
  wedding organisers 49
Orthodox Church 209
outfits 82–93
  accessories 89
  beach weddings 90, 91
  bridal attendants 45, 87, 92
  bride's mother 92–3
  civil ceremonies 90
  emergency repair kit 89
  going-away outfit 44, 53, 90
  groom, best man and ushers 45, 53, 91
  wedding dress *see* wedding dress and accessories

page boys 92
parents
  bride's father 63, 133, 174
  bride's mother 59, 62, 64, 92–3
  divorced parents 8, 10, 64, 70, 71, 171, 172
  groom's parents 64
  introducing 13
  receiving line 64–5, 171
passports and visas 52, 57–8
pensions 197–8
periods 54
personalising your wedding 7, 24, 145
photographs and video 51, 61, 120–8, 186
  average costs 45–6
  checklists 126, 128
  digital photography 125
  insurance 125
  package deals 121, 122–3
  popular photographs 123–4
  reportage style 121
  style of photography 120–1
  video 126–8
post-nuptial agreements 8, 18
postponement 75
pre-nuptial contracts 8, 17–18, 191
Presbyterians 209
prohibited marriages 212–13

Quakers 22, 51, 137, 210, 211

reception 149–83
  average cost 46–7
  cake cutting ceremony 173, 178
  cost-cutting 47
  entertainment 178–82
  flowers 99
  food and drink 159–69
  halls 154
  home-based 158–9
  hotels 151–3
  leaving 106, 182–3
  marquees 99, 156–8, 186
  organising 149–69
  receiving line 64–5, 170–1
  seating plan 54, 55, 171–3
  stationery and decorations 169
  time and duration 149
  timetable 170
  toastmasters 169, 173
  toasts and speeches 173–7
  venues 150–9
  wedding book 75
  see also catering
register offices 22, 51, 66, 98, 113, 143–6
Relate 9, 201
religious ceremonies 7, 8, 20–2, 51, 129–42
  Church of England 129–35, 142
  church fees 44, 55
  church flowers 98
  form of service 52, 205

Hindu 138–9
interfaith marriages 21–2
Jewish 137–8
music 52, 59, 108–11
Muslim 141
Nonconformist or Free Church 137
order of service 130–4
preparation sessions 21, 129
Quaker 137
readings 113
rehearsals 52, 55, 60, 141
Roman Catholic 21, 136–7
in Scotland 21, 51
seating plan 134
service of blessing 72, 142
signing the register 134–5
Sikh 139–41
rings 13–17, 53, 61
  alternatives to 17
  antique rings 15, 187
  average costs 45
  birthstones 14
  caring for 16–17
  custom-made 15
  engagement rings 13–14
  gold and other metals 14–15
  men's rings 16, 45
  returning 19
  valuations and insurance 17, 185, 187
  wedding rings 14–15, 16
Roman Catholics 21, 136–7, 204, 208, 211

Sale of Goods Act 1979 190
same-sex marriages 29
savings and investments 196–7
Scotland
  civil weddings 23
  legal requirements 204, 207–8
  religious ceremonies 21, 51
  second marriages 25, 211
  wills 199–200
second marriages 8, 10, 24–5, 210–11
  civil weddings 211
  service of blessing 142
  toasts and speeches 176
ship, marrying on board 23
Sikhs 22, 139–41, 209
speeches 61, 173–7
  at second marriages 176
  best man 175
  bride 175
  bride's father 174
  groom 174–5
  planning and delivering 176–7
stag and hen parties 55, 60, 62
stationery
  average cost 47
  order of service sheets 53
  reception 169
  see also invitations
Supply of Goods and Services Act 1982 190
surname
  changing to husband's surname 56
  composite surnames 56
  informing others 57
  keeping maiden name 56
  man's change of 57

taxation 191–7
  married couple's allowance 192–4
  mortgage interest tax relief 195
  savings and investments 196–7
  tax-free gifts 195–6
  transferring surplus allowances 194–5
themed weddings 7, 24, 90
timetable 50–6, 58–9
toastmaster 51, 169, 173
toasts 173–7
transport 51, 56, 59, 61, 103–7
  average costs 45
  borrowing cars 105
  checklist 104, 107
  horse-drawn carriages 106
  leaving the reception 106
  parking arrangements 105
  vintage and veteran cars 104, 105
  wedding cars 45, 103–5

United Reformed Church 21, 137, 209
ushers 59, 60, 61, 62, 65, 112
vaccinations 53

VAT 37
video see photography and video

wedding book 75
wedding day timetable 58–9
wedding dress and accessories 82–9
  average cost 44
  buying 82–3
  cleaning and storing 88
  fittings 53, 54, 86
  hiring 44, 88
  made-to-measure 44, 83–7
  second-hand 44, 83, 86
  shoes 53, 89
  train 84
  underwear 53, 89
  veils, headdresses and hats 46, 53, 88, 97
wills 198–200
winter weddings 52

Which? Holiday Destination

A country-by-country guide to the most popular holiday venues around the world, this revised edition includes forthright, thumbnail descriptions of resorts in over 60 countries. It also covers the range of activities on offer to help you decide whether that resort is somewhere to take the family or to have a romantic break away from it all.

Paperback   624 pages   210 x 120 mm   £12.99

The Which? Hotel Guide

Following a rigorous annual selection process based on visitors' reports and professional inspection, the Guide presents readers with a huge choice of characterful places to stay at throughout England, Scotland and Wales, including over 50 London hotels. All the 1,000-plus recommended addresses – from modest B&Bs to the grandest of grand hotels – offer exceptional hospitality, including genuinely friendly service and the highest standards of cleanliness and comfort.

Paperback   736 pages   210 x 120 mm   £15.99

Which? Way to Buy, Sell and Move House

This bestselling book covers: the legal side of buying and selling a house, from exchange of contracts to completion; mortgage options; buying and selling at auction; valuations and surveys; getting the best from your estate agent and solicitor; expenses – what to expect and how to keep them to a minimum; insurance cover; and organising and surviving the move. A separate chapter covers the different system in Scotland.

Paperback   320 pages   216 x 135 mm   £10.99

Which? Way to Buy, Own and Sell a Flat

The book includes information about collective enfranchisement (tenants' right to buy the freehold); the individual tenant's right to buy a new lease; and the implications of the new legislation on covenants. A separate chapter deals with differences in the Scottish system. Whether you are a first-time buyer, or are having problems in a flat that you own or want to sell, this accessible guide takes you painlessly through the process

Paperback   288 pages   216 x 135mm   £10.99

Available from bookshops, and by post from Which?, Dept TAZM,
Castlemead, Gascoyne Way, Hertford X, SG14 1LH
or phone FREE on (0800) 252100
quoting Dept TAZM and your credit card details

Acknowledgements

This book began life as talks for the spirituality course that ran through the heart of weekly life in the community at Trinity College, Bristol. It was developed by the then Principal, David Gillett. When he left to become Bishop of Bolton I took over the teaching of it.

The course was not taught as an academic subject alongside doctrine, mission or biblical studies. There were no essays, exams or credits.

Each Wednesday morning, after an act of worship, the community stayed in chapel for an introductory talk on some aspect of spiritual life and prayer. The hour and a half that followed up to coffee was then kept as silent space for prayer and reflection. This was a vision for spiritual formation as the integrative heart of all studying, training and shared life.

Teaching that course was easily the most fulfilling aspect of my time at Trinity. So these pages owe substantial debts of gratitude – most of all to David Gillett, for his original vision, for his own teaching and example and for his generous blessing upon this book. Thanks also to my faculty colleagues for one of the warmest and most enriching experiences of team I have ever had. Thanks to generations of student community at Trinity, now in Christian ministry in this country and beyond, who entered into the course so richly, shared their own insights and made the course part of their own pilgrimage. And special thanks to a variety of friends who read and commented on various chapters and themes in this book, among them Roger Hurding, Jeff Leonardi, Tim Marks, Philip Seddon, Mary Staunton and Rachel Whitehorn.

Simon Kingston has once again been a fellow traveller as well as a wonderful editor at SPCK. I am also indebted to his colleague Gordon Lamont for his help with the text.

Last, but never least, I owe thanks to my family – to my sons Joshua and Simeon for their enthusiasm and encouragement, and to my dear wife Jackie, once again my shrewdest critic and, as ever, my dearest friend in pilgrimage.

To

David Gillett
Anne Long
&
(the late) Brother Ramon SSF

friends
mentors
and pioneers
in the ways of the Spirit

in
grateful debt

Introduction

On learning to sing in a strange land

A large department store in the centre of Birmingham advertises a 'Spirit Zone' on its store guide. And there it is – a mobile display unit on the first floor. What would you expect to find on offer? There are crystals, aromatherapy goods, CD music for relaxation and various New Age trinkets. That much might be expected. A range of dolls is also on sale: Moses, Jesus and Harry Potter are in stock. On the presentation boxes is printed a selection of teachings and sayings from each of the characters. The Ten Commandments and Sermon on the Mount are there. On the shelf above them are some 'adult' party games, packets of phallic-shaped pasta and soft 'toys' in various erotic shapes.

What does all this reveal? First, that spirituality is available as a consumer accessory. You can buy it – between Men's Clothing and the high-class Food Hall (with its bottled scorpions in vodka and the chocolate-coated worms). Second, the choice of goods makes revealing assumptions about what spiritual life actually is and what it includes. Sexuality, sensuality and spirituality are mixed up on the same shelves. So too are therapy, theology and utter trivia.

So at first sight this is spirituality for the curious affluent, a leisure activity for the bored stimulated by the endless distractions of the consumer market. The choice of what goes into this zone at all is itself completely arbitrary. The 'Spirit Zone' reflects a society without roots in any particular understanding of philosophy of life, prayer or God.

For all that, there is an underlying longing for spiritual life in contemporary culture that should be taken seriously. It is evident in the profusion of alternative therapies, spiritualities and meditation techniques on offer. Spirituality is a subject of continuing interest in popular lifestyle magazines. It is now asked to contribute to serious debate about holistic approaches to health care, education and the work environment. In such a culture the historic riches of Christian spirituality are as relevant as they have ever been. The opportunities are great and varied.

But Christianity is itself facing huge and unsettling challenges. This widespread interest in spirituality is surfacing at a time when the church in the Western world is in serious decline. It is struggling to be an effective presence in a culture that has steadily cut itself off from its roots in a once great Christian civilization and is unable to recognize its own perils.

There is an urgent search on for strategies for growth and mission and much talk about 'fresh expressions' and 'new ways' of being church. It is a time of rapid change that is both exciting and disorientating. No one yet sees what kind of Christian Church will emerge out of this. Like people travelling into unfamiliar country, many of the familiar landmarks of faith by which we navigated and knew ourselves before God and the world are no longer there or seem to have lost their meaning. Language, culture and whole patterns of belonging are changing. We will be exploring, searching and experimenting for the foreseeable future. We are learning to sing in a strange land (Ps. 137.4).

When it comes to our spiritual life there are dangers as well as opportunities in such a time. But a key priority for anyone going on an important journey is to know what to take with them and what to leave behind. What is essential and who decides this? A certain pragmatism can take over in communities feeling the threat of decline and pressures to change. Out of the need to be 'relevant' and noticed, core values and ways of expressing faith can be diluted, abandoned or packaged into something more 'marketable'. But rather than challenging the assumptions of the world it may end up simply mirroring it. What is offered is little more than 'a frantic spirituality for a frantic age' (Robert Warren). Relevance is a very slippery goal in such a fast-changing society.

It is disturbing and revealing to hear that the criticism of the church by spiritual seekers outside it is no longer that it is 'boring', 'out of date' or 'irrelevant'. It is criticized instead for being 'unspiritual'.

Jesus often taught that the things of most value are not lying around on the surface of life. Like that hint of something buried in a field there are hints and clues everywhere. But we must be willing to be distracted. We must break our routine, be inconvenienced and go out and buy a spade (Matt. 13.44). Our dilemma is that there are few areas in our culture that know how to nurture depth and honour the time that is needed to cultivate it.

This kind of depth is hard to measure. It takes time that we may not feel we have. It involves a lot of searching and digging and much of it happens in the dark. When so much needs to happen on the surface there is real pressure to neglect the hard, steady work of putting down deep roots for our living and praying. There are no easy answers for this. But it is an urgent priority – a necessary irrelevance. 'Superficiality is the curse of our age. The doctrine of instant satisfaction is a primary spiritual problem. The desperate need today is not a greater number of intelligent people, or gifted people, but for deep people' (Foster, *A Celebration of Discipline*, 1998, p. 3).

How to get the most from this book

This is a book for explorers and all who want their spiritual life to go deeper. It is for those wanting to know what to take with them as they seek to travel faithfully in a strange land. It is not a formal textbook or a comprehensive study of spirituality (some of those are suggested as further reading).

Spirituality is a huge subject and this book offers only a selection of subjects for study. Nor are they always the most obvious ones. I have omitted some for the simple reason that they are already well covered elsewhere. But those that are included are carefully chosen. Some familiar topics appear in unfamiliar places in the book. I also include some aspects of spirituality that are important but often neglected. At the end of each chapter suggestions for reflection, prayer or activity are made. These are offered as stimulants for thought and discussion where this is helpful. Where that is happening naturally they can be cheerfully ignored. You can choose your own route through this book. The sections are not listed in any order of importance and the numbering of the chapters is only for ease of reference. Your personal areas of interest or concern may determine the best place to start.

The five sections of this book together suggest a definition of what a vision for Christian spirituality must include (an outline of each section follows below). Although it is very exciting to find 'spirituality' so widely talked about, the word needs a health warning on it. It is too easily narrowed down to mean the bit of us that prays, goes to church or enjoys scented candles. It is used in contrast to other parts of our lives such as work, or home, or relationships. But human beings are not for dividing up like department stores and spirituality is not a separate zone within us. When Christians use the word they are really talking about the whole experience and business of living and how it relates in every part to the life and will of God. It is therefore a spirituality that is concerned with integration with the whole of life, not separation from it.

Then and now
This section illustrates the gift of history for the spiritual journey. A careful honouring of the past is vital for spiritual formation. We have come from somewhere and we are going somewhere. We need to know our roots. This is why the Bible places such stress on remembering. 'Stand at the cross-roads,' urged Jeremiah at a time of acute confusion and crisis for his people. 'Look, and ask for the ancient paths, where the good way lies; and walk in it, and find rest for your souls' (Jer. 6.16). History will help us to discern, for example, what are truly significant insights in the present time, and what are passing enthusiasms or even distractions. Above all, the historic 'cloud of witnesses' (Heb. 12.1) is given as a source of constant encouragement, inspiration, warning and wisdom.

Life together
The chapters in this section explore the central place of community and shared life for spiritual formation. Christian spirituality is for living in community. It is not available as a private pursuit of prayer or spiritual development. It is frankly too tough to go it alone. To respond to the demands of the gospel I need the support, wisdom and challenge of a community. It is no coincidence that the first action of the earliest Christians was to shape themselves into communities of radically shared life (Acts 2.42). Their experience may make us question how we approach choosing what communities or churches we belong to. These were communities united by a common experience of the overwhelming love of Christ and the life of the Spirit. They had not chosen each other. God had called them together. They were clearly communities of great cultural and racial diversity. In a fragmenting contemporary society (and church) increasingly grouped by common interests, lifestyle or age groups, there is a profound challenge to another way of living.

Becoming who I am

This section explores the relationship between spirituality, humanity, identity and the stages of our life journey. Christian spirituality is concerned with the whole of our humanity offered, consecrated and transformed in the life of God. It is a pilgrimage into our true identity restored in Christ. This means learning to pray with all aspects of what makes us human – our personal story, sexuality and the stages of life.

When you pray . . .

This section looks at some of the ways we actually pray and our understanding of what we are doing. Though there is no right or wrong way to pray, we can easily get the impression there is! The chapters in this section explore some of the very varied ways in which we express our prayers, such as intercession, praying with the Bible and understanding the neglected gift of liturgy.

In the midst of life

The title of this section could well have provided the title for the whole book. Christian spirituality is lived in the midst of this world. It is not to be separated from it. There is something rightly this-worldly about following Jesus. It is for engaging with all of life. And it is in the midst of life that God is to be found. The salvation we seek is not an escape from this world but includes it all. We must learn to be his spies. The vision at the end of the Bible is not merely for a transformed humanity but for a new heaven and a new earth (Rev. 21.1).

So wherever your point of entry into this book, don't stop there. Let it lead you into the vision and adventure of the greater whole.

This is an invitation to go exploring.

THEN AND NOW

Insights from Christian history and tradition

1 A way in the wilderness

The spirituality of the desert

A young man was sitting in a church service one Sunday and a verse from the Gospel reading stood out like a command. 'Sell what you own, and give the money to the poor, and you will have treasure in heaven; then come, follow me' (Mark 10.21). He was 18 years old. He took this teaching literally and immediately gave away all he owned and lived a life of poverty, manual labour and prayer in his home village. He put himself under the guidance of an older man. The year was 270 and his name was Antony.

Fifteen years later the call came to deeper, more solitary prayer. He withdrew into the wilderness and became a hermit, living in a cave on a barren escarpment high up above the Red Sea coast of Egypt. You can visit the cave today – and the monastery at the foot of the mountain that bears his name. As his reputation for holiness and wisdom grew he was much sought out.

Antony has come to be regarded as the founding father of hermits and monks and his influence continues to be felt to this day. The word hermit comes from the Greek *eremos* which means 'desert'. Monastic life is traditionally described as the 'eremitic life'.

What did they think they were doing?

In the third and fourth centuries, in the deserts of North Africa and the Middle East, there was a significant movement of Christians withdrawing from 'the world' and seeking God in a life of radical renunciation, simplicity and prayer. Stories about them have been told ever since. They fascinate and repel and are easily misunderstood. But because they stand outside all traditionally organized and 'civilized' ways of being church they pose tough reminders of the radical heart of Christian life and prayer.

To withdraw from the world and go into the desert could be a very negative and self-seeking thing to do. How did they understand this call into solitude?

It was, above all else, a longing for God. Like Antony, these men and women were seeking Christ before all else. It was also, therefore, a symbolic protest against an increasingly worldly church. Once the Roman emperor Constantine and his whole empire became 'officially' Christian, a church that had been terribly persecuted suddenly became a respected part of the institution. What would guard it in faithfulness now that all spoke well of it? Withdrawing is not always the answer. There have been Christians in every age who have decided their church is hopelessly compromised and have gone off to start a 'purer' version down the road.

The Protestant theologian Karl Barth saw this movement in a more positive light. He was no fan of monastic life but described the way of the desert as 'a highly effective and responsible protest and opposition to the world, and not least to a worldly Church, a new and specific way of combating it, and therefore a direct address to it'.

This was a strategic withdrawal from church and world, not an abandonment. Christian solitude is never separation. The way of the desert is a critical but loving withdrawal from the surface of life to engage and struggle with it in prayer at a deeper level – in the world but not of it.

The wilderness of God

The God of the Bible is the God of the desert. There is no path to God that does not pass through the wilderness. There is no significant leader in the Bible whose own spiritual formation did not involve significant time in the wilderness. Abraham, Moses, the People of Israel, Jacob, Elijah, the Prophets, John the Baptist, and of course Jesus himself, all spent extended time there.

The language of prayer and worship in the Bible is full of desert imagery. 'My soul thirsts for you; . . . as in a dry and weary land where there is no water' (Ps. 63.1).

The very identity of the people of Israel as God's people was forged in the heat of the desert. In later years of affluence, careless believing or apostasy, the prophets would look back with longing to those desert wanderings as a golden age of faith, of pure love and true obedience (see Jer. 2:2).

The desert is central to the understanding of spiritual life in the scriptures and in Christian discipleship. So what are the marks of Christian life forged in the wilderness?

Exposure

The real desert is a tough, unsentimental teacher. It is no respecter of good intentions. The desert is a place of emptiness and death. It represents human helplessness and powerlessness at its most extreme and that is what makes it such a powerful place of encounter with God. In the desert you leave behind all your familiar securities. You come to a place of confessing your absolute need and the emptiness of all you have been placing your trust in.

The desert is a place that weans us off addictions and false dependencies. If your god is not the true God the desert will find you out. Only the true God can sustain you in the wilderness. This offers one insight into why the people of Israel spent so long in the wilderness after their exodus out of Egypt. Recalling the story of the Exodus and the long wandering in the wilderness that followed, it has been said that it took Israel one night to come out of Egypt, but it took 40 years for Egypt to come out of Israel. The wilderness is a place of judgement. In the desert we are confronted with the sheer depth of our need of conversion.

Testing

In the experience of Jesus the wilderness was a place of tough preparation for ministry.

At his baptism, Jesus united himself with our sinful humanity. The Father affirmed him as his beloved Son and the Spirit descended on him. But he was immediately *driven out* by the same Spirit to meet the devil in the wilderness. The word is the same as that used for casting out demons (Mark 1.12).

His struggle in the wilderness directly followed his naming, anointing and empowering for ministry. God had even booked the devil to do the testing! For Jesus the wilderness was a vital part of his life in the Spirit and the preparation for his ministry. And so it is for his followers.

In the early days of charismatic renewal, when many people were receiving a life-changing experience of God's love and power, the leaders of the movement noticed something puzzling. People who had received these blessings were later coming back in bewilderment. They were now speaking instead of dryness, a sense of God's absence and of struggles against temptation. There was a sense of confusion and isolation from church and friends and a feeling of guilt that they must have done something wrong, failed or sinned for this to be happening.

But the same Spirit who blesses also drives us into the wilderness at times to forge in us our true name and identity in Christ and to strengthen us for service. Without a positive understanding of the place of wilderness we will always be tempted to resist the wilderness and try to force our way back to the blessings we once enjoyed. Whole churches can get stuck in this way, wearily repeating the patterns of worship and prayer that were once so exciting but are no longer renewing. In the desert, driven by the Spirit, we too will enter into tough battles with our allegiances and priorities, our passions and longings and the discerning of evil. It is therefore a vital training ground for Christian disciples.

The desert then is a place of conflict and struggle with evil, but always in the life of the Spirit.

Simplicity

If you have ever travelled in the desert you will know there is no room for luxuries and non-essentials. Life is reduced to bare essentials. The desert teaches us our priorities.

Waiting

Nothing happens fast in the heat of the desert. There is a different understanding of time and it involves a lot of waiting. A world addicted to ever faster ways of doing things finds such a place deeply frustrating – a waste of time in fact.

The story goes that a desert father was visited by three men who wanted to talk to him. He showed them to a nearby cave and offered them hospitality and then left them there – for three years – before going to see what they wanted!

The desert weans us off our addiction to the instant, the immediate. Spiritual maturity requires a quite different sense of time. We are not an age that can come to this truth easily.

Discernment

This was the most highly valued of all the spiritual gifts in desert spirituality. Without discernment we are simply unable to tell good from evil, to unravel what is true and false in our disordered passions, to follow Christ through the sheer confusion of life. By stripping us down to the bare essentials of who we are, the desert is a fertile place for growing the discernment that alone establishes us in true faith.

Silence and tears

There is mistrust of too much talk in the desert. 'Speak a word' was the common request to a spiritual elder. It is not so much that silence replaces words. Rather, through silence, words are allowed to recover their simple power and truthfulness to bless and reveal. So you don't need to say so much. Tears are also a feature of spiritual life in the wilderness as our deepest places, beyond all words, are opened up to God for healing and transformation.

Vigil

Here, at the far end of solitude, was the place where men and women kept watch for the coming of Christ. They waited in the night of faith, between wonder and bafflement, faith and fear. Like the ancient guards on the walls of the city longing in hope for the first signs of the new day, they looked out into the night, watching for the first signs of light on the horizon that herald the coming of Christ.

Three essentials for desert spirituality

Stability

'Stay in your cell and your cell will teach you everything' was the well-known advice. The cell represents a geographical and psychological location where the important battles may be fought. Staying put in one place is a vital antidote to the endless search for the new stimulation, excitements and spiritual experiences by which we avoid facing our personal insecurities. In the cell we learn to face ourselves as well as God.

Conversion of life

Constant meditation on scripture and particularly the Gospels was at the heart of desert faith. It took with radical seriousness the teaching of Jesus that human beings can only live by 'every word that comes from the mouth of God' (Matt. 4.4).

Obedience

The wilderness is a dangerous place. The way of the desert was not a place for spiritual DIY or individual heroics. It needed experienced guides. The willingness to live in obedience and submission to others was central to this way of life. Patterns of shared life varied in the desert but at the centre was the 'Abba', the spiritual elder, whose word was followed absolutely. Their often idiosyncratic sayings, riddles and highly parabolic teachings and sayings were collected, memorized and carefully acted upon (see Ward, *The Sayings of the Desert Fathers*, 1981).

The wilderness, the church and the world

The way of the desert is a living tradition and it is drawing people once again. Over the last 40 years there has been huge growth in people seeking quiet places and retreats. Within traditional monastic communities there has been a steady increase in the numbers of men and women feeling called to more solitary or hermit life. All this is happening at a time of steep church decline and huge outward challenge for the church. Alongside the demands of mission and costly engagement with the world 'out there', there is a corresponding move to the desert and to the secret life of prayer.

Christian prayer has been described as 'a preference for the desert' – a preference to the driven, distracted superficiality of so much living around us. You don't need to go the Sahara. The desert is wherever life is sterile and lost to the sources that will renew it in hope. The inner city can be a desert. So can rural communities.

Whatever else will be a feature of the emerging life of the church in this century, it will need to be rooted in the way of the desert. Only such a spirituality can lead people away from a religion of easy answers and guard the depths that sustain and renew. The demands of this age are perilous without a corresponding deepening of prayer and radical consecration of life.

One minister prepared a list of questions he would use to help him discern the heart of any church community that invited him to join them. These included, 'Is its wilderness deep enough? Is its desert dry enough?'

For thought, prayer and activity

1   If you went into the desert seeking one of the spiritual fathers and mothers
    (a) What would you be seeking?
    (b) What questions would you want to ask them?

2   When have you been 'in the desert' and what form has the desert taken in your life?

3   Choose a difficult and challenging time in your life and write down a list of words or short phrases that describe the experience.
    (a) What did it feel like?
    (b) What words or images sum up the experience?
    (c) How did the experience change you?
    (d) What can you see that is good that came out of the experience?

4   As you reflect on the main features of faith in the desert
    (a) What does your own spiritual life most need at the moment?
    (b) Does this tradition suggest changes or resources that might begin to meet that need? (Remember, the changes need not be major ones. In the spiritual life, it is often the smallest changes that become the most significant ones.)

5   Can you write your own 'rule of simplicity' for your daily life?

Further reading

Louth, Andrew. *The Wilderness of God* (London: Darton, Longman and Todd, 1991).

Nouwen, Henri. *The Way of the Heart* (London: Darton, Longman and Todd, 1999).

Williams, Rowan. *Silence and Honey Cakes* (Oxford: Lion, 2004).

2 The Lord is here

Spiritual roots in Anglican spirituality

When I was a vicar in London I remember looking around the congregation one Sunday morning and realizing that in terms of spiritual background and church membership there were at least eight Christian traditions represented. They ranged from English Free Church to Syrian Orthodox. For many people today denominational allegiances are irrelevant. We join a church where we feel welcomed and at home, where we sense some affinity with the faith and vision of the community and where children are loved and cared for – largely regardless of its historic identity.

That may be the starting place, but if our spiritual life is to grow and deepen we will need to put down our roots into that church. We need somewhere we belong. That will involve developing a critical appreciation of the particular historic expression of the church in which we pray and worship, with its distinctive theological emphasis and way of expressing things. This is easily neglected. A great deal of the contemporary spiritual searching is lived out of a kind of restless wandering. Without that rootedness our spiritual lives will be another expression of pic'n'mix consumerism that drives our appetites for its own ends.

This chapter explores the vision for spiritual life found within the English Anglican church. Like all the churches in Western Europe, it is facing huge challenges and searching for ways to rekindle the fire of its spiritual life and mission amidst the dying embers of a once great Christian Europe.

In the beginning – some history and theology

What became 'The Church of England' did not start at the Reformation. Neither was it simply a reaction to perceived Catholic errors or the outcome of dubious political compromise (though both these factors were significant in the process). It was very important to its sixteenth-century founders that they were not just leaving Rome and doing their own thing. They believed they were part of the 'One Holy, Catholic and Apostolic church'. But they were exploring a fresh expression of its particular life and calling.

The worldwide Anglican Communion

The Church of England spread through the world initially in response to the pastoral needs of its citizens and armed forces serving abroad in what was the British Empire. Today it is part of a worldwide Anglican Communion of Churches. In many places it is experiencing courageous growth, often in the face of persecution and poverty. There are nearly 77 million members worldwide.

Ancient and modern

The name 'Church of England' refers first to a geographical reality rather than the institution it later became. There were Christians in the land for 400 years before Augustine arrived at Canterbury in 597 on his Roman mission. Early Anglo-Saxon documents reveal a church that had links with the Roman church but whose way of life and spirituality had many close affinities with the insights that, much later, the Reformation would seek to re-establish. This was a church that was returning to its spiritual roots in the Bible, in the teachings of the early church Councils and in the vision of faith in its own land.

Reformed and Catholic

Unlike most other Protestant churches at the Reformation, the Church of England chose to retain aspects of the Catholic tradition it was separating from. So it calls itself 'Reformed' and 'Catholic'. It holds together continuity and discontinuity. If this sounds difficult – it is! This church continues to live with almost impossible diversity. So it includes people who consider that the process of Reformation was woefully incomplete and that this is the source of all our troubles. Others long and pray to return to 'our true home' in Rome. Both claim to be the true heirs of the original Anglican vision.

East and West

The emergence of the Anglican church was guided by an exciting renewal of biblical and theological study. The newly invented printing press was a stimulus for this. Explorations into the worship and theology of the earliest Christian churches – East and West, Greek and Latin – shaped the vision of the church. In the way it thinks and prays, the Anglican tradition has a great deal in common with the Eastern Orthodox, a spiritual tradition that takes its biblical, theological and spiritual foundations with utmost seriousness.

Sacred and secular

Two qualities derive from the emergence of the Church of England out of the murky political world of Henry VIII. It was an unplanned birth – in part an almost accidental result of the king's need for an heir and his consequent marital problems. Compromise and collusion was thus part of its earliest experience of the world; it has struggled ever since to shake off 'the infection of political spinelessness' (Gordon Mursell). With some honourable exceptions through its history, it has always been better at accommodating and conserving than at confronting with a radical, prophetic voice.

A more positive quality is that it became a church that has always refused to separate the spiritual from the secular. It is a 'this-worldly' spirituality in a thoroughly biblical way. It expects to be as fully involved in this world as the next. Even the peculiar relationship of the Church of England to the State has its roots in the theology of creation and also of incarnation. It was an Anglican archbishop, William Temple, who famously described the Christian faith as 'the most material of all religions'. At its most faithful, its spirituality is directly involved in politics and social action. William Wilberforce, Lord Shaftesbury, Josephine Butler and Archbishops Trevor Huddleston and Desmond Tutu are immediate examples of this.

Creation and redemption

In the prayer of General Thanksgiving from the Book of Common Prayer we say to God, 'we bless thee for our creation, preservation and all the blessings of this life; but above all for thine inestimable love in the redemption of the world by our Lord Jesus Christ, for the means of grace and the hope of glory'.

Creation and redemption are celebrated side by side as God's gifts. In the Protestant tradition there has been a tendency to stress redemption more highly and to treat the created, 'fallen' world with deep pessimism. On the other hand, parts of Catholic tradition have tended to over-spiritualize this world, its political and church order. Together with the Eastern Orthodox tradition, Anglican theology has sought to see 'the whole world as sacrament, and to claim the potential within heaven and earth for glory, all waiting to be revealed' (Michael Marshall). As in the Orthodox church, Anglican theology has understood the Incarnation as fulfilment of creation, not simply a divine rescue act undertaken when everything else had failed – though of course human sin makes it neces-sary as a tragic redemption. (For related material see Chapter 19.)

It is not surprising that such a church keeps throwing up artists, musi-cians, poets and hymn writers – such as John Donne, Thomas Traherne and George Herbert. It is no accident that many nineteenth-century Anglican country parsons were distinguished as local natural historians. Alongside a robustly practical pride in 'sanctified common sense', it also has deep roots in the mystical traditions of theology and prayer, repre-sented by writers such as Evelyn Underhill.

Here are found some of the roots of an instinctively inclusive and extraordinarily diverse spiritual tradition. It is not easily analysed and is best understood by praying and worshipping with it. This church does not claim a doctrinal system or 'orthodoxy' of its own but draws richly and deeply from across the historic Christian traditions. It is completely in character that when Anglicans published a compilation of their best spir-itual writings they should choose for a title a line from a *Methodist* hymn: *Love's Redeeming Work* (Rowell, Stevenson and Williams, 2004).

The Anglican tradition is perhaps best pictured as a bridge. Within its own life and vision it connects widely diverse and often separated parts of the Christian Church. In so far as bridges are only needed where there are divides, perhaps this church only exists in order to do itself out of a job.

Praying in the Anglican tradition

For all people
Anglican spirituality is strongly inclusive and community-based. To an extent Anglicans are willing to take faith on trust. This is a church that seeks a strong centre while being happy to keep the edges blurred. Although it has not always been faithful to this aim, it was originally

intended to be a genuinely lay spirituality. Cranmer deliberately took the complex monastic patterns of prayer and developed them for use in the outside world of daily work and faith. The Church of England was born out of a passionate vision for a praying nation.

It was a spirituality for all of life. The local parish system was developed to enable the care of everyone, in every part of life, from cradle to grave. It still provides a Christian presence in areas that would otherwise have none.

It was a social spirituality – a vision for a community that meets to pray and study the Bible and support each other in the way of the Lord.

> 'You are here because God wants you to be here. And God's wanting you to be here has been mediated to you through centuries of mixed and imaginative witness . . . Be thankful for that witness, and how it has made the reality of God's welcome complete for you.'
>
> (Archbishop Rowan Williams on his understanding of what it means to belong to the Anglican church)

Word and sacrament

The Bible is central to Anglican life. Its liturgy is almost solid scripture. Through its lectionary cycle of readings it commits itself to a regular reading of God's Word.

A spirituality with a strong theology of creation will also be instinctively sacramental. God's life is immanent in all things. The Anglican founders shared the unease with the Reformation partners about the Roman Catholic theology of the mass. Yet it never went the way of replacing the altar with the pulpit and reducing the sacraments to mere symbols. Local practice and theological emphasis vary considerably. But it holds together and celebrates the Word and sacrament. Both are reverenced as a means of grace but not confused with the one who they reveal. Whenever the Word is opened, water or wine poured out, bread broken, we believe Christ is present and makes himself known. (See Chapter 8.)

Mind and spirit

Anglican spirituality is a thoughtful spirituality. When the risen Jesus appeared to the disciples to commission them and send them out into the world, we read, 'they worshipped him; but some doubted' (Matt. 28.17). The Anglican tradition has always had room for doubts, encourages believers to be honest and expects praying to be questioning and thoughtful. It seeks the consecration of mind as well as heart and will.

Rhythms and seasons

This is an increasingly neglected area but along with the older Christian traditions the structure of Anglican spiritual life is rhythmic and seasonal. Like the seasons of creation these allow for the offering of all our living and the faithful contemplation of every season of the Spirit – winter as well as summer, autumn as well as spring. It frees us from the burden of endlessly guilty striving after the excitement of spring or the endless high summer that we feel 'real faith' should really be about.

Form and spontaneity

One of the features of the newer services in the Church of England is the degree of flexibility available within the shapes of worship. It was once suggested that 'let all things be done decently and in order' was possibly the only verse in 1 Corinthians 14 known to the Church of England! But the dual impact of the charismatic movement and the growing informality of the prevailing social culture has been changing this. Worship is now marked by variety and flexibility. If anything it is 'form' that is now regarded with the suspicion that was once reserved for 'spontaneity'. (See Chapters 16 and 17 for related material.)

Consecration of the ordinary

The English Anglican church is famously hard to excite! It has a very poor track record in responding to the more disturbing moves of the Holy Spirit – much to its own loss. But even here a neglected virtue may be found. It is to do with how we manage the sheer ordinariness of much of daily living. The monastic world has long known the importance of how we manage our boredom in our spiritual life. A great deal of contemporary spirituality is driven by a terror of the ordinary and so is marked by a compulsive search for 'excitement'. There is an important strand in traditional Anglican worship that is hardly reflected in modern song writing:

> The trivial round, the common task,
> Would furnish all we ought to ask, –
> Room to deny ourselves, a road
> To bring us daily nearer God.
> (John Keble, 1792–1866)

This kind of humble, prayerful offering of ordinary daily routines is a characteristic of Anglican spirituality. Even they become 'a road to bring us daily nearer God'. Such an offer is not to be despised.

Going into exile – the challenge of a changing world

When St Peter wrote a round letter to a cluster of churches in Asia Minor (modern-day Turkey) he greeted them as 'exiles' and 'aliens' (1 Pet. 1.1 and 2.11). The words emphasize a very transitory existence, a lack of roots and real belonging. These were resident aliens, non-citizens. The idea of Christians as sojourners in the world so resonated with their condition that *paroikia* (a place of refuge or exile) became a common term for a Christian community in any place. What is interesting is that this is where the English word 'parish' comes from. How the word has changed! In this land the parish boundaries are the most fixed and permanent signs of belonging. In New Testament terms the understanding of parish and parishioner was shaped by the experience of enforced mobility, vulnerable exile and disorientating change. Within this experience was the call to hope, to pray, to serve and to learn to sing the Lord's song in a land far from home (Ps. 137.4).

The Anglican church is long established in a land that has now lost its Christian heritage and does not know how to mourn its loss. What patterns of worship, prayer and witness will emerge to renew faith is still unknown. It is a spiritual tradition in profound transition. The parish community of the faithful will have to recover the original spirit of the word. 'We must take into the exile the feeling of being at home' (Simone Weil).

For thought, prayer and activity

1 'A great deal of the contemporary spiritual searching is lived out of a kind of restless wandering'.
   (a) Is that your experience?
   (b) How important is the sense of history and being rooted in a particular expression of the Christian faith to your spiritual life?
   (c) What would help you to strengthen your roots?

2   If you belong to another Christian denomination
   (a) What points of agreement or disagreement do you find in this chapter?
   (b) Are there things you would wish to add or question?

3   The Anglican tradition is 'best understood by praying and worshipping with it'. Create your own spiritual scrapbook of prayers, collects and liturgies from this tradition.

4   'Perhaps this church exists only to do itself out of a job?'
   (a) Do you agree?
   (b) What would this mean in practice and what positive things could you do to help bring this about?

5   Have you ever deliberately visited churches with a different approach to worship and prayer from your own church? If not, why not try it for a while – perhaps visiting one a month? Wherever possible take time to reflect with them on their particular expression of spiritual life.

Further reading and resources
Bunting, Ian (ed.), *Celebrating the Anglican Way* (London: Hodder and Stoughton, 1996).
Giles, Richard, *How to be an Anglican: Let Me Count the Ways . . .* (London: Canterbury Press, 2003).
Ramsey, Michael, *The Anglican Spirit* (New York: Church Publishing, 2005).
Rowell, Geoffrey, Stevenson, Kenneth and Williams, Rowan (eds), *Love's Redeeming Work: The Anglican Quest for Holiness* (Oxford: Oxford University Press, 2004), see 'General Introduction: The Anglican quest for holiness', pp. xxiii–xxxiii and 'Introduction', pp. 3–12.

www.cofe.anglican.org

3 Power in the name

The Jesus Prayer in the Orthodox tradition

One reason why the Christian faith spread so fast in its early history was the efficiency with which the Roman Empire imposed its order upon otherwise very diverse regions.

When the Empire began to collapse in the fourth century the cracks began to appear. Across the Mediterranean region Greek, Latin and Semitic cultures began to reassert their distinctive identities and seek their own centres of power again. A mixture of politics, ecclesiastical ambition and cultural and theological differences led, in AD 1054, to a major split in the Christian Church that exists to this day – East from West.

In the centuries that followed, these two parts of the church developed in relative ignorance of each other. The 'Orthodox church' refers to the ancient Christian churches across Eastern Europe, the Mediterranean and North Africa. Its cultural origins continue to contribute to its distinctive

---

A brief history of the Jesus Prayer

Fourth to eighth centuries   The prayer develops its distinctive form and use among men and women in the deserts of the Middle East and North Africa.

Fourteenth century   Now an established part of Eastern monastic spirituality – strongly associated with Mount Athos, Greece.

Eighteenth century   Popularized in eastern Europe by St Nicodemus, who edits the *Philokalia* (a collection of sayings and writings based on the Jesus Prayer).

Nineteenth century   Becomes central to Russian spirituality through the influence of St Seraphim of Sarov.

Twentieth century to present day   Gains wide prominence as a central feature of Orthodox spirituality.

character. Orthodox worship is strongly liturgical and sacramental and displays a highly developed sense of ritual. It has a profound theological tradition. In Western societies, marked by superficial informality, immediacy and rootlessness, the sense of antiquity, of deep mystery and holiness is powerfully attractive and there is a growing interest in this spiritual tradition.

Many people first meet the Orthodox tradition through its icons. But another distinctive feature of its spiritual life is the 'Jesus Prayer'.

Praying to Jesus

I was kneeling in a dark chapel lit only by the flicker of candles and oil lamps. In the frescoes on the walls I felt rather than saw the shadowy company of the saints surrounding us as we prayed. Behind me a deep voice with a strong East European accent began to pray. 'Lord Jesus Christ, Son of God, have mercy on me, a sinner.' Over and over he repeated it. After a while the prayer was taken up by a voice on the other side of the chapel, and then another. But the words remained the same.

I began to be aware of the extraordinary power of this ancient prayer. It seemed to weave its seamless thread around and through the centre of my being, into the community and into all the world beyond. It was a prayer without beginning or end. It seemed to rise out of an abyss of human longing and hopefulness. Everything was included in that endless cry for mercy and faith in the name of Jesus.

> The tax-collector, standing far off, would not even look up to heaven, but was beating his breast and saying, 'God, be merciful to me, a sinner'.
> Luke 18.13
>
> A blind man was sitting by the roadside begging. [When he heard that Jesus was passing by] he shouted, 'Jesus, Son of David, have mercy on me!'
> Luke 18.35–8

This ancient prayer combines the petitions of two unnamed people found in Luke chapter 18. In these stories both people cry one repeated prayer from the depths of their helpless need. Together these simple prayers symbolize humanity's deepest need before God – for forgiveness, for healing and for spiritual vision. They also combine two contrasting moods in prayer. One is humble and penitent, hardly daring even to ask for anything. The other is vigorous, bold, persistent – almost demanding!

From a very early stage in the Church's praying these two prayers became merged: 'Lord Jesus Christ, Son of God, have mercy on me, a sinner.' Over the centuries this prayer developed with small variations. The form we have here took shape in the fourteenth century and is best suited to rhythmic repetition.

The Jesus Prayer was also practised as a way of seeking to be faithful to the command of scripture to 'pray without ceasing' (1Thess. 5.17). This is not to be understood as endlessly 'saying prayers', but as a response to the call to live our lives in sustained contemplation of Christ, his love and will.

The theology of the Prayer

The centrality of Jesus
This simple petition is a prayer of incredible completeness. These brief phrases manage to summarize all God's actions in Christ – his birth, baptism, transfiguration, cross, resurrection, ascension. 'Jesus' is the earthly name of the one who took flesh among us: God with us. The titles 'Lord' and 'Christ' acclaim his victory and exaltation through the cross, his resurrection and his ascension to the right hand of the Father. 'Son of God' is the title of the eternally-begotten one – the exact 'icon' of the Father.

And as no one can truly call Jesus 'Lord' except by the power of the Holy Spirit (1Cor. 12.3), this prayer is offered through and in the whole life of God the Holy Trinity.

A prayer of penitence and longing
'Have mercy on me'. We honestly confess our unworthiness and sin. But this is not a grovelling in any sense. In the mercy of God is found the promise of our transformation. In this prayer we turn away from our sins, but we also turn towards the light of God's presence. Nor is this just a private prayer. It is a prayer of love and longing for the fulfilling of all life in his mercy.

A prayer of faith
'Lord Jesus Christ'. At the heart of this prayer is a deep reverence for the name of Jesus. In ancient cultures the task of naming was deeply significant; this is so in the Bible. In Hebrew thought, to invoke someone's name or to act in the name of another person makes them effectively present.

There is therefore deep significance in the very mention of a name. Everything true of earthly naming is incomparably more true of the divine name: the power and glory of God is present in the divine Name. So we name Christ in his true glory. The starting place of this prayer is not ourselves but worship and holy reverence.

With all God's people

Let me offer a spiritual health warning and an encouragement: the Jesus Prayer is powerful. It is not a technique or magic. It is not to be used carelessly. As a discipline of prayer it is best used alongside the disciplines of regular reflection on the Bible, in the fellowship and mutual encouragement of fellow pilgrims, and in worship with all God's people.

With all creation

Though this prayer begins with our sense of personal need and longing, those who pray with it find they grow into a sense that this is a prayer all creation is praying. We are crying out together. (Romans 8.19–27 suggests this connection too.) In this way it becomes a prayer of intercession and some will naturally begin to add the names of people and situations in place of 'me' as they pray the prayer. Others prefer to pause after every so many repetitions and pray for others.

Out of the depths

Those with long experience of this prayer never speak of it as a technique but suggest there are three levels or depths for us to grow into as we pray.

- From the lips. This is the starting point. It is a verbal offering of love and obedience, not dependent on thoughts or feelings.
- With the mind. We are consciously and thoughtfully praying the prayer.
- From the heart. This is the goal. Something much deeper than words and feelings is now going on. Lips are silent, the mind becomes quiet, prayer fills the 'cave of the heart', the centre of one's being. We are beginning to pray out of our truest selves. And it will be no longer us praying but the Spirit praying in us and through us. There is a gradual flooding of dry and arid corners of our lives and depths. A refining, sanctifying, burning love indwells our depths.

Like all praying, it is hard work and there is no neat progression. But in God's grace we keep praying with longing love to be drawn into the prayer of the heart – to be found in Christ.

Beginning to pray the Prayer

Breathing
It is a rhythmic prayer so the rhythm of our own breathing is a very helpful way of sustaining and pacing it. For example, say 'Lord Jesus Christ, Son of God', as you breathe in; 'have mercy on me', as you breathe out.

Jesus Prayer rope
A circular knotted rope is commonly used with this prayer as an aid to attentiveness and a practical way of keeping count without having to think about it (one knot per repetition). Most prayer ropes have a bead after twenty-five knots. Having said that, the goal of the prayer is not quantity of repetition but quality of attentiveness. As one early saint teaches, 'do not trouble about the number of times you say the prayer. Let this be your sole concern, that it should spring up in your heart with quickening power like a fountain of living water' (St Theophan).

Focus and posture
Some find a lighted candle, a cross or an icon is a helpful focus. Whatever posture is used it is important to be relaxed but alert.

Repetition
This idea worries some people. It is best understood as a repetition of loving attentiveness; a discipline of remembrance and awareness enabled by frequent repetition of a single phrase or idea. It is therefore not the same as the mindless, empty repetitions that Jesus warns against (Matt. 6.7).

There are times when one word or phrase says it all – 'I love you', 'sorry', 'thank you'. But these words will still be inadequate to express what fills the heart. It is not surprising to read that repetition is a feature of worship in heaven. 'Day and night without ceasing they sing, "Holy, holy, holy, the Lord God the Almighty"' (Rev. 4.8).

Distractions

These are natural. The repetition of the prayer may act on your concentration like the lead on a dog taken for a walk. The dog is eagerly and continually distracted by everything, pulling this way and that. The lead lovingly but firmly pulls the dog back on to the path. Don't fight the distractions – just return to the prayer.

Alone or together?

Either way of praying is possible. There is no right or wrong way to do this. A suggestion would be to start with a few verses of scripture and perhaps the Lord's Prayer and then begin to pray the Jesus Prayer.

Part of the gift of the prayer is its simplicity. You don't have to think of 'the right words to say' and the given words have a directness that we might not otherwise have the confidence to express. If you are praying in a group you may decide to go round the group each taking a turn. After each person has led for a while they may close their turn by offering a simple summary prayer after which the next person takes up the prayer.

The heart of divine love

The story is told of a monk on Mount Athos called Staretz Silouan. His job was to supervise the migrant workers who worked in the monastery workshops. Many were very poor and had left their families in rural Russia to earn money and send it home. He would organize them and then go and pray for them as they worked – using the Jesus Prayer. He prayed for one young worker, Nicholas, who had left his wife and young child.

'In the beginning I prayed with tears of compassion for Nicholas, for his young wife, for the little child, but as I was praying the sense of the divine presence began to grow on me and at a certain moment I lost sight of Nicholas, his wife, his child, his needs, their village, and I could be aware only of God, and I was drawn by the sense of the divine presence deeper and deeper, until, of a sudden, at the heart of this presence, I met divine love holding Nicholas, his wife and his child and now it was with the love of God that I began to pray for them again, but again I was drawn into the deep and in the depths of this again and again I found the divine love for them . . .' (Bloom, 1989, 202–3).

For thought, prayer and activity

1   Try praying the Jesus Prayer – perhaps for five minutes each day using the rhythm of your breathing. You can pray it anywhere – but a regular time (while travelling to work or during a coffee break, for example) is helpful. It can also be prayed in a group with each person taking a turn to lead it. Beware of trying to analyse what you are doing or how it feels. It needs time to find a rhythm in our depths.

2   (a) Reflect on the place of:
            Penitence and longing,
            Faith,
            Being with God's people,
            Being with all creation,
                  in your life.
      (b) What place does each have and what do they mean to you?

The Jesus Prayer offers a helpful way of managing distractions in prayer. Be loving towards your distractions. Do not fight them. They are natural. But we do not need to be pulled around by them. Let the repetition of the prayer pull you back on to the path.

Further reading

Barrington-Ward, Simon, *The Jesus Prayer* (Oxford: Bible Reading Fellowship, 1996).

Barrington-Ward, Simon and Brother Ramon SSF, *Praying the Jesus Prayer Together* (Oxford: Bible Reading Fellowship, 2001).

Hubbard, Keith, *In the Name of Jesus* (Cambridge: Grove Books, 2000).

Ware, Kallistos, *The Orthodox Way* (New York: SVS Press, 1998).

4 Fire from heaven

The Spirit of Pentecost

On 9 April 1906 in a warehouse on Azusa Street in down-town Los Angeles, the Holy Spirit fell in power. To this and other awakenings of the Spirit around the world around the same time, the Pentecostal church traces its origins. The initial revival in Los Angeles lasted for three years. During that time, seven days a week, three times a day, the warehouse was packed for special services. People travelled across the world to experience what was happening. Within two years the phenomenon had spread to over 50 countries.

The pastor of this warehouse church was an unlikely revival leader. Bill Seymour was the gentle, one-eyed son of ex-slaves. He had studied the Bible at the nearby Baptist College (where the first signs of revival had caused controversy some years before). But in that segregated world Seymour had to listen to lectures through an open window (or in the corridor if it was raining). This self-effacing teacher had the endearing habit of putting a wooden shoebox over his head to 'make space for the Spirit'.

What was happening at Azusa Street?

They believed that what they were seeing and experiencing was a continuation of the outpouring of the Spirit foretold by the prophet Joel (chapter 2) and first experienced on the day of Pentecost (Acts 2).

They believed this was not to be the establishing of another denomination but a gift for the whole Church. Seymour himself said, 'We are not fighting against people or churches, but we are seeking to replace dead forms and dogmas with a living practical Christianity.' The vision was ecumenical. Another early leader expressed the hope that 'as a Pentecostal movement we would lose ourselves in the great body of Christianity'.

The manifestations of this outpouring constituted a prophetic sign of a social revolution – a foretaste of a new society. The gift of tongues that character- ized the revival was itself a sign of social revolution and integration between races, between nations, between men and women, rich and poor. Early Pentecostals were prominent in social protest and campaigned at some cost for the abolition of slavery, emancipation of women and civil rights. This spiritual revival was a sign that the end of the world was approaching and the return of Christ at the end of time was immanent.

> Afterwards, I will pour out my spirit on all flesh; your sons and daughters shall prophesy, your old men shall dream dreams, and your young men shall see visions. Even on the male and female slaves, in those days, I will pour out my spirit.
>
> Joel 2.28–9

Two early divisions

Seymour's church, with its mixed race membership, was already controversial in a society practising rigid segregation. Immediate opposition to what was happening came from Charles Parham, the principal of the Baptist College.

When he visited Azusa Street he was appalled by the sight of blacks and whites, men and women, sprawled together on the floor helpless in the power of the Spirit. Parham was a convinced racist (and a member of the Ku Klux Klan), who believed in segregation.

Still in its infancy, the movement split. By the time the 'Assemblies of God' was founded in 1914, led by Parham, it was dominated by whites. When Seymour died in 1922 not one Pentecostal paper mentioned the fact. More recent writing and studies in the Pentecostal movement have been trying to re-establish the roots of the Pentecostal faith in the vision and teaching of Seymour.

The beginnings of the English Pentecostals

Just a year after Azusa Street an Anglican vicar in Sunderland, Alexander Boddy, held some revival meetings at which a Norwegian Methodist pastor, T. B. Barratt, spoke and ministered. Both had had personal experi- ence of revival and knew something of events in Los Angeles. What the events in America, Oslo and Sunderland had in common was the influence of the revival in Wales in 1904. On 1 September 1907 Barratt began a series of meetings from which, with much quieter beginnings, the same spiritual awakening became evident.

There was not the racial issue among the English Pentecostals; rather the struggle was across social class. Boddy was a middle class Anglican vicar in a movement that, as elsewhere, developed outside the established churches among poorer, less educated communities (Wakefield, 2004).

The Anglican Boddy is one of the honourable exceptions. The historic Christian denominations generally distanced themselves from the Pentecostal movement. Factors included racial prejudice, a suspicion of enthusiasm and the miraculous and the problem of relating across very different cultures. Many of these factors are still influential today. For most of its history, the Pentecostal church has developed in isolation from the encouragement and partnership and resources of the mainstream churches.

The roots of Pentecostal spirituality

The particular character of the American revival could be explained in part as a fusion of two powerful spiritual traditions. It was a meeting of African spirituality – holistic, strongly community based and intuitively open to the reality of spiritual life – and the Wesleyan Holiness movement. As it grew other influences shaped it but certain core characteristics remain central to its character and vision.

A spirituality in search of a theology?
Until more recently the Pentecostal movement has been slow to produce its own theologians. It means that the 'Pentecostal *experience* may be far richer than the Pentecostal *explanation*' (Chan, 2001, p. 10). There are several practical reasons for this. Pentecostal churches were most often found among the least educated parts of the community. As many there entered an experience of spiritual life they had never known in traditional churches, the movement naturally stressed the immediacy of life in the Spirit and a corresponding suspicion of the intellect. But even if they had gone looking for theological resources it was not obvious where they could have found them. The Holy Spirit was a neglected subject among theologians in the mainstream churches. The Pentecostal experience was more likely to be studied by sociologists.

A spirituality of the 'little folk'
Inspiration for this comes partly from the song of Mary, the unknown young village girl who sings of the beginning of a new kingdom in which the lowly will be exalted and the injustices of the present order will be cast down (Luke 1.51–2). The idea is also found in the blessing Jesus pronounces upon the 'meek' in the Sermon on the Mount (Matt. 5.5). The trouble is that the English translation 'meek' means something quite different and altogether less radical. The revolutionary implication of this blessing is therefore missed. Jesus is blessing the *anawim* (the Old Testament word behind the English 'meek'). The *anawim* are the radically disinherited and powerless who have no share or say in the way the world's resources are shared. Jesus says that they are the ones who will inherit the earth. The present order will be judged and overturned.

A supernatural spirituality
There is strong stress on the need to be filled with the power of the Holy Spirit. It is through the presence of this same Spirit that the community is guided and inspired through dreams, visions, prophecy and empowered to minister healing and work miracles. Worship and prayer may be enriched by singing and speaking in tongues inspired directly by the Holy Spirit. Where Pentecostalism has become integrated into mainstream church life it is usually called the charismatic movement. *Caris* means 'grace', *mata* 'gifts'. The name refers to the both the source and expression of divine life among God's people (see Chapter 16).

A revolutionary and celebratory spirituality
There are good reasons why this denomination has attracted more than its share of persecution around the world. With its commitment to maximum participation, the narrative character of its theology, the dialogical approach to teaching, the mix of order and spontaneity in its worship, it points towards a form of community that liberates, reconciles and transforms the present order.

The celebration at the heart of its spiritual life is not easy for the outsider to understand. In reality it is deeply subversive. This can be illustrated by a story from South Africa, at the height of the struggle against apartheid. A young white man is smuggled into a black township for an evening. He describes himself as a 'tired white radical'. He is full of the seriousness of 'the struggle', the urgency of the movement, the price to be paid, the suffering to be endured. But all around him laughter, dancing, singing and sheer human vitality deepen with the night.

He can't cope. It all seems wrong. Inappropriate. He sits there feeling miserable. And then someone finally sits beside him, chiding him gently. 'Don't you see,' he says, 'the revolution is in the dancing.'

A playful spirituality

Jean-Jacques Suurmond suggests that one of the greatest gifts of the Pentecostals to the Western church is the restoration of the place of play in our relationship with God. We have become over-serious, over-adult. He connects this to Jesus's insistence on the necessity of child-like trust and spontaneity. To those concerned that this might trivialize faith he points out that while it is possible to be serious in play it is not possible to play while being serious. But the idea can be taken further. We play because we are God's image. There is a theological strand in the Bible that suggests that 'wisdom' has a playful character (Suurmond, 1994, pp. 29–37).

In Proverbs 8 these words are put into the mouth of wisdom, describing the creation of the world:

> Yahweh created me at the beginning of his work
> . . . when he laid the foundations of the earth
> then I was with him as the apple of his eye
> and I was daily his joy;
> constantly playing before his face,
> *playing* in his inhabited world
> and rejoicing in the human race.

(Prov. 8.22–31, my italics. Translation by G. von Rad, 1970, pp. 151f. I have changed 'rejoicing' to 'playing' in this passage. English translations seem reluctant to use this legitimate and in many ways more appropriate translation.)

Jesus likened himself to the figure of playful wisdom. He once compared his ministry to the frustration of trying to start a children's game in the market place that no one else wants to join in. 'I piped and you wouldn't dance, I wailed and you would not mourn' (Luke 7.32).

An embodied, holistic spirituality
Its African roots help to explain this. Unlike so much spiritual life in Western Christianity, this is a tradition that does not fear the body. It is an emotional and sensual spiritual tradition – though not without an often highly conservative moral code of behaviour to contain it in the holy vision. I reflect that despite a childhood in Sunday schools singing all those 'action choruses' that children are supposed to find enjoyable, it was not until I spent a year, as a young adult, worshipping in a Pentecostal church that I began to discover the place of my body and senses in my faith and worship (see Chapter 11).

A 'Third World' spirituality
This may yet be where the profoundest gift of the Pentecostal church lies hidden.

The Jewish theologian Abraham Heschel, writing out of the experience of another people who understood the diaspora, persecution and exile, once compared the black peoples to the biblical character Joseph. Joseph was sold into slavery but in God's providence and mercy became the saviour to those who had betrayed him so long before.

The phenomenon of the Pentecostal movement

It is the fastest growing part of the church in the world – presently 400 million members and growing by 20 million a year. By 2010 they will constitute approximately half the Christian population of the world.

- They are found among the poorest and most vulnerable peoples of the world.
- They are perhaps the most persecuted Christian group.
- 66 per cent live in the developing world.
- 50 per cent live in severe poverty.

The Pentecostal movement is established in 8,000 ethno-linguistic cultures, worshipping in over 7,000 languages. Today there are five strands across the world:

- Black Pentecostal churches
- White Pentecostal churches
- Charismatic renewal (Pentecostal insights expressed in the main-stream churches)
- Western independent charismatic groups
- Third World independent charismatic groups.

For thought, prayer and activity

The function of the Pentecostal movement is to restore the power of expression to people without identity and power of speech, and to heal them from the terror of the loss of speech.

(Jean-Jacques Suurmond)

Pentecostalism is essentially a gift from the Third World to the West with its poverty of feelings, in bondage to privilege and affluence and its fear of the body.

(Jean-Jacques Suurmond)

1   Have you ever worshipped in a Pentecostal church? If not, why not do so?

2   Learning from the Pentecostal vision of God.
   (a) Write down a series of words that capture the positive and distinctive qualities of this movement.
   (b) Circle those words that reflect, in some part, aspects of your approach to spirituality.
   (c) Put a box around those words that do not seem to reflect your beliefs or practice.
   (d) What does this exercise tell you? Are there boxes that you'd like to turn into circles?

3   'While it is possible to be serious in play it is not possible to play while being serious.'
   What part does play have in your life and in your spiritual life?

Further reading

Chan, Simon, *Pentecostal Theology and the Christian Spiritual Tradition* (Sheffield: Sheffield University Press, 2001).

Clarke, Clifton, *Introducing Black Pentecostal Spirituality* (Cambridge: Grove Books, 1997).

Rad, G. von, *The Wisdom of Israel* (London: SCM Press, 1970).

Suurmond, Jean-Jacques, *Word and Spirit at Play: Towards a Charismatic Theology* (London: SCM Press, 1994).

Wakefield, Gavin, *The First Pentecostal Anglican – The Life and Legacy of Alexander Boddy* (Cambridge: Grove Books, 2004).

5 Beneath the cross of Jesus

Spirituality in the Evangelical tradition

In 1984 an annual conference of evangelical clergy took the theme of spirituality. The first three speakers represented Catholic, Orthodox and charismatic spiritualities respectively (the latter more familiar but still a newly emerging force at the time). It was the first time many of us had heard the subject discussed by speakers who belonged to the tradition they spoke of. I remember feeling quite caught out by how attractive and exciting the first two speakers were. All three communicated a compelling sense of mystery, of holiness and a vision for new depths of spiritual life. Last of all came evangelical spirituality. The speaker stood up and without preamble began, 'Well, there are eight features to evangelical spirituality'. He proceeded to list and explain each of them with characteristic biblical precision and clarity. It sounded disappointingly cerebral after what had gone before. But in the discussion that followed there was further surprise. The Russian Orthodox priest (who despite the power of his address had given every impression of hating being there at all) stood up and congratulated the evangelical speaker. 'I agreed with everything you said and wish I could have expressed it as clearly myself.'

It was a highly significant affirmation for two reasons. First, the real uncertainty at the time was whether evangelicals had a spirituality at all! In fact it was a tradition with deep spiritual riches but it was not accustomed to articulating them in this way. Second, the fact that a Russian Orthodox priest could recognize and affirm the central features of the evangelical tradition challenged its own historic assumptions about its distinctiveness and the need for separation. Here was a call to evangelicals to engage in critical openness with the spiritual life of the wider Church, and to enter more deeply and faithfully into the depths of its own tradition.

From there to here

Here are some of the historic strands of evangelical spirituality.

The Reformation of the sixteenth century
God in his grace justifies the sinner and gives free access into his presence where all serve as priests.

The word 'evangelical' was first used as a self-designation by Lutherans at the time of the Reformation. Evangel means 'gospel'. The roots of evangelicalism are therefore found in spiritual awakening shaped around the doctrine of justification by faith. Salvation is understood as a gift of grace rather than something earned by human works. The implications of this for a relationship with God were profound. Spiritual life relaxed. God could be approached more as Father and less as Judge. The believer was encouraged to approach the Father as a beloved son and daughter, not as a slave (Mursell, 2001, pp. 167–8).

It is important to note that all this was worked out in direct conflict with the Roman Catholic Church of the day. That has given evangelical spirituality an important double emphasis ever since. This is tradition that both witnesses *to* something – to what God has done for us in Christ and a conviction about the kind of community that brings into being – and also dissents *from*. It is a tradition that fiercely guards the truth of the gospel as it has received it and will distance itself from teaching that distorts it. Being 'not Catholic' remains a significant factor in its approach to expressions of spiritual life and prayer.

The puritans of the seventeenth century
God in his grace enables and requires a transforming personal spirituality – to wrestle and fight and pray.

The puritans were an uncompromising reform movement in the seventeenth century at a time when the spiritual life of church and nation was widely thought to be weak, decadent and in need of renewal. Their approach to spiritual formation reflects this concern. Among their leaders were John Owen, Richard Baxter and Richard Sibbes. John Bunyan's *The Pilgrim's Progress* is one of the most famous books from this period. Under the leadership of Oliver Cromwell puritans engaged in direct opposition to the monarchy. They believed that political power rests with the people not in the absolute authority of a king. They were a heavily persecuted movement. Their writings on the spiritual life remain a significant influence on evangelicalism to this day.

The evangelical awakening of the eighteenth century
God in his grace creates a joyful fellowship between himself and his people.

The eighteenth-century spiritual awakening is the birthplace of contemporary evangelicalism within the Anglican church. It built on puritan writing and spirituality and was widely read. George Whitefield, the Wesleys and the former slave trader John Newton are among the best known leaders. Their impact was huge – and opposed by the institutional church of their day. Hymns from this era include 'Amazing grace', 'How sweet the name of Jesus sounds' (both by Newton) and 'O for a closer walk with God' (Cowper). These capture well the character of the movement. It was direct, uncomplicated, personal and devotional. There was an accompanying stress on personal conversion, holiness of life, the supreme authority of scripture and the priority of evangelizing the lost.

Mission, holiness and social action in the nineteenth century
God in his grace grants holiness to the consecrated believer.

Personal holiness of life was a distinctive teaching emphasis of the Keswick Convention, an annual Bible week that began in 1875 and continues to this day.

God in his grace enables us to work energetically to lead others to Christ.

It was also a period of pioneering missionary initiatives across the world led by such people as Hudson Taylor (China) and Henry Martyn (India).

God in his grace calls us to be salt and light in the world, working for the transforming of society.

In this country, the evangelical Anglican William Wilberforce led the political fight for the abolition of slavery. Lord Shaftesbury and Josephine Butler campaigned on issues of poverty and social deprivation.

This was a significant period of growth and influence for evangelicals in the nonconformist wing of the church. These include the various forms of

Primitive and Wesleyan Methodists, Congregationalists, Baptists and Quakers. The Baptist preacher Charles Spurgeon was arguably one of the most significant church leaders in the second half of the century. Appallingly persecuted by the institutional church of the day, evangelical nonconformist spirituality was marked by deep personal piety and social action.

To the present day

For the first 60 years of the last century evangelicals were a beleaguered minority. They kept themselves separate, contributed very little to the political, social or theological debates of their day and were experienced by the watching world as defensive and reactionary. Many of their most gifted leaders were abroad on the mission field (men and women – whose ministry was not always welcomed in this tradition). Today the evangelical wing of the church is in a place of unprecedented influence and strength and leadership. This represents a remarkable turnaround.

Evangelicals within the Anglican church today offer an interesting example of what happens when a once persecuted minority becomes a respected majority. There are significant tensions within the tradition and much talk today of a crisis of evangelical identity. Evangelicalism has always been a diverse tradition though within strictly held conventions and with the core belief in the centrality of scripture. The conservative evangelical wing represents a quite aggressive restatement of Reformation and puritan principles. It is deeply disturbed by what it perceives to be present trends in the wider church. A large number would call themselves 'open evangelicals'. The title expresses a degree of distancing from historic separatist tendencies of past generations (and the present approach of some conservatives). Theologically the stress on the cross is now expressed alongside the doctrine of the incarnation. There is a commitment to critical and creative involvement at all levels of church life, theological debate, church government and leadership, social and political involvement and the world of other faiths. The charismatic movement has influenced all parts of the church and is influential in both the conservative and more open wings of the movement. The centrality of the Word is now appreciated afresh, interpreted through the dynamic life of the Spirit.

Some features of evangelical spirituality

Evangelicalism is a hard tradition to summarize with any precision today, but certain core features in its spiritual life are foundational.

A spirituality of the Word

It has always been a Bible-centred spirituality. This has been expressed through a strong emphasis on the preaching of the Word. The sermon is highly esteemed. But so too is the believer's own relationship with the Word of God. This is a spirituality based on the knowledge and learning by heart of scripture as the living Word of the Lord.

Contemporary evangelicalism tends to emphasize the 'Word' at the expense of the sacraments which tend therefore to be given the role of a visual aid. There is an impatience with and suspicion of sign, symbol and mystery. This has not always been so. Past generations of evangelicals have reverenced Holy Communion in terms that would sound very 'Catholic' to evangelicals today (Seddon, 2004, pp. 17–21 and see Chapter 8 in this book).

A cross-centred spirituality

'We preach Christ crucified' is the motto often printed above the pulpit or on the church notice board of evangelical churches. Central to this tradition is a belief in objective atonement resulting in an intensely personal encounter with Christ at the cross. Worship, adoration and service flow out of deep indebtedness to Christ. There is therefore a strong stress on original sin and the Fall.

A practical and missionary spirituality

The priority of evangelism and outreach shapes evangelical approaches to Christian living. It has always been a robustly outward-looking, practical approach to living the faith. It is uneasy if it is not 'up and doing'. Prayer meetings are for intercession. Indeed it can be described as a spirituality of intercession (Gillett). In such a tradition the idea of 'spirituality' can sound suspiciously passive and inward-looking.

Partly for this reason it has tended not to produce great art, music or literature. This is not its priority. 'I decided to know nothing among you except Jesus Christ, and him crucified'(1 Cor. 2.2) is the approach evangelicals understand well. This is a tradition once mischievously complimented for its willingness 'to embrace bad taste for the sake of the gospel' (Richard Holloway)! Among open and charismatic evangelicals there are signs of a growing appreciation of the place of creative arts and an openness to wider approaches to spirituality.

An unfashionable spirituality

To this day, in parts of the world, evangelicals have costly experience of being marginalized and of holding to certain core gospel truths against the prevailing mood of the day. They are not embarrassed to be unpopular by insisting on the centrality of more uncomfortable aspects of the gospel message such as the reality of sin, the centrality of the cross, self denial and the final judgement. It can therefore be experienced as a spirituality of great gentleness or unnervingly hard certainties, but it does expect its followers be clear about what they believe and why.

Devotion to Jesus

Evangelical faith is centred on a deep personal devotion to Jesus, who makes a free gift of his love, forgiveness and presence to all who turn from their sins and trust in him. Their hymns celebrate this tirelessly. 'What a friend we have in Jesus, all our sins and griefs to bear' (Joseph Scriven).

A spirituality of new birth

It is a spirituality of radical personal conversion and change centred on the Pauline epistles. Paul's clear-cut sense of 'then' and 'now' most closely relates to the evangelical experience of conversion. 'If anyone is in Christ, there is a new creation: everything old has passed away; see, everything has become new!' (2 Cor. 5.17). Nonetheless, some evangelical traditions have a strong sense that conversion of life to Christ involves journey and spiritual struggle.

Assurance

Assurance of faith is central to the understanding of evangelical spirituality. The opening line of a favourite evangelical hymn captures it well: 'Blessed assurance, Jesus is mine' (Fanny Crosby). Core biblical texts include, 'We want each one of you to show the same diligence, so as to realize the full assurance of hope to the very end, so that you may not become sluggish, but imitators of those who through faith and patience inherit the promises' (Heb. 6.11–12 and see also 2 Pet. 1.10). Paradoxically it is a gift that must be wrestled with to makes it ones own. There is no suggestion that someone who lacks assurance is not a Christian. But without such an assurance the believer will always be struggling to find the boldness that Christian prayer and service requires.

Late in his life, the saintly evangelical leader of the nineteenth-century church Charles Simeon was having his eyes bathed by his personal assistant. When his assistant had finished he asked Simeon if his eyes were more comfortable. 'He said, opening them and looking up to heaven, "Soon they will behold all the glorified saints and angels around the throne of my God and Saviour, who has loved me until death, and given himself for me; then I shall see him whom having not seen I have loved; in whom, though now I see him not, yet believing I rejoice with joy unspeakable and full of glory"; and turning his eyes towards me, he added, "Of the reality of this I am as sure as if I were there this moment"' (Gillett, 1993, p. 65).

No presentation of evangelical faith and spiritual formation would be complete without a challenge and an invitation. In obedience to Christ and out of love for the lost the question must be asked – 'Do you know how much Christ has done for you?'

*   *   *

The core emphases of evangelical faith

1   The finality of Christ
2   Centrality of the cross
3   Authority of scripture
4   Necessity of conversion
5   Assurance of salvation
6   Priesthood of all believers
7   Dependence on the Spirit
8   Commitment to mission
9   The call to holiness

For thought, prayer and activity

1   (a) What, for you, are the most significant features of this tradition
          and its approach to spiritual life?
     (b) Which qualities are you most drawn to?
     (c) Are there features you struggle with? Can you say why?

2   At different stages of history evangelical faith can be seen to have had
     different emphases and senses of priority. What do you consider to be
     the priorities for faith and spiritual life in the challenges of the world
     today?

3   'A spirituality of the Word': This tradition is uncompromising on the
     centrality of the Bible for spiritual life and formation. But it varies in
     how it expresses this. How would this tradition speak to your own
     discipline of regular reading and reflecting on the Bible?

4   How do you respond to the question: 'Do you know how much Christ
     has done for you?'

Further reading
Cockerton, John, *The Essentials of Evangelical Spirituality* (Cambridge: Grove
     Books, 1994).
Cocksworth, C., 'Holding Together: Catholic Evangelical Worship in the Spirit',
     Anvil Journal, Vol 22:1 (2005).
George, Timothy and McGrath, Alister (eds), *For All the Saints: Evangelical
     Theology and Christian Spirituality* (Louisville, Ky.: Westminster John Knox
     Press, 2003).
Gillett, David, *Trust and Obey: Explorations in Evangelical Spirituality* (London:
     Darton, Longman and Todd, 1993).
Gordon, James, *Evangelical Spirituality: From the Wesleys to John Stott* (London:
     SPCK, 1991). Includes some of the leaders from the Methodist, Free Church
     and Baptist traditions.
Skeats, David, *Experience of Grace: Aspects of Faith and Spirituality in the Puritan
     Tradition* (Cambridge: Grove Books, 1997).

LIFE TOGETHER

Spiritual life in community

6 Into the unknown

Spiritual life and community

If someone were to ask you 'What community are you part of?' what would you reply? Does it sound a strange question? You probably belong to more than one. The word can describe very widely diverse patterns of relationships, but it commonly includes two important qualities. It will describe a group (or groups) of people with whom we have a sense of shared vision, values and purpose, and among whom we seek to give and receive the love, encouragement and support we need to sustain us in the challenges of living. This might be the family, close friends, our immediate neighbourhood or local church. For others it might be a number of networks defined by work, special circumstance or shared interest. Each is a community. The question may also make us aware that despite having any number of relationships and contacts we have nothing that feels as close and committed as the word suggests. Community is something we are searching for.

It was the quality and depth of their shared life that made the first Christians such a compelling presence in the world. 'See how these Christians love each other!' The evidence is that finding and sustaining community in today's society is a real struggle.

Yet not many courses and books on spiritual life pay much attention to the importance of community. All too often 'spirituality' is pursued as a private journey or shared in like-minded groups. We are missing something. The Christian vision of community is central to spiritual formation, prayer and faithful discipleship. It springs from two simple truths about ourselves and about God. First, it is not good for human beings to be alone (see Gen. 2.18). We are made for community. Second, we meet God in the community of the Holy Trinity – Father, Son and Holy Spirit. In every age God's people have sought out the patterns of living and belonging that enable them to grow faithfully in the will of God, to support each other in need and danger, to resist the prevailing pressures of their times and to witness to God's love in the world.

What might be the distinctive marks of such communities in our age? To explore what this might mean we draw on the life and writings of two wise guides who pioneered contrasting expressions of community to meet what they saw as the challenges of their time.

Dietrich Bonhoeffer

Dietrich Bonhoeffer was a pastor and theologian in Germany through the deepening crisis in the 1930s. Alarmed by what he saw as the compromise of his own church in the face of Hitler, he formed the Confessing Church and founded a new theological college. He ran it on radically new lines – a community of shared life, worship and prayer where Christ's call to discipleship was taken seriously and practised together. For Bonhoeffer, community was a response to the need for truth, moral clarity and resistance to evil. It was a prophetic sign. In 1937 he published *Life Together* – a summary of his vision for the community and its practical outworking. It has stayed in print ever since. The English edition is now in its twentieth reprint. It is a radical and subversive vision for Christian living in the midst of a world of political crisis, close to devastating conflict. Soon after the book came out the Gestapo closed down the college and arrested a number of the former ordinands. Bonhoeffer himself was imprisoned in 1943 and remained there until his execution in 1945.

Jean Vanier

Jean Vanier's vision for community grew from the time he began to share his home with people living with significant mental or physical handicap and who had often experienced abandonment and terrible neglect. In 1964 he founded the first of what became the L'Arche communities. In these communities people of various handicaps and learning difficulties live as equals with able-bodied people. He still leads the movement that now has 124 such communities around the world, offering places of love and dignity to some of the most rejected in human society. These are communities founded on shared weakness and acceptance of human frailty rather than strengths and competitive achievement.

Welcome

Christian community is a gift of God. It is not a human idea or invention. This is Bonhoeffer's starting place. It begins in 'divine welcome' and therefore has a source of life and purpose unlike any other. The Church comes into being solely because the love of Christ is present in the world and people are drawn to him. He is Lord and he knows what he has in mind in calling us. 'As the Father has loved me, so I have loved you . . . You did not choose me but I chose you', said Jesus (John 15.9, 16). We are here at God's pleasure and sustained in his love. In an age dominated by personal preference and consumer choice this is a challenging and subversive truth.

Unknown

The Church is a community that has its origin in the mystery of God's love and call. It doesn't begin or end with us. So there is always something about the life of Christian community that can feel a bit out of control. The vision for our life together belongs to God and not to us. We are a holy mystery. 'Beloved, we are God's children now; what we will be has not yet been revealed' (1 John 3.2). It is God who has called us together. We must learn to see each other as Christ sees us. 'From now on, therefore, we look at no one from a human point of view,' says Paul. 'If anyone is in Christ, there is a new creation' (2 Cor. 5.17).

We also come into this community with our own wounds, uncertainties and incompleteness. So this life together will need patience and care to work out.

We have not been here before. The theological college where I once taught worked very hard at the community life. But I noticed that with each passing year we were questioning the corporate disciplines of our life together more and more. It was not that we lacked commitment but it did feel as if we were coming from such independent lifestyles and assumptions that we had less and less idea of what shared life really required. 'Contemporary society is the product of fragmentation', says Vanier.

Love

This is obvious, surely? But Vanier observes that a society based on competition, independence and self-preservation will find this way of life very difficult. 'To have had cerebral palsy or meningitis is a tragedy but this is not the real sickness. The way these people have been treated shows a deeper disease. The real sickness is to have a heart made for love – and not to love.' Christian love is a cross-bearing love. It is the primary call to all who follow Jesus. 'This is my commandment, that you love one another as I have loved you' (John 15.12).

Henri Nouwen joined a L'Arche community for the last years of his life. He was an internationally known speaker and writer but suddenly he was in a place where he was unknown for all that. His gifts were irrelevant. They could not be the basis on which he was to recognized or loved. He was just 'Henri'. Although he had longed for such unconditional love he wrote movingly of how hard it was to accept it. This way of love asks us to learn to accept each other for who we are. Christian community is never ideal. It is no use wishing we were somewhere else. Vanier writes, 'We should not seek the ideal community. It is a question of loving those whom God has set before us'.

Reconciliation

Forgiveness and reconciliation are at the heart of Christian community. Bonhoeffer warns that our first instinct will be to strive to be a community of the 'devout'. We will put on our Sunday best, our most acceptable words and actions. We will strive to be saints. It may be very well intended and can look very pious but this is not yet Christian community. That happens when we accept that we are actually a community of the *un*devout. This is a community that is not living by a self-created image of holiness or piety or social respectability – but is a community of forgiven sinners who live by God's grace and mercy together. Vanier writes, 'If we come into community without knowing that the reason we come is to discover the mystery of forgiveness, we will soon be disappointed.'

This was exactly my experience of community in the Lee Abbey Fellowship in North Devon. Like many I came with heady idealism about what living together as Christians might be like. But I soon realized why so much of the New Testament was written to guide those communities through their struggles, conflicts and the need to forgive each other!

Are you prepared to learn to live in fellowship, being open to be known for what we are, accepting one another in Christ, and saying of others nothing that could not be said to them personally, if love and wisdom required it?

I am.

(One of the promises made on joining the
Lee Abbey community, North Devon)

Gratitude

For St Paul, a hallmark of Christian life together is sheer gratitude. 'As you therefore have received Christ Jesus the Lord, continue to live your lives in him . . . abounding in thanksgiving' (Col. 2.6–7). Never mind that so much of his time was spent sorting out the problems. The church never ceases to be a place of God's generous grace and must be received as such. Bonhoeffer is uncompromising on this. 'If we do not give thanks daily for the Christian community in which we have been placed, even where there is no great experience, no discoverable riches, but much weakness, small faith and difficulty, if we only keep on complaining to God, we hinder God from letting our fellowship grow according to the riches which are there for us all in Jesus Christ.'

Whatever their gifts or limitations, people are all bound together in a common humanity. Everyone is of unique and sacred value and everyone has the same dignity and the same rights. The fundamental rights of each person include the rights to life, to care, to a home, to education and to work. Since the deepest need of a human being is to love and to be loved, each person has a right to friendship, to communion and to a spiritual life.

(From the L'Arche charter)

Without walls

At the height of the struggles against apartheid in South Africa a multi-racial community was founded in Cape Town. It was called 'The

Community of the Broken Wall'. This picks up one of most dramatic ways the New Testament speaks of what Christ has done for the world. A wall of division has been broken down. There is now no division between ourselves and God and between each other. 'For he is our peace, [who] . . . has broken down the dividing wall' (Eph. 2.14). When such a basic divide is removed there is no limit to the possibilities of shared life. The image of a community without walls confronts one of the biggest temptations of community living. It is perilously easy to create a private, insular world of like-minded people and to shut out all those who don't fit in.

In a community without walls, people will meet others who are seriously different from each other. It will not be a safe, insular network of the like-minded. It is harder and harder in our world to find the kind of place where we learn to talk and listen and meet each other in our real differences.

Even in the midst of a society facing powerful evil and in deep moral and spiritual confusion, Bonhoeffer still insisted that Christian community is to be lived in the midst of it all – without walls. Jesus did not withdraw into safe seclusion but lived in the midst of his enemies to bring them to peace. So must his followers. So life together, says Bonhoeffer, is never to be taken for granted or presumed as a right. Where it happens it is a gift and sign of 'gracious anticipation' of the Kingdom of peace, justice and love that will one day be fully revealed and for which we live and long.

For thought, prayer and activity

1 What communities do you belong to?
   (a) Make a list and then write the name of each community in the centre of a piece of paper and surround it with the qualities of that community and the gifts you receive by being part of it.
   (b) Add the demands and responsibilities of the community in a different colour.
   (c) Reflect on what these community maps tell you. Do they encourage you to make changes to the way you live with your communities? Do they indicate that there are some things that you want from community life that you're not getting at the moment?

2 Reflect on your life in community under the headings of this chapter: welcome, unknown, love, reconciliation, gratitude, without walls. How does your community life reflect each of these?

3 Dream a dream of your 'ideal' community life. What would be its features and qualities, what would it look and feel like to live in?

4 What would Bonhoeffer and Vanier highlight as core features of Christian community?

Further reading and resources
Bonhoeffer, Dietrich, *Life Together* (London: SCM Press, 1981).
Vanier, Jean, *Community and Growth* (New York: Paulist Press, 1989).

www.larche.org.uk

7 Seeking shapes for living

Values, disciplines and a rule of life

In his classic book *The Shape of Living*, David Ford describes life in today's world as a series of successive and stressful experiences of feeling overwhelmed. We are being swept along by powerful and competing pressures on our time, relationships, choices, money and beliefs. We have lost the patterns and rhythms of belonging that give shape and meaning to our living. Something is fundamentally out of control. The cost to our relationships and our quality of life is plain to see.

We will need to find some structure for the way we live to help us recognize and resist such pressures, to deepen our contemplation of God and to find a way of creative, faithful discipleship. It won't happen by chance. This is what has traditionally been called a rule of life.

What is a rule of life?

The word 'rule' can be off-putting. It sounds impersonal and authoritarian. Human and spiritual progress is surely not for measuring against the precise straight edge of a ruler. Holy living is not a matter of submitting to a set of rules. But there is wisdom in seeking some means of assessing whether we are making any progress in our Christian living. This is responsible discipleship.

It may help to suggest other ways of picturing our relationship to a rule of life.

A rule of life is

A way of grace

'there is no condemnation'

To be lived in mercy

'love is the fulfilling of the law'

A means of growth and transformation

'follow me'

Rule as scaffolding

The job of scaffolding is to offer a secure containing structure that enables the real building to happen within it. The scaffolding is not itself the real building of course. It enables the real building to happen. Nor is scaffolding meant to draw attention to itself. It is only needed to enable a chosen work to be successfully completed. When that has happened it is entirely disposable.

Rule as punctuation

Read a paragraph aloud from a magazine or newspaper, ignoring all the punctuation – pauses, commas, full stops etc. It sounds chaotic and the sense of the passage is quickly lost. In the same way our lives need punctuating – pauses, full stops, breaks, commas – to help us make 'sense' of our living and discern where its deeper meaning and significance lies.

The Rule of Benedict

The best known Christian rule is the Rule of St Benedict.

Not much is known about Benedict, but he founded his most famous monastery at Monte Cassino, in Italy, in the early sixth century. There he set about writing a guide or rule for community living. Although it has come to be associated with specialist monastic living it was in fact written as a rule for lay people. Offering a sustainable and nurturing shape for Christian community the Rule of Benedict was a hugely renewing gift to a society struggling through the violent turmoil of the Dark Ages.

In the increasingly chaotic and unstable world at the start of the twenty-first century Benedict's writings on relationships, money, authority, community, work, lifestyle, prayer and personal development seem as timely as when they were first written.

Rule as guidepost and support

The Latin word for rule is *regula*, which suggests a signpost or handrail. This is a gentler and more nurturing picture of a rule. It is something that offers support and gives direction in my journey of life and faith. A handrail is a support when travelling over uneven terrain. It is something to lean on.

Starting from the heart

A rule of life is a chosen commitment to a personal or corporate shape of living. It provides us with a practical structure to help us to live from those values and beliefs that are most important to us. It helps us, under God, to take responsibility and to be accountable for the way we live. So a starting place may be the question 'What is most important to me?' What do I want for my life and those I share it with? What are my core values – those moral, social and spiritual convictions that are non-negotiable and that I wish my life to be fashioned around? Where is my centre? What do I find there?

In the Bible this is a question about where my *heart* is. This question has to come before any decisions about what we are going to do with our lives. 'I can only answer the question "what am I to do?" if I can answer the prior question, "of what story do I find myself a part?"' (Alasdair MacIntyre).

These are big questions. We should not be discouraged if approaching them feels rather daunting. And it is important to realize that we are not starting to answer them from scratch. We don't come to this discussion like a blank sheet of paper. We have been influenced and shaped by the values of the world around us from long before we could think and choose. This means we will not be fully aware of how we have come by the present shape of our living and the convictions that underlie it. The answers lie deep within us and we need help to bring them to consciousness to make them more truly our own. (See Chapter 10.)

What we are trying to draw out here could be called our personal mission statement.

Developing a personal mission statement

What areas might your mission statement include?
This must be, in the best sense, a thoroughly worldly exercise. It is not to be narrowed to a private set of religious or church-centred disciplines. It involves the whole of our living and being human. How we pray is intimately connected to how we live.

We are seeking the core principles that shape all our relating – to family, spouse, ourselves, church, work, our enemies, our friends, possessions, money and time.

An example of a personal mission statement

(These are extracts from the mission statement a woman with a dual vocation to working career and family life. She is seeking to sustain a faithful and creative relationship between them.)

I will seek to balance career and family as best I can since both are important to me.

My home will be a place where I and my family, friends and guests find joy, comfort, peace and happiness.

I will exercise wisdom in what we choose to eat, read, see and do at home. I especially want my children to love, to learn and to laugh – and to work and develop their unique talents.

I will be a concerned and responsible citizen, involved in political process to ensure my voice is heard and my vote is counted.

I will act on situations and opportunities rather than be acted upon.

I will try to keep myself free from addictive and destructive habits. I will develop habits that free me from old labels and limits and expand my capabilities and choices.

My money will be my servant, not my master. My wants will be subject to my needs and my means.

Except for long-term home and car loans, I will seek to keep myself free from consumer debt.

I will spend less than I earn.

I will use what money and talents I have to make life more enjoyable for others through service and charitable giving.

(Covey, 1992, p. 107)

Begin with the end in mind

As a way of beginning to detect your core values try these two exercises:

Imagine you have died and at your funeral three people share their memories of you: a member of your family, a colleague at work and a close friend. What would you most want them to remember you for?

Write your own obituary. Where would you wish to see it published and what would you most want it to contain about you?

You *choose*

Approach all these questions as if God is leaving it to you to decide your values. This is *your* responsibility. This is not to suggest that God's place in our values is not important. But it can be tempting to over-spiritualize the process and hide behind variations of 'Well, I just want what God wants'. More than just being a likely cop-out in this context, it is also a very dangerous assumption!

Invite the discernment of others

We need the help of those close to us in preparing this – people who know us, love us and will speak the truth to us. The more something matters to us, the closer it is to us, the harder it may be for us to recognize our relationship to it.

A personal rule of life

You might find it helpful to use a rule of life chart like the example printed on page 63. You may wish to adapt the categories. For example, someone with school-age children may well find their year is shaped more significantly around term times and holidays rather than regular weeks and months.

In each box you are invited to make a time commitment. Where appropriate you might also suggest at what point of the day or week your commitment might be fulfilled. It is important to be aware of when your energies are freshest or at their lowest in the day, for example. Where possible this should influence the choices you make for your use of time.

1   As you work through the chart pray for guidance and wisdom.
2   Seek a pattern that is possible, achievable and sustainable. This is important. 'Pray as you can, do not try to pray as you can't' (John Chapman). This is not a place for spiritual heroics! If ten minutes prayer a day is what is realistic then start by seeking to be faithful to that.
3   Avoid the language of legalism – 'I must', 'I should'. This too quickly

	Personal	Family	Friends	Work	Church	Leisure
Daily						
Weekly						
Monthly						
Annually						

A rule of life chart

becomes a source of condemnation. Instead use phrases like: 'I will seek to . . .', or 'with the help of God I will . . .'

4   It is important to honour responsibility to those with whom we share our lives. If you are married it is important to discuss your ideas with your spouse. The commitments we make in our rule of life should not be at the expense of others.

5   Remember your rule is concerned with the *whole* of life. Nothing is irrelevant. Beware of narrowing it to the 'spiritual' or 'Christian' bits of life.

6   Whilst it is important to plan a rule that is sustainable and realistic, it is right to plan an appropriate element of challenge for growth.

(a)   Ponder your present prayer life and your relationship with God. What would you dearly like to see change over these next few months? What might enable that to happen?

(b)   Are there some things which you have tried to improve on over the years and always just missed it? Give thought to why this is. It is worth looking at, say, one of those areas this year. Would talking it through with someone else give you a new perspective that could make a difference?

(c) If you feel challenged to take on something extra in your life what other things will you give up or reduce to make space? These other things may be just as worthy and godly but they are not what you sense God is calling you to make your main focus at this time.

7 Review the rule. Include, as part of your rule, a commitment to review how it is going – perhaps every six months or certainly each year. If you find that you have not been keeping parts of your rule you might consider:

(a) Was this a realistic commitment in the first place? If not, how could it be helpfully revised to encourage my growth rather than plan for failure?

(b) Have any changing circumstances in my life been a factor?

(c) Have I been living carelessly and do I need to confess this for what it is?

A community rule

Whenever the New Testament talks about patterns and shapes of living it speaks of something shared in community. The Rule of Benedict was a *communal* way of life. Within the support, encouragement and challenge of shared life each individual found strength to live faithfully to their own unique vocation in Christ. In fact my personal rule of life will express a conviction about where and how I live community. And I will need the support of community to live it faithfully.

For this reason some find it helpful to be linked to a specific community as part of their rule. The Iona and Taizé communities are popular examples of this. The rule may include an annual retreat to the community house for refreshment, teaching and renewal of discipleship. Traditional monastic communities such as the Franciscans have a 'Third Order' where people living outside of monastic life can share in the life and prayer of the community. Drawing up a rule of life is always part of such a commitment and the guidance of a spiritual director is an important part of this.

> 'As for those who will follow this rule – peace be upon them, and mercy . . .'
> Gal. 6.16
>
> 'Join together, my friends, in following my example. You have us for a model; imitate those whose way of life conforms to it.'
> (Phil. 3.17 REB)

A community rule of life might be very helpful for local church communities. It is quite common for churches to have their own mission
statement these days. What is less common is to find churches that have
gone on to think and pray through together a shared, sustainable shape of
living that might make that vision realizable. Without an agreed boundary
to its life and mission, church life proceeds on the assumption that Christian time and energy can extend limitlessly into an ever-increasing range
of worthy projects. That this is all 'for God' just makes the burden worse!
The result is corporate exhaustion, guilt and frustration. Communities
burn out too. In the face of yet another new challenge there is something
very liberating about being able to say, 'I can see this is important but after
careful thought and prayer we have agreed that we believe God is calling
us to put our time and energies into other things at the moment. So we will
have to say no.'

A rule, in the end, is a way of freedom.

> The issue at stake is the whole shape of living. To attend to that is no
> easy matter . . . but it is hard to imagine any adequate way of coping
> that does not try to answer the big questions about life, death,
> purpose, good and evil. We do not need to drown in what over-
> whelms us. Nor is the solution to fiddle with some of the details,
> important though they are. While doing justice to both the over-
> whelmings and the details, the main task is to stretch our minds,
> hearts and imaginations in trying to found and invent shapes of
> living. It is a task as old as the flood and as modern as the computer.
>
> (Ford, 1997, p. xvii)

For thought, prayer and activity

1 This chapter suggests far-reaching ways of discerning the rhythms and
   shapes of our living. Take time to work with the suggestions for a
   personal mission statement and personal rule of life. If you already
   have such a rule, is this is a helpful time to review it?

2 Take a way of life that you find strange or even alien – for example, a
   very strict solitary monastic rule or a nomadic lifestyle. It could be any
   way of living valued by those who follow it, but which does not appeal

to you. Enter into it imaginatively and try to see it from the point of view of its adherents.

(a)   Can you begin to understand its attractions?

(b)   Are there things you can learn from it and try to incorporate into your rule of life?

Further reading

Chittister, Joan, *The Rule of Benedict* (New York: Crossroad, 2001).

Covey, Stephen, *Seven Habits of Highly Effective People* (New York: Simon and Schuster, 1992).

Ford, David, *The Shape of Living* (London: Hodder and Stoughton, 1997).

Miller, Harold, *Finding a Personal Rule of Life* (Cambridge: Grove Books, 1985); reprinted in *Building Your Spiritual Life: the Best Contemporary Writing on Christian Spirituality* (Grand Rapids: Zondervan, 2003).

8 In the breaking of the bread

Communion, sacrament and the spiritual life

At the centre of the Christian life is a meal. But not just any meal. 'Do this in remembrance of me', said Jesus (Luke 22.19). The first Christians simply called it 'breaking bread', recalling the last supper Jesus shared with his disciples on the night of his betrayal. There 'he took a loaf of bread, and when he had given thanks, he broke it and gave it to them, saying, "This is my body, which is given for you"' (Luke 22.19).

Followers of Jesus have broken bread in faithful obedience ever since. Whether in secret in concentration camps or publicly in the open air; around a simple kitchen table or in solemn ritual at the high altar; offered to the privileged rich and the destitute poor alike; marking a believer's first steps of confirmed faith or as a final gift on the lips of the faithful dying, this same meal of bread and wine – body and blood of Christ – has sustained and renewed the people of God throughout its history.

The breaking of bread is specifically mentioned as part of the day by day life of the New Testament Church, in the context of radically shared life, the teaching of the apostles and acts of service in the wider community (see Acts 2.43–7). One story more than any other illustrates the transforming power and significance of this meal for the early church. On the first Easter day two disciples were walking home to Emmaus. They were utterly despondent at the death of Jesus. Although they had heard rumours of the resurrection they had no understanding of what had happened. Jesus joined them but they did not recognize him. We are told he gave them a (long) Bible study as they walked. At the end of the journey they invited him to stay in their home. There, at the meal table, 'he took bread, blessed and broke it, and gave it to them. Then their eyes were opened, and they recognized him' (Luke 24.28–31).

Christ makes himself known in the breaking of the bread. It is a place where eyes are opened, where faith is renewed and divine life and purpose are revealed.

This meal is clearly more than a memorial of an event past. This meal is more than a symbol like, for example, a wedding ring. It is certainly more than a kind of visual aid. Nor is it simply a sign pointing to a reality found elsewhere. It is what the Bible calls an act of remembrance. During the Passover meal these words are spoken: 'In every generation, every person is duty bound to imagine him/herself to have personally taken part in the exodus from Egypt. It says in Torah, "You shall tell your son on that day that it is because of what God did for me when I came forth from Egypt".' Remembering is a living participation in that same story of deliverance and salvation.

The word the historic church chose to convey this is 'sacrament'. It has attracted more than its share of complex philosophical or crude mechanical explanations. A sacrament has been more helpfully described as like the experience of encountering the expression on someone's face. We look and find ourselves looked upon. The smile, the eyes, convey the living personality behind the face. A sacrament is a sign that carries with it the living reality of what it signifies. It came to be defined as 'an outward and visible sign of an inward and spiritual grace' (Augustine).

So why is it that few contemporary books on spirituality, prayer or Christian life mention sacraments or communion at all? The best known introduction to Christian faith, the Alpha course, completely omits it. Contemporary worship songs show little interest in it. For a great many people today an encounter with Christian worship and prayer will be a non-sacramental experience.

There are a number of reasons for this and they centre around four false polarities.

Creation versus redemption

Though the word is Latin and is therefore not found in the Bible, the understanding of sacrament is rooted in a biblical theology of creation. The God of the Bible reveals his character, love and will through this material world. Even in the work of salvation creation is not bypassed or superseded. The Creator becomes creature and lives among us.

This material world, consecrated through prayer and blessing, is always a means of grace. The world itself is a sacrament. It is mistake to think that loyalty to the gospel of our redemption requires us to treat creation with suspicion. (See Chapter 19.)

Catholic versus Protestant

In the Catholic tradition the reverencing of Christ in the sacrament at communion has always been central to its spiritual life. A moving expression of this is found in a church in the centre of Bristol. The community there keep a chain of silent prayer for the city that surrounds it. The church is kept simple and uncluttered. It is a place of waiting, watching and longing. Candles lit by pray-ers flicker softly in the sanctuary. The central focus for worship and intercession is a large consecrated communion wafer on the altar – the sacramental sign of the presence of Christ. The church is next door to the central bus station and its grounds host a hostel for drug addicts. Here is a moving place of prayer alongside life at its most transitory and fragile.

The understanding of communion remains a major point of division between Catholic and Protestant traditions of the church. A strong anti-Catholic prejudice can surface that makes it very hard to discuss the idea of sacrament at all for fear of sounding Catholic. I recall one minister firmly declaring, 'If I never move my hands during the communion prayer it is because I don't want to give any impression that anything is happening on that table!'

Of course there are differences between the traditions that we must continue to engage with. But it is not true that Reformed, biblical, 'true' faith is non-sacramental. Martin Luther and many of the Reformers, for example, retained a strongly sacramental understanding of communion and a belief in its centrality in the Christian life. (See Seddon, 2004, pp. 17ff; for a fuller introduction to a Catholic understanding of communion and sacrament see Leech, 1995, Chapter 4.)

Word versus sacrament

In reaction to the Catholic practice of placing the altar at the centre of worship, Protestant churches often put the pulpit and Bible there instead. This witnessed to the vibrant rediscovery of the Word of God in the life of the church. But this too can lead to a false polarization. Luther never saw the 'Word' replacing 'sacrament'. For him the sacrament was a 'visible word' – not an illustration that needed a sermon to *really* explain it. He is not alone. The Scottish Reformed pastor Robert Murray M'Cheyne could describe the laid prepared communion table as 'a sweet, silent sermon'. The Communion service is its own exposition.

On the road to Emmaus (mentioned above), Word and sacrament interweave. Jesus leads the two disciples through a careful Bible study, 'beginning with Moses', explaining the meaning of all that had happened (Luke 24.27). A story-teller in a 'Word'-centred tradition would have recorded this Bible study in detail as a matter of priority. But we are told nothing of what Jesus said. Instead the focus moves to a moment at supper where Jesus takes, blesses, breaks and shares the bread, as he did at the Last Supper (24.30). It is here that he is recognized – in the breaking of the bread. Eyes opened, the disciples return with new understanding to what they had heard earlier. 'Were not our hearts burning within us on the road, while he was opening the scriptures to us?' (24.32). Word anticipates sacrament and sacrament reveals the Word. They belong together.

Mission versus worship

A church seeking to reach outsiders will rightly consider how to welcome people into its worship. But that is not the same as assuming that everything must be made as immediately 'relevant' and accessible as possible. Add this thinking to an already non-sacramental worship culture and the communion service is easily assumed to be an excluding obstacle as the main act of worship. There are a number of dangers in this approach. First, worship that is organized to impress outsiders is no longer true worship – which is offered to God alone. Second, worship that is self-consciously trying to simplify, be relevant and accessible becomes obvious and will quickly tire. There is a difference between relevance and resonance. When worship resonates, people draw near.

Third, these assumptions sound suspiciously like the prevailing pragmatic consumerism of our culture and may reflect, in part, the struggles of a church that needs deeper roots in own history and theology (see Chapter 23 and Rolheiser, 1998).

Finally, is it true that communion is excluding? Hospitality is a central feature of the Passover service and Hebrew culture on which the Christian communion service is based. Many of Jesus's parables tell of feasts from which it is insiders who are excluded and to which outsiders are indiscriminately welcomed (Luke 14.12–24). Evangelists from the Catholic traditions simply do not understand the problem in the first place. For them, as for St Paul, the sacrament of communion is supremely the place where the gospel is made known. 'As often as you eat this bread and drink

the cup, you proclaim the Lord's death until he comes' (1 Cor. 11.26 and
see Cottrell, 1996 and Ward, 1999).

Keeping the feast

What does the sacrament of bread and wine contribute to the task of
spiritual formation?

Creation

The sacrament of communion anchors our spiritual life in this physical
world. There is no salvation on offer that is not ultimately the transformation of all creation (Rom. 8.19–22; Rev. 21.1). Some of the earliest false
teachings the church struggled with denied precisely this truth.

Incarnation

The sacrament of communion anchors spiritual life in a living participation in the incarnation, death and resurrection of Christ. 'This is my
body.' The same false teachings about creation also claimed that Jesus did
not really become a human being, but only appeared to be. Christian
spirituality involves costly embodiment (see Chapter 11). By contrast
popular spirituality today is ecstatic (literally 'out of matter') rather than
incarnational.

There is something wonderfully down to earth about the sacrament of
communion. It doesn't matter what I am feeling or thinking. It does not
depend on me. I reach out with empty hands and Christ comes to me.
Something is given and received.

Community

The sacrament of communion anchors us in community. This is a *shared*
meal celebrated at the invitation of Christ. We did not choose this community. It comes with following Jesus. We are part of something much
bigger than ourselves. Communion is not a private meal with God.

Justice

The sacrament of communion anchors spiritual life in a world of injustice.
This dramatic dialogue is sometimes used as the bread and wine are
brought to the communion table.

What do you bring to Christ's table?

We bring bread,
made by many people's work,
from an unjust world
where some have plenty
and most go hungry.

At this table all are fed,
and no one is turned away.

Thanks be to God.

What do you bring to Christ's table?

We bring wine,
made by many people's work,
from an unjust world
where some have leisure
and most struggle to survive.

At this table all share the cup
of pain and celebration,
and no-one is denied,

Thanks be to God.

These gifts shall be for us
the body and blood of Christ.

Our witness against hunger,
our cry against injustice,
and our hope for a world
where God is fully known
and every child is fed.
Thanks be to God.

(Brian Wren in Morley (ed.), 2004, p. 170)

To share this meal is to join the struggle for God's Kingdom of justice and equality on earth.

Reconciliation

The sacrament of communion anchors spiritual life in the gospel of reconciliation. Some communion services include something called 'The Peace'. Before breaking bread together the community are invited to renew the bond of peace with each other. Among the Christian Masai tribes in Africa the peace is expressed by passing a tuft of grass from household to household (they are herdspeople and grass is a symbol of their shared vocation and livelihood). If there is division between any part of the clan the grass cannot be passed on and they do not proceed to break bread together.

Foretaste

The sacrament of communion anchors spiritual life in the hope of heaven. The bread and wine are a foretaste of the great feast to come. Jesus himself spoke with longing anticipation of that feast (Luke 22.16, 18). In the communion liturgy the community are invited to come forward to receive with these words:

> Jesus is the Lamb of God who takes away the sins of the world.
> Happy are those who are called to his supper.

The words combine the declaration of John the Baptist at the beginning of Jesus's earthly ministry (John 1.29) and a passage at the climax of the book of Revelation (19.6–9). The supper referred to is actually a marriage feast. Jesus is the bridegroom. The world is a wedding. We are being invited.

*   *   *

Preparing for communion

The practice of taking time to prepare to receive communion is not as familiar as it once was. It is a helpful discipline we could do well to recover. The New Testament teaches us not to receive communion without careful self-examination (1 Cor. 11.27–8).

Fasting
Some Christians have the discipline of fasting before communion so that the bread and wine are the first food and drink to pass their lips that day. (This is obviously easier for those attending an earlier service of communion.)

Reconciling
Part of preparation will be to review recent behaviour and relationships. There may be people we need to seek out to forgive or say sorry to.

Reading
It may help occasionally to read again the story of the Last Supper or another passage of scripture.

With open hands
This is a sacrament in which Christ gives himself to us. More important than our own thoughts and longings are what he wants to say and give to us. Imagine your hands open before him – in self-offering and to receive from him. Take time to listen and ask him to speak.

*   *   *

For thought, prayer and activity

1   Think back over memorable meals you have shared with others: perhaps a family celebration, an intimate time of deep sharing or a meal in an unusual setting with good company. Dwell on and enjoy the qualities of sharing food with others. Perhaps make some plans to do this again soon!

2   The chapter focuses on Holy Communion but the word 'sacrament' can refer to other times of special consecration, such as baptism or marriage.
  (a) Are there other moments, events or places in your life that you remember as having a sacramental quality, and that have spoken to you of God's presence and blessing in a significant way?

(b) What might it mean to approach all of life as 'a hidden sacrament, waiting to be revealed'? (See pages 19–20.)

3 Do you take communion? Following what you have read in this chapter, could you approach communion differently, or prepare for it with greater care?

Further reading

Conway, Stephen (ed.), *Living the Eucharist: Affirming Catholicism and the Liturgy* (London: Darton, Longman and Todd, 2001).

Culling, Elizabeth, *Making the Most of Communion* (Cambridge: Grove Books, 1998).

Howard, Geoffrey, *Dare to Break Bread: Eucharist in Desert and City* (London: Darton, Longman and Todd, 1992).

Miller, Charles, *Praying the Eucharist: Reflections on the Eucharistic Experience of God* (London: SPCK, 1995).

Seddon, Philip, *Gospel and Sacrament: Reclaiming a Holistic Evangelical Spirituality* (Cambridge: Grove Books, 2004).

9 As it is in heaven

Prayer, personality and community

The brief glimpses we have into the life of heaven reveal a community of strikingly different creatures apparently united around the throne of God in timeless worship. Any worship leader who has struggled to cater for the mutually contradictory tastes of earthly congregations would love to know the secret!

> In front of the throne there is something like a sea of glass, like crystal. Around the throne, and on each side of the throne, are four living creatures, full of eyes in front and behind: the first living creature like a lion, the second living creature like an ox, the third living creature with a face like a human face, and the fourth living creature like a flying eagle. And the four living creatures, each of them with six wings, are full of eyes all around and inside. Day and night without ceasing they sing, 'Holy, holy, holy, the Lord God the Almighty, who was and is and is to come.'
>
> (Rev. 4.6–8)

In Christian imagination these four creatures have long been linked to the distinctive character traits of the four Gospels: the lion to Mark, the human face to Matthew; John to the eagle and Luke to the ox. They have also been used to explore personality differences in prayer and spirituality. What follows is based on an original idea by David Gillett and draws on the writings of Ruth Fowke (2002). Her wise and accessible use of the Myers-Briggs Personality Indicator makes her book one of the most helpful on this subject. The application of creatures to types is my own here and only intended as an imaginative way in to discussion.

Like a lion

Lions are hunters for truth. They pace the world of faith seeking to track and grasp its true meaning. They are precise creatures, thinking through everything carefully and asking questions until they arrive at an answer. They are concerned for intellectual integrity in faith. They always look for the underlying principles and will not let other creatures get away with lazy thinking. Other creatures may think that lions don't really pray at all. What lions do looks more like an academic Bible study. But they remind the community of the commandment to 'love the LORD your God with all your *mind*'. This commitment is not necessarily remote theorizing. Their convictions may lead to social action and campaigning for causes they believe are expressions of principles of faith. In worship they tend not to enjoy too many songs – especially if sung more than once. They can be suspicious of the emotions – just as the other creatures may be suspicious of their brains!

Like an eagle

Eagles enjoy variety and their interests can range widely. They are inspirational creatures to have around. They tend to live in their imagination, can fly high and so have a way of seeing and articulating the wider picture of what is going on. The practical detail will leave them impatient and they get bored quickly if they are not allowed to take flight again. They can be very disciplined at times and not at others. They can be very unaware of others.

Prayer for the eagle is a kind of musing with God. They are at home with silence. Praying may need few words. In Bible reading they will usually enjoy parables and stories more than the factual parts of scripture. They may appreciate liturgy but a phrase is likely to lift them up and away in contemplation like a bird freewheeling on thermals.

Like an ox

Oxen are solid and strongly grounded. They are very reliable. They draw near to God through being in touch with the real world around them – things that can be seen, smelt, heard, touched and tasted. Holy Communion may also be very important for this reason. They are focused, practical, factual and straightforward creatures. They are not much interested in the past or the future. What matters is the present and they are wholly given to the 'now'. They do not like to miss their daily 'quiet time' (or equivalent prayer discipline). They probably use a prayer list. Bible study notes work well for oxen as they know what is expected of them. Some oxen like traditional worship, some like new worship, but they rarely like both. They tend to know what they like and may be somewhat uncomfortable with other forms of worship. Oxen pay attention to detail and are therefore often very observant creatures. They prefer things orderly and predictable and need continuity. They usually value liturgy, written prayers and perhaps sacramental ritual. Tangible sensory symbols such as candles, pictures or a cross will be helpful to them. In prayer *how* and *where* something is done may be as important as *what* is done. So place and bodily posture are important too. Overall they can be most deeply moved by the sense of God's nearness in all things.

With a human face
Creatures with a human face are people- and relationship-centred. They pray and live from the heart. They long for authentic faith and that for them means that *experiencing* God directly is more important than any knowledge about him. Feelings and emotions are very important. They have a deep love and longing for peace and harmony. Conflict around them can make them very anxious and they will be very concerned to stop everything to try and 'make it right'. They are not so moved by abstract theology. They will relate to God as 'Father' or 'Saviour' more readily than as 'Logos' or 'Word' for example. As with each of the praying types their strengths may also become their weaknesses if stressed to the exclusion of any balancing insights. But they will remind the community of the reality of God's immanent presence and the call to worship him 'with all our heart'.

Meeting the creatures

This works as a very effective way of enabling communities and groups to become more aware of the variety of personality and spiritual expressions in their community.

The spirit of this exercise is exploratory. It can be quite affirming to discover that our own rather ugly duckling attempts at prayer in fact belong to a recognizable and respectable species! Rather than resting on the sense that 'this is me and my way of doing it' we can also be encouraged to use these insights as a way of exploring and trying out expressions of prayer and faith that we have not been aware of before.

The first task is to read the scripture and then the description of the creatures. Then encourage people to name the creature they most identify with. They may find parts of themselves in more than one species. This is not a problem. We are all cross-breeds to varying degrees. But for the discussion that follows encourage them to go with the strongest identification.

Now invite everyone to gather with others of the same species. This is always an interesting moment. The relative sizes of each group may be quite revealing. This will be influenced in part by the historic spiritual tradition of the church and the species of its present or recent leadership. If any one group is particularly dominant or looks like an endangered species it will be important to ask what might be missing from the *whole* life of the community prayer as it is presently being expressed.

Let each species take time sharing from their personal or their preferred expression of faith and spirituality. This can be wonderfully encouraging. You thought only you had this struggle or were moved by such things.

Creatures are then invited to visit other species and spend time sharing with them. This is a chance to seek to understand and learn from approaches that are different from our own, as well as helping others to understand us.

Four golden rules must be observed in this exercise.

1   In the Kingdom of God size is never a measure of importance. If one group is much smaller than the others that is not an excuse for ignoring them. The reverse is true. They need listening to more carefully.

2   Naming not labelling. Using categories like these is only helpful if they spark recognition and lead to a liberating and developing sense of our distinctive gifts and potential. All too easily they become ways of confining people to boxes with labels on. This exercise is an invitation to reverence our personalities as gifts of God for the enriching of the whole life of the community.

3   Beware of comparisons. Have you noticed how everyone else at prayer meetings looks deeply in touch with God and full of concentration?

They are thinking the same about you of course. It has been said that prayer is like sex. We easily assume that everyone else is better at it and doing it more!

4   Differences are not deficiencies. God has made us all different. This is the way he likes it to be. But it is quite possible to find ourselves in a church whose routine ways of expressing prayer and worship are simply not ours. If everyone else around seems to be happy and full of faith it is easy to feel that this must be our problem. Perhaps we are just different and we have something distinctive to give as well as to receive in the variety of the community we are part of.

Introvert and extrovert

There is one other important factor in the discussion. The degree to which creatures are introvert or extrovert will influence the way they express their spiritual life. But the words are commonly misunderstood. In Western society extroversion is regarded as healthy and introversion is generally thought of in negative terms. No one describes their child as 'a healthy *in*trovert'.

Rightly understood, these categories describe where we draw our main energies from. An introvert may be very sociable but will need personal space and times of withdrawal to resource those encounters. The opposite will be true for extroverts. They will need the energy that people and activity give them to resource their times alone.

By contrast the world of spirituality writers and teachers is heavily populated by introverts. It is extroverts who are often left feeling guilty and inadequate. Extrovert patterns of prayer will often include activities such as prayer walks, creative arts or group discussion. This is not to be confused with activism. It is not true that extroverts can't be still or appreciate silence, but they will need the resource of their active engagement to resource their silences. Introvert patterns of prayer will usually draw more on silence and solitude. Contemplative prayer groups and retreat may well be an important part of the prayer life of introverts. It is not true that introverts avoid people and outgoing activity. But they do need the resources they find more in silence to energize those encounters.

Out of the shadows

No one's personality is ever summed up in one creature. We all have sides to our personality that we choose to meet the world with and that we live in for most of our lives. We also have sides to us that tend to stay more hidden. These are sometimes called our 'shadow' sides. The word is easily misunderstood. It does not mean sinister or sinful. But they may be parts of our whole personality that we are less comfortable with and have spent less time getting to know. We may not yet appreciate what gifts they may to give us in our own journey into wholeness.

When it comes to growing in prayer it may help to spend time looking at the approaches of the other creatures and trying some of them out. For example the lion, so at home in the world of thinking, might be encouraged to consider what insights the heart might have to offer. The high-flying vision of the eagle needs the rich wisdom of the down-to-earth ox to discern more surely what it sees.

We are told that the apostle Peter had such spiritual life within him that sick people tried to lie close to where he was passing so that his shadow might fall on them and heal them (Acts 5.15). Our shadows are not usually expected to be a source of wholeness for others. We probably expect the reverse. In a way that the story may not have intended, we have a beautiful parable here of a life now fully integrated and whole in the power of the Holy Spirit.

Enriching the whole

The richness of the spiritual life of any Christian community will depend on its willingness to welcome and actively nurture the distinctive variety of praying personalities God has placed in its midst. This needs time. We must learn to understand and value expressions of prayer and faith that may be very different from our own.

There is no 'right' way to pray. We all are seeking the patterns that are authentic to our personalities, that will deepen our relationship with God and so become a gift for the enriching of the whole.

With a myriad of subtle variations and quirks, each of these creatures is present in us and to us. Each has its own capacity for intolerance of other types and of obsessive preoccupation with its own needs and preferred ways of doing things. And each will find its fullest joy in the rich variety of creatures that also surround the throne to the worship and praise of God.

*   *   *

Notes on personality profiling and prayer

The Myers-Briggs Personality Indicator is one of the best known and most widely used approaches to personality profiling. It is based on the work of Carl Jung, who summarized human personality under four main features. These features relate to each other in a variety of different ways. Jung's concern was to find ways to assist the complex tasks of integrating them into a whole. He saw the developing of spiritual life as central to this process.

Another popular approach is the Enneagram. It is not based on any established psychological model and is therefore more interpretative in style. Personality profiling methods are only ever *indicators*. They are not to be used as labels. They can be helpful in indicating ways of understanding our personality and the ways we relate to each other and to God. But they must not be used to confine us. At their best they will also indicate where we may seek to grow and develop as more fully human beings.

*   *   *

For thought, prayer and activity

Hopefully, you have found a group of people to explore this with.

1   Meeting the creatures. Does this exercise help you understand some of the differences in the people who share your spiritual life?

2   (a) Can you set yourself a challenge of learning, experimenting with, praying in a new way, embracing aspects of other traditions?
     (b) Can you pray through movement, through drawing, out-loud or with long periods of silence, for example?

3 (a) Choose one of the creatures that feels like a very different charac-
        ter from you.
   (b) What can you learn from it?
   (c) Take a feature of its approach to prayer and pray with it yourself
        for a while. (It is already part of you in fact.)

Further reading

Duncan, Bruce, *Pray Your Way: Your Personality and Prayer* (London: Darton,
    Longman and Todd, 2000).

Fowke, Ruth, *Finding Your Prayer Personality* (Oxford: Abingdon, 2002).

Innes, Robert, *Personality Indicators and the Spiritual Life* (Cambridge: Grove
    Books, 1996).

Metz, Barbara and Burchill, John, *The Enneagram and Prayer* (Denville, NJ:
    Dimension Books, 1987).

BECOMING WHO I AM

Identity, personhood and spirituality

10 With unveiled faces

Human identity and spiritual formation

Imagine you have arrived somewhere for a meeting. Coffee is finished and it is time for introductions. In the familiar way of these events we are each asked to give our name and say 'two sentences about ourselves'. What do you say?

Of course it will partly depend on the context of the meeting. At a professional training seminar we will probably say more about our life at work. In a social group we may talk about our family and personal interests. It is never an entirely comfortable exercise, is it? Attempts at humour and nervous laughter cover over the awkwardness.

We choose what we say to the group about ourselves very carefully. There may be things that are very central to who I am (and even to my place within that group) that I will choose not to share because they are too personal or make me feel too vulnerable. There are parts of my life I will only risk sharing when I am sure I can trust the people I am with.

The exercise does work on the assumption that I will have a response I can make to the question of 'who am I?' But what if I can't? I remember sitting in one such group at a time of considerable personal confusion. I could think of nothing to say that did not feel trivial, and I resented being put on the spot in this way. In the event, I managed something acceptable, but what had actually come to mind were phrases from a favourite psalm: 'Such knowledge is too wonderful for me; I cannot grasp it. I am fearfully and wonderfully made' (Ps. 139.6, 14, my paraphrase).

Let us approach the same task with a different question: 'When did you first discover you had a face?' The answer is not immediately obvious. The question is another way of asking when we first began to develop a sense of our own identity and personhood. The simple answer is: 'when someone first gave me theirs'.

I have a favourite photo of my son Joshua. Just one day old, he is lying on his back, being dried after a bath. He is helpless, vulnerable and utterly dependent. He can contribute nothing to what is going on, nor communicate anything of his needs. His life can only be received and sustained as a free gift of another. My wife is bending down to him. He is gazing into her wide, warm face with total concentration. What he makes of what he sees there is no way of knowing. The image and identity of another is being gifted to him. In those first hours of his new life, as he responds to a face whose likeness he so intimately shares, he is beginning to know himself.

We know ourselves, for good or ill, through our relationship with the lives of others. Long before we can make choices for ourselves, we have already been acted upon and powerfully shaped by the circumstances, desire and will of others. We are even given our own name by others. So deep is the individualism that shapes our contemporary assumptions about ourselves that this truth is not just a surprise: it may even feel unwelcome and intrusive. But we are the fruit of lives, stories and desires that are not our own.

And have you ever considered what an extraordinary and hazardous amount of living has gone before us that we might emerge at all at this point in history?

> For 3.8 billion years, a period older than the Earth's mountains and rivers and oceans, every one of your forebears on both sides has been attractive enough to find a mate, healthy enough to reproduce, and sufficiently blessed by fate and circumstance to live long enough to do so. Not one of your pertinent ancestors was squashed, devoured, drowned, starved, stuck fast, untimely wounded or otherwise deflected from its life's quest of delivering a tiny charge of genetic material to the right partners at the right moment to perpetuate the only possible sequence of hereditary combinations that could result – eventually and astoundingly, and all to briefly – in you.
>
> (Bryson, 2003, p. 3)

So the answer to the question 'who am I?' is a complex one. The problem is not where to start but where to stop! To discover what makes me uniquely and recognizably me involves tracing patterns of intimate interconnectedness and dependency in which ultimately the whole universe has a part. Not only am I born into this world, it seems the world is contained in me. To be a human being is to be in relationship.

Searching for identity

In past generations our sense of personal identity and belonging would have been found through participation in a society that had a shared consensus about its vision and values. Within it we could begin to know ourselves and explore our place and vocation in the world. That social consensus has long ago collapsed. The defining identity on offer today is that of a consumer. The irony is that consumer culture, priding itself on offering ever more choice, actually offers us little alternative in this respect. We are all customers now. In a rampantly materialist culture my 'self' is no longer regarded as something given or revealed. We have to create it for ourselves. We are identified by what we buy, choosing our identities much as we choose the clothes we wear. And like clothes, the fashion constantly changes.

One very helpful book on human identity in contemporary society is called *Crossing the Unknown Sea* (Whyte, 2001). The title reflects the uncertainty of the task we face. We are seeking to know ourselves in very new contexts. Old ways of defining ourselves by the work we do or the roles we fulfil are no longer available. So our sense of who we are remains uncertain and is required to be constantly changing. We may even have a portfolio of identities, each appropriate to different contexts of our living – our work, home, spirituality or leisure. Each is an attempt to cope with one or other of the shifting roles that make up our lifestyle. The question 'but which is the real me in all this?' not only remains unasked, but is regarded as irrelevant.

The consumer market continually exploits the needs of this uncertain self. But it can only offer us strategies for distraction, or for soothing our superficial needs. So we are working and playing ever harder but have to add more layers of activities onto our lives without getting nearer the question of who we really are and what all this living is really for.

The social cost of this is more evident by the day. By any measure of social health, our current way of life is clearly bad for us. Social analysts and counsellors alike speak of 'consumptive disorders'. Symptoms include chronic boredom, alienation and the inability to concentrate for more than short periods at a time. They also bring a sense of meaninglessness, low self-esteem and an increase in violent behaviour. The diagnosis of depression has increased tenfold in Western countries in the last 30 years. Stress is now one of the top five causes of health breakdown.

Our dilemma is the same as that of the Invisible Man. Having lost our identity we are invisible to ourselves and each other. Lacking true substance we use our hectic activities and choices to clothe, disguise and bandage our non-existence. Now at least there is something to be seen. But our lives are increasingly lived at a distance from our true selves. What is actually needed is another way of being – another way of knowing ourselves (Whyte, 2001, pp. 60–1 and Runcorn, 2002, Chapter 8).

The roots of human being

The Bible draws very similar conclusions about our elusive self-knowledge but insists that the discussion must start from a more fundamental truth. Our life and identity can only finally be found as we share in the greater life of God. So the creation stories at the beginning of the Bible insist on a number of core truths about what it means to be a human being (see Runcorn, 2001).

We are someone else's idea
'In the beginning God created . . .' (Gen. 1.1). Some other source of life chose to bring us into being and continues to sustain us. That is the only reason we are here. We are therefore dependent creatures. Our very existence depends, moment by moment, on the will of this 'Other'.

We are finite creatures
The name Adam means 'earth creature' (2.7). We are from the dust and to dust we shall return. We are mortal and finite. Who expects anything from dust?

We are gift
The one who brings us into being chooses to give us to ourselves. We are not robots. We can think and feel and make choices. Life in this world is possible not prescribed. It is all left remarkably open.

We are becomers
We are unfinished. We are lives in process. On the wall of Chartres Cathedral in France there is a sculpture of God creating Adam. Adam has half emerged from the dust of the ground and is resting (or has slumped)

against God's knee, which he is clutching strongly with his left hand. The sculptor has chosen to freeze the action at mid-point. Adam is not yet a complete human being. He is halfway between death and life, being and non-being, dust and divine image. And so are we. We are always human *becomers* – growing, journeying, exploring.

We are social creatures
'It is not good that the earth creature is alone' (Gen. 2.18). In the goodness of all the breadth of new creation this is the one thing that is not good. This *aloneness* is not because something has gone wrong. It is because humanity is made for relationships and community. We are made for each other. Our personal wholeness and fulfilment is to be found in community.

We are free – and therefore responsible
This freedom is underlined in a particular way. One place in creation is forbidden to Adam and Eve: the tree at the centre of the garden. This is God's. Freedom exists in the presence of boundaries. We are asked to respect God's own freedom and what is God's alone. Neglect of freedom has real consequences (Gen. 3.3ff).

We are divine
The second creation story has an extraordinary scene. A creature has been shaped out of the dust of the earth and there it could have stayed, a created but lifeless model. But God himself comes down to this dust creature. He breathes his own breath of life into its nostrils, 'and Adam became a living being' (Gen. 2.7). The life that Adam receives is divine life. So we are dust – but we are dust that can dream. We are creatures with immortal longings. Our story can only be fully known in God's own story. We are made his image. This is our glory and our dilemma.

We are in exile
As the creation story ends in the wellknown tragedy of disobedience, its consequence is played out in a very familiar way. There is a radical loss of identity. Adam and Eve can no longer face themselves or their world. They cover up and hide from themselves, from one another and from God. And so, in the cool of the evening, the garden is haunted by the sound of God calling as he seeks what he has made – 'Where are you?' (Gen. 3.9).

Beginning again

In the helplessness and confusion of our loss, love comes down to us. One way of expressing the significance of the coming of Christ in our humanity is that he gives us his face. And so it is that 'the New Testament breathes an air of astonishment' (Philip Seddon). Men and women stumble into the wonder and glory of knowing themselves for the first time, transformed, with unveiled faces, named and loved in the gift of the Father revealed in the face of Jesus.

The love of Jesus, growing close to his image, is not a replacing of one identity by another. In his reconciling love we are given back our true selves. In his grace we can now become truly who we are.

But it is a process that is still full of mystery. 'See what love the Father has given us, that we should be called children of God,' writes John; 'and that is what we are. Beloved, we are God's children now; what we will be has not yet been revealed. What we do know is this: when he is revealed, we will be like him (1 John 3.1–2).

These verses suggest so much. Our true identity is received as gift – 'see what love the Father has given us that we should be called his children'. Our true identity will only be fully known in the fullness of God's own life. Then we will know even as now we are fully known – for 'what we will be has not been revealed'. Our true identity is revealed in the face of Christ. We receive it in trust – 'when he is revealed, we will be like him' (1 John 3.2).

Christian discipleship means learning to trust to Jesus with the secret of who we are becoming.

Where are you?

So there are two contrasting reasons why the question 'who am I?' remains an elusive mystery.

First, I am still deeply a part of the confusion of a fallen world, so long accustomed to hiding and covering up that I am helpless to imagine myself in any other way.

But second, the full mystery of who I am will only be known in the fullness of the life of God. Our lives are hidden with Christ in God (Col. 3.3). There is a place where my true self is known and loved and kept safe. Rowan Williams suggests that this necessarily remains hidden. If we were given too much sight of it we would only plunder and misuse it. So 'our lives are hidden in him, our deepest integrity and joy kept from our greedy eyes by being drowned in his glory' (Williams, 2002, p. 50).

And where else would you rather find yourself?

For thought, prayer and activity

1   A journey of self discovery needs to begin with three questions.

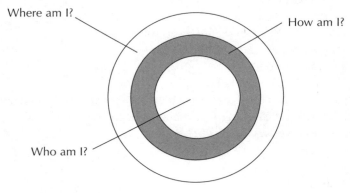

Where am I?

How am I?

Who am I?

Where am I?
These are the things about me that are givens – things I did not choose and cannot change. These include the family I was born into, my genetic make-up, my cultural and racial mix, and my natural gifts. What would your answer to this question include?

How am I?
These are areas where I can make choices and negotiate how I live my life. I take personal initiatives. I can accept or reject things. I make friendships with some and not others, and invest my time in certain things and not in others. I may conform to things around me or I may rebel.

Who am I?
This is the person I most truly am before God. I may be hidden under many layers. The outer parts of my life may not reflect the truth about me at all.

2   Look through your photo collections and choose five pictures that tell you most about who you are (or imagine which picture you would choose if you had one).

3   Which of these statements resonates most with you?

> We are someone else's idea
> We are finite creatures
> We are gift
> We are becomers
> We are social creatures
> We are free – and therefore responsible
> We are divine
> We are in exile

4   Choose one of the above that particularly strikes you and think about it by focusing on the feelings it engenders, the memories it invokes, and the challenges it poses.

Further reading

Clément, Olivier, *On Human Being* (New York: New City, 2000).

Mursell, Gordon, *Praying as Exile* (London: Darton, Longman and Todd, 2005).

Runcorn, David, *The Creation of Adam: Seven Guided Reflections from Genesis* (Cambridge: Grove Books, 2001).

van Swaaij, Louise, *The Atlas of Experience* (London: Bloomsbury, 2000).

Whyte, David, *Crossing the Unknown Sea: Work as a Pilgrimage of Identity* (London: Penguin Putnam, 2001).

11 Flesh and spirit

Praying in the body

'Sit still. Hands together. Eyes closed,' was the Sunday school ritual. I learned at a very early age that my body was a distraction where God was concerned. It needed firm handling if 'praying' was going to happen properly.

The relationship of our bodies to the spiritual life will have been shaped by a variety of influences and attitudes. At the start of this exploration it may help to ask ourselves what we bring to the discussion.

- What place has my 'body' and 'flesh' had in my spiritual pilgrimage?
- What do I most seek for my body – and from it?
- 'The Word became flesh' – how important is this truth to me in my relating to my own physical being?
- Are the issues different for men than for women – and if so in what ways?

Flesh, bodies and God – a difficult relationship

Here, in this place, we flesh; flesh that weeps, laughs; flesh that dances on bare feet in grass. Love it. Love it hard. Yonder they don't love your flesh. They despise it.

This is flesh I'm talking about here! Flesh that needs to be loved. Feet that need to rest and dance; backs that need support; shoulders that need arms, strong arms I'm telling you . . . *You* got to love it, *you!*

(From a sermon by a preacher to fellow slave plantation workers in the USA, in Toni Morrison's novel *Beloved*, 1997, pp. 88–9)

Christians included a strange declaration in their Creed. They said they believed in and wished for the resurrection of the body. As if the body were the only thing of any importance. That's the way it is: in this body, so small, so ephemeral, a whole universe lives . . .

God's desire is revealed in our bodies.

But a strange thing happened. We began to look for God in perverse places. We thought to find God where the body ends: and we made it suffer and transformed it into a beast of burden, machine for labour. And we became cruel, violent, we permitted exploitation and war. For if God is found beyond the body, anything can be done to the body.

(Alves, 1990)

'It is difficult to be on equally good terms with God and your body,' wrote Etty Hillesum. Is that your experience? For much of its history the Western Christian tradition has insisted that flesh and spirit must be kept apart. A perverse and destructive dualism between spirit and matter has infected so much of the understanding of the Church that we have been left with little positive use for the body at all. Body and flesh have been treated in two particular ways as a result.

First, they are simply treated as inferior. So they suffer from neglect in the Christian life. For evidence of this some will look no further than the sheer discomfort of traditional church pews and kneelers. The spiritual life and the world of the mind were thought to be the 'higher' goal. In pursuit of this the flesh holds us back or, worse still, leads us astray. So the body is treated as an inescapable burden, to be towed around in this mortal life while the 'spirit' within longs for its freedom. Like resentful children knowing instinctively where they are not welcome, our bodies get bored, fidget and cause a distraction. The body is a temporal nuisance.

There are signs that this attitude is changing. Books on the spiritual life are much more likely to include advice on posture and encouragement to use the senses as we pray.

Second, body and flesh have been treated as an enemy. The 'flesh' was treated as the source of all that is fallen and sinful. Holiness therefore required a renunciation of the flesh and its disordered desires. All too easily in Christian vocabulary the word 'flesh' is used negatively. It implies something illicit or forbidden, rather than warm living embodiment. These attitudes are the more surprising in a faith that uniquely claims the doctrine of the incarnation at its heart. 'This is my body, given for you.' We meet God in our human flesh. Christian discipleship is therefore about taking flesh, not renouncing it.

The heirs of such an ambivalent tradition are probably going to need help to know what to do with their bodies and the powerful range of energies and passions contained there. This unease continues to contribute powerfully to contemporary anxieties about sexuality. It also lies behind at least some of the difficulties in accepting the place of women as equal partners with men in Christian life and ministry.

The Bible on body, flesh and spirit

When the Bible speaks of body and flesh we need to be sensitive to what is being said, what is meant and what its context is. Much damage and hurt is caused when this is ignored.

For example, what do you make of this selection of verses?

'My *flesh* faints for you' (Ps. 63.1 – and in some translations *flesh* here is translated *soul*).
'The glory of the Lord shall be revealed and all *flesh* shall see it' (Isa. 40.5, literal translation).
'The Word became *flesh* and dwelt among us' (John 1.14).
'Who will rescue me from this *body* of death ?' (Rom 7.24).
'But you are not in the *flesh*; you are in the Spirit' (Rom. 8. 9).
'Present your *bodies* as a living sacrifice' (Rom. 12.1).
'Your *body* is a temple of the Holy Spirit' (1 Cor. 6.19).
'I punish my *body* and enslave it' (1 Cor. 9.27).

The same words are used to teach strongly contrasting truths about our human existence before God. In one place 'flesh' refers to unredeemed, fallen human nature (Rom. 8.9). But in Ezekiel God's people are promised a heart of flesh (Ezek. 36.26)! What St Paul calls 'flesh' Ezekiel calls 'stone'. Neither implies any suspicion about physical existence. Both refer to that stubborn, rebellious centre of human living that remains unyielding and unresponsive to the life and will of God.

When the Bible speaks of the body it is referring to the whole person. There is no separation of body, soul or spirit in the Bible. Nor is there any notion of a spiritual, 'real me' living inside this earthly body and longing for its future freedom. The Christian teaching of the Resurrection includes the body. Christian hope is unashamedly physical.

Getting in touch – body and spirit

The body is where we start from
This is such an obvious but neglected observation.

> Movement is our first language. We move in the womb, and experience the movements and heartbeats of our mothers. Rhythm, well-being, joy, anxiety, distress are all communicated through these early movement experiences. Before language even starts to develop, our bodily interaction with our carers gives us the necessary scaffolding to develop person knowledge.
>
> (Sara Savage in Begbie, 2000, p. 77)

And life continues in the body. Our body is something we never grow out of. Life is inescapably physical. The business of living involves the whole of us. Did you know, for example, that only 7 per cent of human communication is verbal?

Pain, healing and embodiment
We learn from people who have suffered particular violence that our relationship to our bodies is central to who we are and to our search for wholeness. Helen Bamber, who has spent a lifetime working with victims of torture, comments that for such people 'cruelty is, above all, an experience of the human body. To live in such a body – one that had been starved, beaten, marked for death – must have been to experience a sharply heightened awareness of the physical self, and to resent any disparagement of it' (Belton, 1998, p. 135). Central to her work of rehabilitation and healing is a reclaiming of 'the good body' and relearning a way of respecting the body and the self with it. The same truth is witnessed in the effectiveness of 'body positive' therapies among people with illnesses that carry particular stigma such as HIV.

Truth, fantasy and reconciliation
The search for embodied spirituality will not only have to live with the prevailing hesitations in historic Christian teaching. It must also find a way of responding to the relentless idealizing of the human body in contemporary culture. This means that relating to our physical being is a continuous

loving act of reconciliation and acceptance of ourselves – and others. It means letting go of unrealistic hopes.

Our bodies are also mortal. They have strengths and weaknesses. They are frail and are not made to last. They can let us down – and we let them down. Nor did we choose them, actually. They are given.

In all this a Christian community that is creative in seeking holistic expressions of prayer and worship will be both a healing and subversive gift to the idolatry and cruelty of cultural pressures.

For thought, prayer and activity

Some of the exercises that follow may seem strange and embarrassing for some of you, but the process may bring surprising insights and rewards if you take the risk.

> You knit me together in my mother's womb. I praise you, for I am fearfully and wonderfully made.
> Ps. 139.13–14

Listening to our bodies
Ask yourself: When am I most alive in my body? When do I most struggle in my body?

Talking to our bodies
For good or ill our life story is mapped on our bodies in some way or other. Our flesh absorbs our joys and our stresses – aches, pains, butterflies and frissons.

Write an imaginary conversation with parts of your body. These may be parts that have carried particular burdens for you in your journey, or brought special joys to it.

Which parts would you want to talk to?

This may bring a realization of ways in which we have been careless about our bodies, or treated them badly. We may need to say sorry.

Meeting, honouring, consecrating our bodies
For many reasons, some of which we have already discussed, it is very easy to live in alienation from our physical nature. This is not for mocking. We may have good reason for our unease. For some it may be very healing to seek a place of personal privacy and to lie or sit naked.

Taking each part of the body in turn, name it, greet it, pray for it and bless it. 'God be in my . . .'

Another way of expressing this is in the bath or the shower where the physical sensation of being warmly soaked or poured over can be a vivid picture of the reality of God's love for us in our flesh.

Praying with our bodies
On your own or in a group pray the Lord's Prayer without words – using movement, mime or any actions you choose.

Embodying the Word
I once attended a most unusual Bible study. As the publicity said 'wear loose clothing' it was obvious we were in for something different. The person leading it was a man who believed that the split between body and spirit in Western Christianity carried such profound and damaging consequences that he would not now lead a Bible study that did not include physical movement. For 40 minutes we were encouraged to move around the room in whatever way we chose, to a background of music and scripture reading. 'And the word became flesh and dwelt among us.'

Love your body.

You are a body:
not a no-body,
nor just any-
body,
but some-body.

The Body is the dwelling place
of the whole-making Spirit

(Cotter, 1989, p. 61)

Further reading
Some of the books for further reading in Chapter 12 will also be helpful.

Coakley, Sara (ed.), *Religion and the Body* (Eastbourne: Kingsway, 1988).

Cotter, Jim, *Prayer at Night* (Sheffield: Cairns Publications, 1989). The final section, 'Cairns for the journey', contains a variety of prayers and meditations on the themes of embodiment, sexuality and human passions.

Runcorn, David, *Rumours of Life: Reflections on the Resurrection Appearances* (London: Darton, Longman and Todd, 1996). See especially Chapter 6, 'It's flesh I'm talking about here – the resurrection of the body'.

Savage, Sara in Begbie, Jeremy (ed.), *Beholding the Glory: Incarnation Through the Arts* (London: Darton, Longman and Todd, 2000). See especially Chapter 4, 'Through Dance: fully human, fully alive'.

The Way: Review of Contemporary Christian Spirituality, Vol 35, Number 2 (April 1995). The whole issue is on the theme of 'Embodiment'.

12 Sexuality and spirituality

Prayer and passion

In the story of creation at the beginning of the Bible only one thing is described as 'not good'. The first human being is alone (Gen 2.18). Something is missing. In the midst of the goodness of that new world is a being who lives with an ache of incompleteness. It is nothing to do with sin at this stage. Nor is this a hunger that God can satisfy. Whether or not he actually knows what it is he seeks, this ache drives Adam out into the world searching for something.

This God-given hunger lies at the heart of our whole response to being alive. We are created with a longing for intimacy. We experience it as an incompleteness. For good or ill it powerfully shapes the way we live and relate. It is a central truth of our human identity that this wholeness we long for is only found as we take the risk of reaching out into relationships with others.

Our vocation is to be makers of love. At times this hunger is experienced as a raw, direct, physical sexual drive. But we also meet it in our capacity for sublime creativity, our sensitivity to beauty and pain, in a desire to reach out into the lives of others, in our search for wholeness, meaning and purpose. All this is involved in our understanding of the word 'sexuality'.

Today the word 'sexuality' popularly refers to the physical aspects of our sexual behaviour and how we express it. This reflects the highly sexualized character of our society. Sexuality certainly includes our desires for experiencing and sharing physical pleasure but it is far more than this. It is concerned with the mystery and gift of our deepest identity as men and women. Our sexuality involves the whole of our being – body, mind, soul and relationships. This means that sexuality and our spiritual life are intimately linked. They need each other (see Runcorn, 2002, Chapter 11).

Christianity and sexuality – a difficult relationship

Let him kiss me with the kisses of his mouth!
For your love is better than wine . . .
Draw me after you, let us make haste.
The king has brought me into his chambers . . .
(Song of Sol. 1.2–4)

It is no secret that through its history the Christian faith has found the relationship between sexuality and spirituality very difficult. Sexual passion and holy living are not usually thought of as partners in Christian discipleship. One is usually thought of as a 'problem' to the other. This relationship continues to be one of the most difficult and divisive issues in the Church today.

The most common way the Church has tried to cope with this has been to keep sexuality and spirituality firmly separate. So our maturing in prayer and faith is achieved by avoiding the world of our passions. The subject appears when there is a need to stress Christian standards of behaviour. There is high price to pay for such a strategy. Unruly and complex though it may be, by avoiding our sexuality we will be cutting ourselves off from our deepest source of God-given creative energies for the very task that needs them most. 'There is, in passion, a power that holiness needs' (Louis Lavelle).

This separation became institutionalized for large periods of the history of the Church by the prizing of celibacy as the holier path for anyone seriously seeking God. But the subject of sex was far from ignored. Christian teaching on spiritual life frequently used the language of sexual love and erotic desire. It is interesting to discover that during the Middle Ages the book of the Bible that was written about more than any other was the Song of Solomon. The instinct to find a metaphor for knowing and loving God in the highly charged erotic poetry of this love song is not wrong at all. But even here there was still a separation. While explicit sexual imagery and language could be used to contemplate the intimacy with God and his love for us, sexual *experience* could not.

Isn't there a missing word in this discussion? We need a way of expressing a vision for living that is between 'promiscuous' and 'chaste'. 'Promiscuous' means 'indiscriminate, careless or casual behaviour'.

'Chaste' means being 'pure from unlawful sexual intercourse'. But this is a negative definition. To be chaste is to be *not* doing something wrong. We have no positive word for our faltering attempts to live as faithful, passionate, sexually alive people. It one thing for a hermit in the wilderness to say to God, 'one thing have I desired', and quite another for someone who has just fallen in love or is married with three children. We are struggling to express a positive vision for sexuality that naturally integrates love for God with and through the raw, erotic earthiness of human passions.

So what might it mean to seek our path to God through and with the richness, mystery and complexity of our sexuality?

The earthiness of spiritual life

Perhaps one of the main gifts of our sexuality to our spiritual pilgrimage is to keep it all down to earth. It may embarrass us, distract us and confuse us, but the sheer, messy earthiness of our sexual passions and energies keeps us praying and seeking God out of real human living. Christian spirituality involves taking flesh, not avoiding or abandoning it.

> Starved of affection, terrified of abandonment, I began to wonder if sex was really just an excuse to look deeply into another human being's eyes.
>
> (Coupland, 1996, p. 35)

Befriending our desires

Our human passions and desires are something positively God-given, not a problem to be solved or overcome. This does not assume that we will be desiring what is right. But it is an important affirmation to start from. It is *disordered* desire that is condemned in the Bible. We are created with powerful and complex needs and longings and appetites. Some are very trivial; others are profound. We must seek a relationship with them. They shape our lives for good or ill. The choice we do not have is to try to live without them.

Listening to our desires

We need to find a way of listening to our longings and passions. Even at a time of intense arousal of desire the answer to the question 'what do I really want?' may not be obvious.

An example of this is the single woman who once found herself, quite unexpectedly, attracted to a married man. She was a Christian. For all the confusion of her feelings she had no wish to pursue a relationship with him and would have considered it wrong. But the attraction was very powerful and she felt extremely vulnerable. She found the courage to speak to a trusted friend. She perhaps expected to discuss strategies for avoiding him or burying the feelings. In fact her friend asked her to take the risk of drawing nearer to her desire. 'Listen to your feelings. What is it that attracts you to this man? You know this relationship is not possible but what are you recognizing in his character, faith and approach to living that you know is important to you? You may be discerning the most important qualities you would seek in the man you marry.' This brave advice led the woman to review the shape of her desires in previous relationships and to find a new confidence in what she was actually seeking in human love and the commitment of marriage if such became a real choice in the future.

Community and sexuality

We seek a Christian vision for our humanity in the midst of a society that reflects deep confusion in the area of sexuality and which has radically abandoned Christian moral teaching and lifestyle. Fearfully held at a distance, exploited carelessly for pleasure, or burdened with impossible expectations of fulfilment in relationships, human sexuality is the place where some of the deepest wounding and confusion in our culture is found. We cannot work this out alone. We need each other.

A Christian vision for sexuality will never underestimate the depths from which we need redeeming. For example, we are now much more aware of the prevalence of sexual abuse and the devastation it causes. 'Sex' is now the top search interest on the Internet. The dangers are real and access has never been simpler. It is clear that the first Christian communities in the New Testament were made up of people who had come from lifestyles that reflected considerable sexual licence (see for example 1 Cor. 6.9–11). The same will be true today. St Paul's reputation for negative teaching about sex needs to be understood in this context. In a fallen world any Christian community will share, in some measure, both its wounds and its compulsions. But alongside the call to challenge contemporary behaviour is the complementary vocation to offer community where people know they will be loved, accepted and listened to as they try to understand where life has brought them.

What will be the marks of such a community?

- A celebrating and reverencing of our shared gift of humanity.
- A sensitive awareness of our mutual vulnerability.
- A compassion for those who struggle.
- A discernment of the reality of sin and evil.
- A prayer for holiness of life.
- Grace to be gifts towards each other's fulfilling in Christ.
- Truth, forgiveness, reconciliation in facing up to disordered and destructive elements in our lifestyles.
- Support in seeking holiness and sustaining new patterns of living and loving.

Sacrament and consecration

Our sexual desires are not only God-given. In the passion and vulnerability of our sexual living we will express, however falteringly, something of the mystery of God's image and the glory, power and even vulnerability of divine desire.

One of the most startling teachings of St Paul is his suggestion that the intimacy of love-making between husband and wife is a sign of the love of Christ for the Church (Eph. 5.28–32). He could not have chosen a more intimate and vulnerable image. We are more accustomed to looking at the love of Christ as an example of how we should be loving and behaving. Here we are invited to reflect the other way round and to ask 'what does our experience of sexual longing and intimate fulfilment suggest to us of the love of Christ?'

Even at its most earthy, then, human sexuality is charged with something holy. It reveals a deeper hunger for intimacy and union with God. As such our sexuality is a sign and sacrament of divine love for the world. It is to be offered as a real presence. 'This is my body – given for you.' At the very moment of deepest earthly intimacy and fulfilment, we are being reminded of a desiring that is quite beyond all earthly living.

The most important thing is not whether we are sexually active or celibate, married or single – but whether we are living in the expectation of Christ's coming Kingdom.

Our sexuality is the playground for prayer. It is where we tumble over our greatest needs and hungers, where the possibility of erotic delight is revealed, the limitations of self-love are exposed, and pride is purged . . . our sexuality remains the place of great personal intensity where we have the capacity to be most open and most closed to God because it remains a place of trouble and torment and also of the greatest earthly blessing and happiness.

(Angela Tilby in Watts, 2002, pp. 94–5)

O God
Giver of life
Bearer of pain
Maker of love
affirming in your incarnation the goodness of the flesh.
May the yearnings of our bodies
be fulfilled in sacraments of love
and our earthly embracings
a foretaste of the glory that shall be
in the light of the Resurrection of Jesus Christ.
Amen.

(Cotter, 1989, p. 65)

For thought, prayer and activity

1   Think about the abusive and 'swear' words that people use.
(a)   How many are related to body parts and sexual activities?
(b)   What does this say about our view of sex and sexuality as a society?

2   'Sexual passion and holy living are not usually thought of as partners in Christian discipleship'.
(a)   Why not?
(b)   Having read this chapter, can you broker a marriage between these two and see how they might support one another?

(c)   If you feel like a writing challenge, describe their relationship as if they were a married couple!

3   Does Jim Cotter's prayer inspire you to write your own prayer concerning sex and sexuality?

Further reading

Cotter, Jim, *Prayer at Night* (Sheffield: Cairns Publications, 1989). The final section contains a wonderful selection of prayers and meditations on human sexuality and passion.

Ind, Jo, *Memories of Bliss: God, Sex and Us* (London: SCM Press, 2003).

Nelson, James, *The Intimate Connection: Male Sexuality, Masculine Spirituality* (Louisville, Ky.: Westminster John Knox Press, 1999).

13 The changing scenes of life

Spiritual development through life's stages

At a very confused and painful stage in my life I remember saying to a friend, 'I don't think I believe any more.'

'You don't sound to me like someone who has lost his faith,' she replied. 'You sound like someone who is having to live out of a new part of himself. You are still a stranger to this "you" that is emerging. So it is not surprising if you don't yet know what faith means.'

'Faith', 'prayer' and 'spiritual life' do not exist as finished products on a shelf that we can acquire and apply to whatever circumstances we face. There is a sense in which the task of living by faith is something we relearn with every change of life. To do so is not a failure of faith (though it can at times feel like that). As we grow through life it is entirely appropriate to expect to find that both what we believe and how we pray will also grow and develop along the way.

Honouring the life journey

A feature of traditional cultures and ancient religions is the care they took to mark and honour the stages of life. 'Rites of passage' (ceremonies and celebrations) marked birth, puberty and the entry to adulthood, for example. Contemporary society has largely lost the significance of this. We are poor at protecting our young as they grow into life. We have forgotten the importance of rituals. We seem to have little patience with the relevance of age in relation to experience or behaviour. We no longer reverence our later years as a source of distilled wisdom.

Faith across the stages of life

Each stage of life has its gift and its cost. Each has its potential and its struggle, a losing and a finding. The transition between one stage and

	Name of stage	Faith characteristics
Stage 0	Primal faith	Infant's trust in mother. Simple pre-linguistic trust. A spirituality fixed at this stage will be focused on personal fulfilment and having one's own needs met.
Stage 1	Intuitive–projective faith	State of unordered but powerful images. The young child constructs meaning to interpret experience but has no concepts to base them on yet.
Stage 2	Mythic–literal faith	Between the ages of 6 and 11, thinking skills develop around a literal interpretation of the world. Storytelling is central. Little abstract thinking yet.
Stage 3	Synthetic–conventional faith	Adolescent develops thinking ability beyond the literal. Stage of conformity to peer groups, beliefs. Can easily continue into adulthood and often does. Spirituality based around stages 1–3 will tend to be conforming and attracted to concrete answers.
Stage 4	Individuative–reflective stage	Young adult develops critical judgement and begins to choose for him/herself. Critical distancing from one's previous value system. Spirituality: potential for opening up or regressing into a new conforming/certainties or moving to an expression of stage 5.
Stage 5	Conjunctive faith	The dissolution of previous certainties sets in. Often mid-life stage. Previous meaning of faith questioned and possibly revised. Stage characterized by 'critical openness'. Spirituality marked by questioning and non-conforming. Seeking to personalize what has been a 'given'. A stage of exploring and integrating.
Stage 6	Universalizing faith	Stage marked by a sense of coming together and of wholeness. (Fowler believed very few people achieve this.) Spirituality: an attraction to and acceptance of paradox and mystery.

Fowler's seven stages of faith

another is often marked by conflict. With each stage of life comes a task – a challenge to grow in some particular way. James Fowler (1980) was one of the first to use developmental theory to discuss the maturing of faith through the life journey. The table on page 110 gives a brief outline of his understanding of faith across the life stages.

Fowler's stages are not without their critics but they offer a helpful starting point. Human development does not happen in a straight line. In fact there are no guarantees of progress at all. Life's hurts or distractions can leave us stuck at times. Under pressure we may regress. Most of us have a mixture of responses depending on what we are facing. When things don't go our way we may still react like a sulking child. At other times we may respond with maturity 'beyond our years'.

God and faith through our life stages

At this point it may help to take the discussion from theory to your own lived experience. Using the spaces below can you draw a picture or symbol, or choose a few words, that express your understanding of God at the key stages of life so far? (Your intuitions of the earliest years may be just as significant.)

If these categories do not helpfully reflect the patterns of your life that you know to be significant, do adapt them.

My childhood image of God

What was going on in your life?

What was important to you and gave your life meaning?

What was faith to you?

My adolescent (or early adult) image of God

What was going on in your life?

What was important to you and
gave your life meaning?

What was/is faith to you?

My present image of God

What is going on in your life?

What is important to you and
gives your life meaning?

What is faith to you?

How my image of God might change/is changing

What about your image of God
might be transformed?

What in your life is calling forth
this new image of God?

It may be helpful to do this exercise with friends and share and pray for each other in the light of what emerges. (I regret I cannot trace where I first came across a version of this exercise.)

An example of faith development in a particular life stage

Observers of human development, in developed and traditional cultures alike, locate a stage roughly between the ages of 40 and 50 as especially significant. This time of transition is popularly called the 'mid-life crisis'. 'Mid-life Crisis' is even available now as a popular board game.

Mid-life transition can actually happen at any stage from the age of 30 onwards. It may arrive in the shock of sudden awareness. 'In the middle of the road of my life I woke in a dark wood where the true way was wholly lost' (Dante). A life crisis or change can be a trigger. When the children grow up and move away from home is often a significant time. However we experience it, it is important to honour it as a natural and important part of our journey into maturing personal integration.

Changes at mid-life

Psychologically and spiritually this stage marks a point at which we start to seek to integrate our inner journey and our outer one. Until now we have been living more on the outside. We have been seeking to establish our place in the world – work, relationships, family etc. None of this is wrong. But it is not our whole story and we are uncomfortably aware that something is beginning to change. The things that have given us our drive and fulfilment no longer fulfil. We may not be sure what we want in their place.

There is a sense of 'looking both ways' at this point in life. Symbolically and chronologically we are moving from life's morning to the afternoon. We begin to be aware that the evening approaches. We are reviewing where we have come from and may become aware of unfinished business, or have regrets about what we have or have not achieved. Life choices and commitments have already been made and we may not be free to change our lifestyle or direction significantly. We may feel very trapped.

We will also be looking forward in a way we haven't until now. There will be a growing sense of our mortality, and the mortality of those around us. And in the midst of all this we are asking with new urgency who we are, what we seek and what we are worth. How do we respond at such a time?

One temptation is to regress. We make an anxious bid to re-enter the world we are in fact beginning to leave. In Tony Parsons' novel *Man and Boy* (2000) a couple are happily married and have just had their first child. At this point husband Harry becomes increasingly restless for a sports car. It is a longing he has had for a long time but never acted on it. He buys one, gives a lift home to a much younger female colleague and, in a curiously unpremeditated way, ends up having a one-night stand with her. It destroys his marriage and family, and the rest of the novel explores his coming to terms with his own actions.

Others may choose this moment to change direction completely and plunge headlong into the new, like the man on the train to work who read a book that so caught his imagination that when he arrived at work he handed in his notice.

For many, there may be no one moment when it all starts and no one issue to be resolved. We just become aware of growing unease and restless questions. The things that have held our living with a certain meaning, satisfaction and security are no longer doing so. There may be no obvious way to respond. The following moods and feelings are fairly typical of this stage:

1　General disillusionment – things that once satisfied us and fulfilled us now feel empty. Could well include prayer and church.
2　Confusion of what we are feeling or wanting.
3　Resistance to stereotypical roles we feel 'trapped' in.
4　Sense of failure.
5　Anxiety and guilt.
6　Sense of loneliness.
7　Feelings of burnout or breakdown.
8　'Last chance' mentality.
9　Disconnectedness.
10　Depression.
11　Restless for change of job or career direction.
12　Concern (perhaps obsession) with the past.
13　Loss of God – at least as we have known him.
14　A move toward interiority – mystery, paradox.

Spirituality, prayer and faith in mid-life

I recall meeting a friend in a Christian bookshop. He had been the leading light of his church for years, full of faith and vision. Now he was searching the shelves for titles like *Renewing your Spiritual Passion* or *Restoring your Dynamic Faith*. It had all gone dry on him and he was desperately seeking a way back. I was reminded of the lament of the psalmist, 'I remember . . . how I went with the throng, and led them in procession to the house of God . . . Why are you cast down, O my soul?' (Ps. 42.4–5). The anguished searching of the lover in the Song of Solomon also came to mind. 'I sought him whom my soul loves; I sought him, but found him not; I called him, but he gave no answer' (Song of Sol. 3.1).

My friend could only interpret what was happening as a failure of faith and assumed his task was to find a way *back*. In fact this struggle may be part of the mid-life journey and a sign of faith at the heart of it. The real task is to discern a new way *forward*, facing the challenge to a new depth and integration of life.

The poet T. S. Eliot was in his middle years when he wrote his famous poem 'The Journey of the Magi', movingly tracing how the journey of faith must lead us through painful disorientation to new beginning. Having met Christ the wise men are 'no longer at ease in the old dispensation'. The old life is closed to them. It is highly symbolic that the Bible records them returning home 'by another route'. There is no way back into familiar ways.

There is an occasion when Jesus speaks to Peter about his vocation. 'I tell you most solemnly, when you were young you put on your own belt and walked where you liked; but when you grow old you will stretch out your hands, and somebody else will put a belt round you and take you where you would rather not go . . . Follow me' (John 21.18–19, JB). These words capture so much of this stage of faith. We are called to new dependency – where before you 'walked where you liked'. We feel ambivalent about it – we find ourselves being taken where we would rather not go. It is a journey into the unknown, guided by another – 'follow me'.

The mystical love poetry of St John of the Cross offers some of the most profound reflection on spiritual darkness. What he called the 'dark night of the soul' is a time when all surface comforts and awareness of God have gone. Mid-life transition is not necessarily the same as the dark night of John's writings, but it offers a way of understanding. It may well feel like a journey in the dark without any of the familiar landmarks or securities. The struggle can have all the symptoms of depression but is actually a profound journey of personal transformation. It is a time that needs great pastoral wisdom. This is God at work. We are being led by 'a way we would rather not go' into new depths of love and contemplation of the Beloved.

Journeying

In all the stages of life we need the support of those around us. We need friends and groups who do not require us to conform to what everyone else is thinking and feeling. We need fellow travellers who keep us honest, who are comfortable sitting in the dark and wrestling with unsettling issues that do not quickly offer answers.

I know of two churches where groups were set up in which there was permission to ask questions never asked before, perhaps because we feared others would assume we were doubting the faith or going off the rails in some way. One group was called 'Agnostics Anonymous' and the other 'Mid-faith Crisis'. Members all sensed an immense relief at being able to talk freely rather than feel the need to toe some Christian 'party line'. The very questions that were feared as potentially destructive of faith became the means of liberating faith for new and more authentic expressions of life and prayer.

For thought, prayer and activity

1   The chapter suggests that we have lost ways of marking significant stages of life's journey. If we were to recover these 'rites', what would be the most important times and events to mark and how might they be expressed?

2   Take time to work with the exercises suggested in the chapter.

3   Living through life changes.
'You sound like someone who is having to live out of a new part of himself (or herself). You are still a stranger to this "you" that is emerging.' Does this wisdom offer ways of living with changes you

may have been facing and their effect on your sense of who you are as a person?

4   Exploring – a further suggestion for reflection.

Windows of your life

The East Window	The West Window
What is starting to rise above the horizon? The earliest beginnings of something? Are there things you should celebrate and welcome?	What is dying off in your life, what is sinking below the horizon? Are there things you should grieve over but let go?
The North Window	**The South Window**
What holds you steady, keeps you coming from, or pointing in, the same direction? What is your value base?	What is warming the creativity of your life, where are the growing tips, what is it in you that wants to develop?

Further reading

Carroll, Patrick and Dyckman, Katherine, *Chaos or Creation: Spirituality and Mid-life* (New York: Paulist Press, 1986).

Fowler, James, *Stages of* Faith (New York: Harper and Row, 1980).

Hay, David and Nye, Rebecca, *The Spirit of the Child* (London: Fount, 1998).

Nouwen, Henri, *Ageing* (New York: Doubleday, 1976).

WHEN YOU PRAY . . .

Ways and understandings

14 Before God with the people on your heart

The prayer of intercession

I was once invited to lead a quiet day at a Christian theological college. My host introduced me and then told a story of some missionaries he knew who used to get up at dawn, spread a much folded map of the world over their living room floor and systematically pray their way across countries and continents. 'They *really* prayed!' he exclaimed, leaving us in no doubt that he suspected this 'Quiet Day' was not real praying at all.

I found the story intimidating rather than inspiring. Their practice was impressive but not one that everyone could achieve or even find helpful. Furthermore, silence, waiting and contemplation are essential if our praying is not to become a busy, repetitive list of needs and problems. It is certainly possible for silence to be a kind of escape (though it never works for very long). But it is equally easy for 'saying prayers' to become a shopping list, or a presumptuous agenda-setting for God.

What that story does remind us is that Christian spirituality is a way of service, not self-fulfilment. When we read that Christ, in glory, lives forever to intercede (see Rom. 8.34; Heb. 7.25), we immediately know that inter- cession lies at the heart of Christian prayer. It means the centre of Christian living and prayer is not about what we seek for ourselves. It is concerned with God's glory and with the needs of others.

For many though, 'the intercessions' remain one of least inspiring parts of Christian worship. When you hear the invitation 'let us pray' what kind of praying do you expect to follow? It is usually time spent verbally asking God for the needs of various people and situations. Intercession is a costly discipline to be faithfully embraced. But there is no one way of expressing it and there never has been.

What is intercession?

To 'intercede' literally means to go between ('inter' – between, 'cede' – go). 'Standing in the breach' is the way the Bible often pictures the ministry of an intercessor. The greater the need the more God seeks people willing to go there. One of the starkest examples is during the time of Ezekiel: 'I sought for anyone among them who would repair the wall and stand in the breach before me on behalf of the land, so that I would not destroy it; but I found no one' (Ezek. 22.30).

So the word says more about *where* we pray than *what* we pray for. Intercession is expressed as a living relationship rather than a way of saying prayers. It involves the whole of us, not just our lips or thoughts. To truly intercede means being willing to enter into a costly relationship with the world around us. Michael Ramsey defined intercession as 'standing before God with the people on your heart'. This also means our praying is inseparable from the way we live.

Intercession involves seeking to be where Christ already is. It is his ceaseless intercession that sustains all our living, holding us before the Father for our healing and transforming. Far from persuading God to get involved where he is not, intercession is a participation in Christ's costly and life-giving presence in the world. It  is such a comforting thought that there is somewhere we are held in a continuous stream of prayer, perfectly understood, in infinite love. Intercession is not speaking or pleading or making requests. It is going to meet someone and to abide with him where he abides, on behalf of others.

I find this very helpfully illustrated in this picture of the cross. Between two painfully broken pieces, the figure of Christ is filling the gap with his own body. His arms are thrust deep into each piece. In his own being he provides a meeting place. Through him the two separated pieces find a way of meeting. So Christ is actually represented as the gift of a space. One of the meanings associated with the word 'to save' in the Bible is 'spaciousness'. Through the intercessory presence of Jesus, we are offered a space in which reconciliation and a new way of belonging to God and to each other are possible.

Finally, it comes as a relief to realize that God fully expects that this kind of praying is beyond our understanding and will leave us tongue-tied. We should be suspicious if it didn't. Jesus encourages us to come to it with confidence and the expectation that God will hear and answer (Matt. 7.7, Luke 11.5–13). But part of the ministry of the Holy Spirit is to help us in our attempts to pray at all. 'The Spirit helps us in our weakness; for we do not know how to pray as we ought, but that very Spirit intercedes with sighs too deep for words . . . the Spirit intercedes for the saints according to the will of God' (Rom. 8.26–7).

Ways of interceding

Times and seasons
Intercession is one activity in the wider pattern of our regular praying. But there may be times when we feel called to make intercession our primary activity. There is wisdom in using the traditional seasons of the Church's year. At times such as Advent and Lent we give particular focus to more disciplined prayer and intercession. We cannot live every part of Christian living with equal intensity all the time. There may also be particular times of need when individuals or groups may feel called to spend more concentrated time in prayer seeking God's presence on behalf of others.

Praying with the whole of us
All our senses can be gifts to us when we pray. We have already noted how intercessions are too often dominated by words. Some will find sight, touch and smell helpful. The use of symbols may also be helpful. Lighting a candle is an ancient expression of prayer and vigil, as is the burning of incense. Mime, movement and dance can be deeply expressive where words are hard to find. Writing a letter or holding an imaginary conversation is another way of trying to discern what prayer is needed in a particular situation.

Some will find using a photograph or praying with an icon is a way of drawing heart and mind into prayer. (See also Chapter 3.)

Watching, vigil and worship

We do not need to know exactly what is going on around us to offer intercession.

One monastic community I know feels a call to pray during the night. The darkness of the night is often when people can be most alone and struggling. It is a time when people may be dying. It is also often when new life is born and love is given and received. The night is full of wonders and terrors and we are most deeply vulnerable even in the act of sleep. Between two and three o'clock every night the community prays in the chapel. I joined them once. Out in the night you could hear the nearby motorway traffic and the noises of the world that did not sleep. What was totally unexpected was that all they actually did for that hour was chant psalms. I kept wanting to ask: 'but when are we going to start praying?' Yet I began to realize that in their worshipful attentiveness to those ancient songs that express the heights and the depths of human longing we were praying for the world. Intercession was a loving vigil, in the worship of God, in the midst of the world's darkness.

Prayer of 'intention'

There will be times we will not be able to consciously pray because we rightly have to concentrate on the task that is before us. The prayer of intention is a way of offering our work or present task as a prayer, asking that the quality and care with which we attend to it may itself be a prayer.

The gifts of the Spirit

If the Spirit is at the centre of our praying, guiding, leading and empowering us, then intercession must include listening – leaving space for the Spirit to guide and prompt in all sorts of creative ways. (See Chapter 16.)

Lists and prayer diaries

The advantage of a prayer diary is that those who need our prayers do not depend on our memory, what mood we are in, or how awake or easily distracted we are. A simple list of names, pausing quietly after each to hold them before God and to listen to the Spirit, may be a very helpful way of interceding. Lists need to be kept to a reasonable length. They need reviewing from time to time and we must be as ready to take a name off as we are to add one.

Interceding together
Jesus talks about the power of agreeing in prayer about something (Matt. 18.19). This is an important but neglected aspect of praying together. Often we discover what others believe is needed in a situation only when they pray their prayer. What if we don't agree with them, or believe that the real need for prayer lies somewhere else?

Life is rarely straightforward. Some issues are painfully complex. It will not be easy to know what to ask for and people in the group may have very different views. This needs talking through together. Only then can we honestly say 'Amen', let it be so, together. Even after agreeing it will still be important to resist the temptation to supply God with the answer or tell him what he should be doing!

Silence and waiting
Recalling his time as a missionary in the Lebanon at the height of the civil war, Alan Amos speaks of the place of silence in intercession. What he says of that situation could be transferred to many other corners of the world today.

> The difficulty is that words have lost their meaning. For instance, if you mention hope, you might as well be talking about despair for all the effect it has on people. Therefore I would talk mostly of waiting upon God and quietly searching for his presence. Real prayer is offering what you can see and grasp of what is happening, however beastly it is, and waiting on God with it, almost as though you have it in your hands.
>
> (From an interview in *Grassroots* magazine, February 1983)

A vocation to intercession
We are all called to intercede but for some it may be a particular calling, which may be costly. The scriptures tell us God looks for people to be intercessors but finds it hard to find them. God laments the lack of an intercessor: 'I sought for anyone among them who would repair the wall and stand in the breach before me on behalf of the land . . . but I found no one' (Ezek. 22.30).

Many of these intercessors and their ministry are hidden from view and rightly so. But two men from very different Christian traditions offer glimpses of this ministry at its most costly and powerful. Both lived and prayed through a traumatic era of European history. Both were recognized as intercessors. They died within two years of each other in the early 1950s.

Rees Howells grew up in a Welsh mining village. As a young adult he had a powerful conversion experience that led him to a radical commitment of his life to Christ. This increasingly drew him into intercessory prayer. He taught that three things were found in intercession that are not necessarily found in ordinary prayer – identification, agony and authority. These are the marks of Christ crucified and Howells understood such prayer as a participation in the intercession of Christ. For him intercession was a participation in the cross of Christ.

Over those same years another young man was growing up in a poor Russian home. He too was powerfully drawn to Christ and became a monk on the island of Mount Athos in Greece, where he was known as Staretz Silouan. For the 40 years up to his death he only allowed himself to sleep in brief 20-minute snatches, sitting upright. His whole life was given to intercession, marked by an almost continuous experience of spiritual warfare and demonic conflict. His biography is not for the faint-hearted! He would have agreed with what Howells wrote about the marks of an intercessor – but he would have added the word 'Glory' above all else.

We can be grateful for God's intercessors hidden in the world. We can pray for them, even if we do not know them. We can pray for the strengthening and sustaining of this way of prayer at the heart of the life of the world. It has never been more needed.

In the prayer of Jesus

The story is told of an American Episcopal priest who shortly after being elected a bishop in her church was diagnosed with cancer. She was someone who had followed a steady discipline of prayer all her life, but now, just when she needed it most, her spiritual life went into darkness and she could find no sense of God's presence or comfort. It was frightening. This continued for some time until one day, as she walked along a beach, she suddenly became aware that 'Jesus was praying his prayer in me.'

If intercession is standing before God with the people on our hearts, we can only be there because Christ is there for ever. In the end there is only Christ praying. It is all held in his living intercession. Jesus is praying his prayer in us.

For thought, prayer and activity

1   Do you find the picture of the crucifixion on page 122 a helpful image of intercession?

2   'For many . . . "the intercessions" remain one of the least inspiring parts of Christian worship'.
   (a) Is this your experience?
   (b) Where does the problem lie?

3   Sometimes we struggle with intercession because one particular way of doing it has been imposed on us.
   (a) Are there suggestions in this chapter that helpfully challenge or creatively develop your understanding of intercessory prayer?
   (b) Can you explore other ways of expressing prayer for others and the needs of the world?

4   (a) If you could meet and talk about intercession with Rees Howells or Staretz Silouan and were free to be completely honest, what personal experience would you share and what questions would you like to ask?
   (b) Imagine how they might reply.

Further reading
Grubb, Norman, *Rees Howells: Intercessor* (Cambridge: Lutterworth Press, 1991).
Sakharov, Archimandrite Sophrony, *The Monk of Mount Athos* (New York: St Vladimir Press, 1983).

15 The joy of being wrong

Confession and forgiveness

Only sinners understand the gospel. Only sinners know their need of it. Of all the names for Jesus, 'friend of sinners' is surely the most unexpected and wonderfully welcome. This is why one book on the subject of sin has the delightful title *The Joy of Being Wrong* (Allison, 1998)! This place of our deepest human disorder and helplessness is where divine love is most fully revealed. Human waywardness and rebellion apparently draw from God a greater revelation of his compassion and mercy. The God whom Jesus reveals has this wildly improbable and even irresponsible love for the lost. After all, what kind of responsible shepherd abandons the whole of the rest of his flock on an open hillside to go looking for one that has wandered off somewhere on its own (Luke 15.3–6)?

Fore-giving love

God's love for us is always fore-giving love. It is given in advance of anything we do or say. We have not earned it. It is love offered without any guarantee that we will choose to accept or return it. This fore-giving love is pure gift. God's desire and intention for us *precedes* any worthiness or repentance.

In the Gospels the people who received this love most freely and joyfully were those outside any religious or social acceptance. By any human expectation these were people who had nothing to offer, or bargain or impress Jesus with, at all. The godly, religiously devout found this kind of love offensive. It made all their attempts at holiness and devotion apparently irrelevant. What is often missed in the Gospel stories is how our 'goodness' may be a greater problem than our sin. It was godly and devout people who arranged the death of Christ.

If God's love is fore-given then our first task is not to come to terms with our sinfulness. It will be to accept the love with which God seeks us.

What is sin?

From the earliest days of the Christian Church, 'I repent of my sins' has been one of the three core promises made at Christian baptism. The first is 'I turn to Christ', the third is 'I renounce evil'. But what is 'sin' exactly? In general terms it can be described as any way of life that falls short of God's will and purpose for us. It is a state of profound separation from God that the Bible often calls 'death' (Rom. 5.12). When we try to be more specific the tendency is to begin to list wrong actions, words or thoughts. But the problem is more basic. Who we *are* always comes before what we *do*. Our choices, desires and actions flow from our sense of personal identity. Our deepest problem is not with what we are doing or saying. The power and significance of sin lies in this profound confusion about our true identity.

Adam and Eve's real wrongdoing was not stealing fruit from God's private orchard, getting caught and punished for ever. Something more dangerous was going on. Adam and Eve were trying to be who they were not. They wanted to be 'like God' (Gen. 3.5). And the consequence of trying to take the identity of another is that they utterly lost their own. Something died in that moment. They ended up ashamed, covering up from themselves and from each other and trying to hide from God.

To say that we are born in sin, in Bible terms, is to say that we live with a radically false sense of who we are. Even with the best of intentions, life must then unfold as a case of tragically mistaken identity.

True repentance

One ancient prayer asks God for '*true repentance*'. This is wise. It is possible to say sorry and not to really mean it, or to hope to make a pious impression. It is possible to say sorry but be hopelessly deluded about where real guilt and responsibility actually lie in the situation. If we do not really know ourselves we will need God's help in the task of recognizing and turning from sin. This is why the ancient desert fathers and mothers took

Dear God,
When we fall, let us fall inwards.
Let us fall freely and completely:
that we may find our depth and humility:
the solid earth from which we may rise up and love again.

(Michael Leunig)

repentance so seriously. They taught their followers to pray for 'compunction'. The word means to pierce or sting. The image is of a balloon being punctured. To have compunction is to have our false image of ourselves pierced, to begin to know ourselves in truth and to turn to God for his forgiveness. The issue is one of truth. It is not a joyless obsession with sin that Christianity is sometimes accused of. True repentance will lead to mercy and new life.

Confession and forgiving

Preparing to confess
Confession and forgiveness will have different significance on different occasions. In daily or weekly prayer there is something rightly routine about praying 'forgive us our sins'. We are trying to keep short accounts. There will be other times when confession needs more careful preparation, thought and action. In the ancient cycle of the Christian year, extended times for deeper self-examination are provided – such as the seasons of Lent and Advent.

Confessing in community
The first Christians were taught to 'confess your sins to one another' (James 5.16). This is one of the neglected teachings in today's church. The more common expectation is that confession is what we do privately between ourselves and God. For some this direct personal relationship is so central that to involve anyone else is thought to be an attempt to take the place of Christ in the ministry of confession. It is true that there is only one mediator between us and God – Jesus Christ (1 Tim. 2.5). But his ministry in the place of human sin may be received in a variety of ways. Far from undermining the work of Christ, shared confession may be an important way he ministers his grace to us. We are not able or expected to go it alone in this ministry. The strength we need to open our personal lives to God needs the encouragement, support and challenge of being part of Christian community. In the Epistle of James this kind of confession is explicitly linked to healing (James 5.16).

It is strange, on the face of it, to find it easier to go directly, in private, with our sins, to a God of awesome perfection and burning holiness, rather than to a brother or sister who shares our struggles and failures. Perhaps we should be more suspicious of our motives for keeping it private. Shared confession of sin and the ministry of forgiveness together lead to a breakthrough to a new kind of community. We are no longer a community of secret sinners struggling to act like saints but a community of forgiven sinners walking in the light of God's mercy (see Bonhoeffer, 1981, pp. 87ff). Down through church history, mutual confession and forgiveness has been a central feature of many great re-awakenings of faith.

When Christians pray the confession together, it is intended to be a *corporate* prayer. It is not there to provide individuals with a chance to confess their private sins to God. If this is true then a Christian community will need to discuss and come to agreement as to what they need to repent of. And what are the limits of this corporate confession? For example, many Christians in the Western world meet in the privileged freedom of an economic system that leaves vast parts of the world in debt, hunger and poverty. What might it mean to 'turn' from our sins in this context? What lifestyle and values and involvement in the world would express the reality of our penitence?

Giving and receiving forgiveness
In the Lord's Prayer receiving forgiveness from God is clearly linked to the willingness to forgive others. In recent years there have been moving stories of forgiveness in the face of terrible suffering and evil – for example in post-apartheid South Africa. They are reminders of the power of the cross of Christ to break through cycles of bitterness and hate and give us the freedom to respond with love and not hate.

For many the experience of forgiving is not dramatic or easy. It may be more like carrying a wound that is deep and that will not heal easily. It is easily bumped into and the pain is awakened again. It is a wound that needs regular and faithful rebinding, cleaning and anointing. Forgiveness is the discipline of rebinding that wound until it is whole.

Sinners and sinned against
We are not just sinners. We all carry the wounds of being sinned against. For some people the impact of the sin of others upon their lives must be acknowledged and ministered to first. This is why ministry in the place of sin needs such care and compassion. Victims of abuse, for example, may very easily believe that what happened to them was their fault. The cross

of Christ is first of all God's identification with innocent suffering in this world – his becoming victim with them. For those who have only heard of the cross as a place that judges them, this discovery is liberating.

One wise pastor ministering in an era of church history noted for its extreme practices of self-denial and harsh disciplines wrote this to someone whose conscience continued to trouble them: 'You should rejoice every time you find an imperfection.' Why? Because sin is not really that serious after all? Not at all. But it is not our discipline or capacity to feel guilt that saves us. Our every failure, confessed to Christ, is an opportunity to be renewed again in the gift of his grace and mercy. And where else do we seek to be?

Personal confession

There is one other expression of confession in community but it tends to be looked on with suspicion. Sometimes called 'sacramental confession' this is the ancient practice of making confession in the presence of another Christian and receiving the ministry of Christ's forgiveness through them. Traditionally, but not always, this person is an ordained minister, or at least a wise and experienced Christian who represents Christ and the church they serve. They are bound to keep what they hear completely confidential. It has been said of this kind of confession that 'all may, none must, some should, few do'. We may seek it for a variety of reasons.

1   To receive absolution and assurance for forgiveness when assurance is lacking.
2   When we need to talk about something which requires the seal of absolute secrecy.
3   When we are suffering some bondage which may be the result of sin.
4   As part of review or seasonal evaluation and reflection on our Christian life.
5   As part of preparation for a major life-change – new job, marriage or ordination for example.
6   In preparation for death.

I was very nervous in seeking this ministry for the first time as none of my friends did it. I asked an older minister whom I trusted and respected. I prepared by writing down what I wanted to say sorry for. Together we knelt down and I prayed my confession to God. I felt embarrassed and ashamed in a way I never normally did when I prayed privately to God. I wept for my sins for the first time. My friend listened carefully, read some scripture verses about God's promise of forgiveness and laid hands on me for the life of the Spirit to strengthen and renew me. He spoke some words that he believed God wanted me to hear and then took my list, tore it up and put it in the bin. I knew I was no longer condemned and left with a quite new confidence of God's love.

Ashes and kites

At the beginning of Lent, Christians traditionally receive the sign of ash on their foreheads with the sober words, 'remember you are dust and to dust you shall return; repent and believe the gospel'. Ashing is a universal symbol of human mortality, of grief and mourning for sin, and of penitence. This is a season for serious reflection and for practising the disciplines that strengthen the fight against everything that denies Christ. Christian living is to be marked by watchfulness and careful self-examination. There are tears to be shed. There is no cheap grace. It is the way of the cross.

But there is another symbol for this season – a complementary one. Some Greek Orthodox communities mark the start of Lent in a quite different way. For them the first day of Lent is treated as the first outdoor day of the new year. Lent is the beginning of Spring ('Lent' in fact means 'Spring'). After the long death of winter, here is the first sign that new life is coming. We must go out to greet it. The community celebrates this day by climbing the nearest hill and flying kites on the fresh spring wind!

Always more important than what we turn *from* is what we turn *to*. Here we meet the Spirit enticing, provoking, driving, inspiring us in the struggle to turn from sin and be caught up into the adventure of divine love.

For thought, prayer and activity

1   (a)   Would 'The joy of being wrong' be an accurate description of your Christian experience of sin and forgiveness?
    (b)   If not, what would be a more appropriate title?

2   What makes facing our sin and knowing ourselves forgiven so difficult?

3   (a) Have you ever 'made confession' in the way this chapter describes?
(b) If not, would this be helpful and is there a wise pastor you could
discuss this with?
(c) What kind of qualities would you look for in a 'confessor'?

4   Do you agree that 'who we *are* always comes before what we *do*' or are
we simply defined by our actions?

5   Does your own approach to sin, repentance and forgiveness need more
ashes or kites at the moment?

Further reading

Dudley, Martin and Rowell, Geoffrey, *Confession and Absolution* (Collegeville,
Minn.: Liturgical Press, 1990).
Moreton, Mark, *Personal Confession Reconsidered* (Cambridge: Grove Books, 1994).
Runcorn, David, *Touch Wood: Meeting the Cross in the World Today* (London:
Darton, Longman and Todd, 1992). See Section B, pp. 39–73.
Tutu, Desmond, *No Future Without Forgiveness: A Personal Overview of South
Africa's Truth and Reconciliation Commission* (London: Rider, 2000).

16 When the Spirit comes

The Spirit in Christian spirituality

It came without warning, shooting high into the sky from out of the depths of the earth. They had struck oil! There is wild celebration.

But it is too precious to waste. It must be gathered, refined and distributed. There is no part of life that will not be transformed by its energy.

The relationship of the Holy Spirit to the Church is not unlike that. In unexpected moments and places in its history, as on the day of Pentecost, its transforming life has broken out on the surface. And, each time, the Church has faced the challenge of receiving this power to renew its life and mission.

There is a tension here. That wild display was at least a vivid sign. There is life here! But left to itself it will just burn out. Its renewing power needs drawing in to the full life of the Church. But at other times the Church has had all the most impressive piping systems for refining and distributing, but is showing little sign that anything is actually flowing through it at all.

When the Spirit comes

The first Christians saw the coming of the Holy Spirit at Pentecost as a fulfilment of a promise:

> I will pour out my spirit on all flesh;
> your sons and your daughters shall prophesy,
> your old men shall dream dreams,
> and your young men shall see visions.
> Even on the male and female slaves,
> in those days, I will pour out my spirit.
> (Joel 2.28–9)

Prophesied in a highly conservative, patriarchal and hierarchical society this is a vision of a radically inclusive community. This divine Spirit gives authoritative voice to people who are more usually denied one. It has a potential for being very untidy and divisive. The presence of such a Spirit will always unsettle the powers that be. So it is hardly surprising to find that the relationship of the Holy Spirit to the church institution has often been an uneasy one. For large periods of the history of the Church the place of the Holy Spirit in the scheme of things has been neglected or carefully controlled. In some medieval Christian art, for example, the Spirit is pictured as a minute bird, hovering inconsequentially between the more theologically 'significant' figures in the Godhead.

But at regular intervals in history the life of the Spirit has broken out and reminded the Church of its transforming mission in the world.

The year 2006 marks the centenary of a spiritual awakening in Los Angeles that was the beginning of the Pentecostal church (see Chapter 4). It represents a continuous sustained outpouring of the Holy Spirit around the world. In the last 40 years this has strongly influenced churches within the historic mainstream denominations where it has become known as 'the charismatic movement'. It has inspired fresh approaches to worship, the sharing of the ministry across the whole community, the ministry of healing and a new confidence to live out the faith and make it known. Movements such as the New Wine network are vital sources of continued encouragement to Christian communities living their faith in increasingly isolated contexts.

There is no one experience of the Holy Spirit. No one way of being a spiritually alive church ever fully expresses it. But the Pentecostal awakening has represented something of a 'rediscovery' of the Holy Spirit and within it three common characteristics are to be found.

Release

My own Christian upbringing was in more traditional churches. Rather than making me more 'spiritual', my own sense of being newly filled with the Holy Spirit was to help me relax with God and with myself more. The encounter began a process of making me more human. Asked what the Holy Spirit had done for him (in what had been a very dramatic encounter), one person replied, 'He took away my dignity!' But he said this with such a broad smile that it was clear that he felt he had been set free, not humiliated, by the experience.

Presence

The ministry of the Holy Spirit is to make real to us our place in the love and life of God. 'When we cry, "Abba! Father!"', writes St Paul, 'it is that very Spirit bearing witness with our spirit that we are children of God' (Rom. 8.15–16). This may be much more than the playful intimacy of family life. The Holy Spirit is gift to our deepest fears and anxieties. There is nothing sentimental in calling God our Abba. In a world like ours 'it is the child's cry out of nightmare' (Rowan Williams).

Expectancy and enabling

Without the Spirit's vitality, Christian living quickly becomes dull conformity to moral rules. One mark of the Spirit's presence is in provoking an edge of faithful expectancy that God is present and active among his people and in his world. But expectancy without enabling leads only to disillusionment. The Spirit enables life in a way we cannot generate of ourselves. To people lacking confidence, struggling to trust and to live in the promises of God, the Holy Spirit is a generous, strengthening presence. This may be experienced in very different ways. For some there is a new depth of worship, a hunger for prayer and love for the Bible. There may simply be an overwhelming awareness of the sheer power of God and his holiness. For others it comes as a gift of tears. For many it brings a new confidence and boldness to live and share the faith. For many it is a quiet, undramatic renewal of life lived in daily consecration to God's will and glory.

In the fellowship of the Holy Spirit

In the liturgical prayer called 'The Grace', that closes many Christian meetings, we pray for the 'fellowship of the Holy Spirit'. What are we praying for?

Spirit of the wilderness

An important starting place is the encounter of Jesus with the Spirit at his baptism. All four Gospels describe how the Spirit descended on Jesus at his baptism 'as a dove'. Down the centuries Christian art has traditionally portrayed the descending Spirit in this scene as a small, delicate, pure white dove. But that is not the kind of dove that is described there. The

Greek word describes a rock-dove. This bird is neither immediately striking nor attractive. It looks like an ordinary English wood-pigeon. Rock-doves like rocky and rugged desert terrain. They make their homes in inhospitable and hostile places where human life would instinctively feel under threat and at risk. This is the bird that mysteriously appears overhead and descends on Jesus as he emerges from the water. This is the Spirit who immediately drives Jesus into the wilderness for a period of tough testing and preparation for his ministry.

Imagining this tough, wild bird roaming freely in the life of the Church and the world challenges our tamer expectations of life in Spirit (see Mitton, 2000, Chapter 1).

Cross and Spirit

Pentecostal and charismatic movements have tended to start from Luke's accounts in his Gospel and the Acts of the Apostles for their understanding of the gift of the Holy Spirit. This has often resulted in an unhelpful separation of Good Friday, Easter and Pentecost, as if Christian maturing involves leaving one stage (e.g. the cross) for the next (Pentecost). By contrast St John expresses the relationship of Spirit and cross in a very different way. When Jesus appears to his disciples on Easter day he helps them to recognize him *by his wounds*. The risen one is the crucified one. Risen life does not cease to be cross-bearing. It is the victorious, crucified and risen Christ who breathes the Holy Spirit on the disciples and commissions them (John 20.19–23). This is John's understanding of Pentecost.

Spirit of community

The Holy Spirit creates community. Here all have a unique place and contribution and no one may claim greater importance than any other (cf 1 Cor. 12.14–26, and see Chapter 6). The Holy Spirit is a shaper and orderer, leading the Church into its God-given order and shape. There is a sense then in which we must lose control of our spirituality. We are to live in obedient openness to the work of the Spirit.

Spirit of creation

Interest in the Holy Spirit in recent years has tended to focus most strongly on the more ecstatic experiences of prayer and worship. This is important and has led many into a more intimate relationship with God. But it needs to be balanced with a 'this worldly' emphasis of the Spirit in creation. The vision is not of an increasing supernatural community, but of a community expressing God's presence across the whole range of earthly life. In the Bible the Holy Spirit is the constantly sustaining source of all life. 'You send forth your Spirit, you *ever* renew the face of the earth' (Ps. 104.30, literal translation). The dramatic outpouring on the day of Pentecost combines both aspects very vividly. The intoxicating experience of the Spirit in prayer and worship spills out of a locked upper room and into the midst of life.

Life in the Spirit

'Be filled with the Spirit' urges St Paul (Eph. 5.18). If we need reminding to be filled with the Spirit it is clearly possible not to be. As someone once said, 'I am filled with the Spirit – but I leak!'

To deepen our praying and strengthen our Christian living we need to be consciously seeking the empowering presence of the Holy Spirit. Where the challenge of this lies will be different for each us. But Jesus encourages us to be bold in asking, knocking and seeking (Matt. 7.7).

So what do you want to ask for?

It may help to ask others to pray with us for the life we seek in the Spirit. It is not always easy to ask in faith and expectancy for ourselves.

Gifts and ministries
The Spirit empowers and gives shape to our Christian living through giving gifts to the Church.

We have gifts that differ according to the grace given to us: prophecy, in proportion to faith; ministry, in ministering; the teacher, in teaching; the exhorter, in exhortation; the giver, in generosity; the leader, in diligence; the compassionate, in cheerfulness.

(Rom. 12.6–8)

There are several such lists in the New Testament. They are not meant to be comprehensive and they are not ranked in terms of importance. But it also is clear from the church in Corinth that the possession of these gifts is no guarantee of spiritual maturity. I can think of a time when the idea of speaking in tongues and other supernatural gifts was so personally exciting that it became a complete distraction to me from following Jesus. But they are not to be ignored either. We are to seek them and to learn to use them wisely for the common good. They are vital equipment for Christian living.

Fruitful living

The gift of the Spirit is to enable the transformation of our deepest character traits and patterns of behaviour. St Paul contrasts the destructive human behaviour with what he calls the fruit of the Spirit (Gal. 5.16–26). The Holy Spirit is as at home in the raw, messy guts of our human experience as in our attempts at godly living (maybe more so!). What is on offer here is a challenging but ultimately transforming gift of grace for earthly living – even at its most dysfunctional and hopeless.

Prayer

The Spirit helps us to pray. 'For we do not know how to pray as we ought, but that very Spirit intercedes with sighs too deep for words' (Rom 8.26). To be involved at a level too deep for words is profound, loving identification. It is hardly surprising that in drawing near to God human words should run out. So how generous and enabling it is that one of the gifts of the Spirit should be a language to pray with. It is a symbolic gift – literally giving voice to those who otherwise would find none at the moment they need it most.

To those who have never come across praying in tongues the idea may sound strange. It is simply a language of prayer given by the Spirit. Praying in tongues involves no loss of consciousness or personal volition. It is one of the ways the Holy Spirit prays in and for and through us.

Leaving spaces for the Spirit

If the Spirit helps and guides us in expressing ourselves before God, we must learn to leave spaces in our praying, our worship and our talking. This is where liturgy and service patterns must not be allowed to control. Some churches have a prayer group that meets before the service to listen to God. When they sense that God is speaking in some way the person leading the service will share this with the congregation. If the picture or message is relevant to someone there they are encouraged to share or pray with a member of the prayer team after the service.

Ministering and discerning

The Holy Spirit 'speaks' to us through all our senses. We may sense that an intuition, a mental picture or verse from the Bible has a particular significance. Perhaps God is speaking. We will need to test this out through the discernment of others. This takes a bit of courage. I remember sitting through one prayer meeting feeling totally weighed down. Everything felt very heavy. But I assumed it was just my own mood. Finally someone else said, 'Is it just me or is there a real heaviness among us? Do we need to talk about this together?' What followed was quite a breakthrough in the life of that group. As we take the risk and share, faith can grow and our ability to hear God will become more sensitive.

On catching fire

Our prayers, Bible reading, worship and acts of service are all fuel for Christian living but they do not themselves give life. The fuel awaits the fire of the Spirit.

The story is told of a young monk seeking advice from an older monk about his spiritual life. 'Abba,' he said, 'as far as I can I say my little office, I fast a little, I pray and meditate, I live in peace and as far as I can, I purify my thoughts. What else can I do?'

Then the old man stood up and stretched out his hands towards heaven. His fingers became like ten lamps and he said to him, 'If you will, you can become all flame' (Ward, *The Sayings of the Desert Fathers*, 1981, p. 103).

For thought, prayer and activity

1   The encounter with the Holy Spirit is described in a variety of ways: as wind, fire, water or, in this chapter, as 'striking oil'.
    (a) What words or images describe your own experience of the life of the Spirit?
    (b) Are there other words or images that you wish were your experience of the Spirit?

2   How might the image of the Holy Spirit as a wild rock-dove change our expectations of the Spirit's presence and ministry in our lives?

3   Which features of the ministry of the Spirit in this chapter most draw you and which leave you with questions or uncertainties?

4   (a) Have you ever worshipped in churches of a more distinctly charismatic tradition?
    (b) Are there aspects of their approach that you find beneficial and that you can incorporate into your spiritual life?

5   (a) As you pray, read through the story in John 20.19–23 of the wounded and risen Christ appearing to the first disciples revealing his wounds and breathing the Holy Spirit upon them.
    (b) Imagine Jesus coming to you and doing the same.

Reading and resources

Leach, John, *The Spirit Comes* (San Francisco: HarperCollins, 2001).

Smail, Tom, *The Giving Gift: The Holy Spirit in Person* (London: Darton, Longman and Todd, 1994).

Stockitt, Robin, *Open to the Spirit: St Ignatius and John Wimber in Dialogue* (Cambridge: Grove Books, 2000).

Suurmond, Jean-Jacques, *Word and Spirit at Play: Towards a Charismatic Theology* (London: SCM Press, 1994).

www.new-wine.org

17 In search of words that raise the dead

The liturgies and shapes we pray with

'Liturgy' is commonly understood to mean a *written* order of prayer and worship. What this brings to mind will vary according to our experience. For some it will be a familiar and secure pattern that has laid a nurturing foundation for our Christian life over many years. For others it sums up everything that is deadly about church as they have endured it. In a discussion between people training for ministry one of them bluntly announced, 'I hate liturgy!' For him it was the very antithesis of freedom and openness to the inspiration of the Spirit. Liturgy, by definition, quenched the Spirit. He was himself a gifted worship leader but it was noticeable that even in his improvised style certain words and phrases were often repeated. There was also a recognizable order to the way the worship would progress. His way of worship was liturgical, actually. It just wasn't written down.

The relationship between word and Spirit for prayer and worship is a subtle one. In a way that reflects the surrounding culture there has been a reaction against 'traditional' liturgy in much church life and a greater valuing of the improvised forms of worship. Word and Spirit are easily thought of as being in opposition to each other. The truth is they need each other. Liturgy gives a framework for the Spirit and the Spirit gives life to the liturgy.

Some history

In common with other ancient religions, Hebrew prayer and worship was liturgical, rhythmic and expressed through dramatic, sacred rituals. The book of Leviticus is a detailed example of the intense care that went into the choice of all actions and words to be offered to God.

In personal devotion, regular times of prayer through the day were familiar in a way more closely associated today with Muslim devotions. Daniel prayed three times a day (Dan. 6.10). The psalmist even speaks of worshipping seven times a day (Ps. 119.164). The spiritual life of Jesus would have been shaped by the ancient formal liturgy worship of his people. It was a practice continued by the first Christians in Jerusalem. Although we do not know the precise form their praying together took we know they continued to attend the Temple 'at the hour of prayer' (Acts 3.1) until they were later expelled.

The glimpses we have of worship in heaven are all liturgical, as 'day and night without ceasing they sing, "Holy, holy, holy, the Lord God the Almighty, who was and is and is to come"' (Rev. 4.8).

Liturgy should always be a living, dynamic and evolving resource. Though some historic forms of liturgy prove very rightly durable, it is the task for each generation of the church to adapt and develop the disciplines of prayer that will sustain and renew the people of God in their vocation.

In Western Europe this was strongly influenced by monastic communities. At the Reformation the monastic cycle of seven services (or 'offices') through the day was taken and adapted into a pattern of prayer for lay Christians to use in their daily living. The three morning offices of lauds, prime and terce were combined to becoming one service of mattins (morning prayer) at the start of the day. None (pronounced 'known'), vespers and compline became one service of 'evensong'. This was accompanied by a lectionary cycle to guide the regular reading of scripture.

In more recent times a huge amount of liturgical revision and experiment has been going on. The variety is now considerable but they have in common:

- greater choice and flexibility of content;
- resources for more creative expression of particular times and seasons;
- the use of contemporary language;
- greater opportunity for participation in public worship;
- spaces for informal or spontaneous contributions.

There are also liturgies that reflect distinct spiritualities such as Taizé, Iona or the Celtic tradition. Some excellent and very accessible prayer resources are available on the Internet. For example <www.sacredspace.ie> offers ten minutes of daily prayer, a Bible reading and reflection, backed up by helpful guidance where needed. It is based on Ignatian spirituality (see Chapter 18).

Liturgy is natural

Liturgy is not something religious in the first instance. We human beings instinctively seek ritual and liturgy to express the things that mean most to us. We see this in the way children learn and explore their world. They thrive within the security of quite set patterns, rules or litanies. Children's rhymes and stories are highly liturgical. Repetition, ritual and rhythm are a vital part of them. Far from confining or restricting a child, liturgical ritual is freeing. It enables a space within which the real play can happen.

Adults too live liturgical, ritual lives. We have a need to order and give shape to our lives. We are creatures of routine. That doesn't mean we are boring. Those daily patterns and habits of eating, sleeping, meeting and working meet a much deeper need than we realize. When the pattern is disrupted by a crisis and our living is knocked out of its familiar shape, we can become very stressed and insecure. We seek the structures that will give our lives the shape they need for the task of living freely. The rhythms and words of liturgical prayer enable this to become a praying shape (see Chapter 7).

The gifts of liturgy for spiritual formation

What do we look for in good liturgy?

Liturgy as a constant
We need the gift of a disciplined pattern that will lead us into praise, penitence, intercession and meditation. We need a resource that is not dependent on our variable levels of inspiration, changeable moods, fallible memories or limited theological understanding. In short we need a shape of praying that is bigger than us.

Liturgy as scaffolding
It offers a protecting shape for our praying. Scaffolding is never to be confused with the real building within it. But it provides a safe structure for the building up of our prayer and worship. Liturgy holds our praying in a shape it needs to mature and deepen.

Liturgy offers sustainable patterns of prayer

It frees us from the burden of having to think what to say and even to work up the feelings of inspiration. That is an important part of its job. It broadens our vocabulary for praying. Some feel that it is a failure to resort to the words of others to pray with. Thankfully we have no requirement that hymn-singing must be made up as we go along. In more informal and spontaneous patterns of prayer the burden of constantly finding fresh ways of expressing worship is a very real one.

Liturgy and the holiness of God

That all the great world religions, let alone the historic spiritual traditions of the Christian Church, should have taken such care over their evolving patterns of liturgical prayer and worship is surely significant. By contrast it may be one of the most damaging losses in a contemporary culture that expects to meet everyone and everything with casual familiarity that we no longer know how to give reverence where it is due. The instinct to create holy ritual and liturgy is very wise. Real care is needed in how we express ourselves and act before the living God. He is a consuming fire. He is not to be approached casually. Annie Dillard may not be exaggerating when she writes, 'I think of set pieces of liturgy as certain words that people have successfully addressed to God without getting killed.'

Liturgy is a way of praying with the Bible

Traditional liturgies are woven almost entirely out of scripture (see Chapter 18). There is nothing wrong with spontaneous prayer and worship but we are no longer a culture with depth of memory and reflection on the Bible that enables rich and nurturing liturgy. We will need help to find the words and phrases we need.

Liturgy and memory

Good liturgy is memorable. It enables us to build up a Christian mind and memory.

I grew up with the Book of Common Prayer. I remember finding it very boring. But it is phrases and prayers from those liturgies that still arise in my heart in times of difficulty and need. There are stories of Christians in prison and labour camps whose liturgical memory of scripture and prayers, built up steadily over the years, sustained them through the hell they were enduring.

Although the pic'n'mix options of much contemporary worship offer a creative variety we need, the danger is that we are losing the very regularity and rhythm through which liturgy does its work and soaks into us.

Liturgy as a means of transport

The job of liturgy is to carry us somewhere. It is not meant to draw attention to itself. We are not meant to be too conscious of it. There is a tension here. The beauty of the very words and phrases that move us to God can themselves take the place of God. Beauty of holiness is not to be confused with the 'holiness' of beauty.

Liturgy as a dance

In its rhythm and use of words liturgy works more like a dance than a recital. Repetition and rehearsal of movements bring the dancer to a place where they no longer consciously think about them and are caught up in the dance itself. Liturgy is learning how to dance.

Liturgy as a way of praying with the whole Church for the whole world

Liturgy nourishes our praying with a theology and vision wider than our own. In the midst of this world, despite our enduring divisions there are words we share and pray together before God. We never pray alone. Even on our own we pray '*Our* Father'.

Liturgy and blessed routine

Daily prayer is not sustainable if we think it must always achieve a celebratory high to be 'real'. It may be better understood as a routine like brushing our teeth. In that sense it is not meant to be exciting. We need somewhere to offer the ordinariness of daily life to God and to confess our needs to him.

In a society that lives at high levels of overstimulation, liturgy can be a gift that anchors and settles us. Monks understood very well the problem of human boredom. But the answer was not to find endlessly new ways of doing things. Boredom is an encounter with our own emptiness. We need to find ways of offering it to God for what it is, rather than going off in search of distractions or to inflict the tedium of our own company on other people.

Liturgy, times and seasons
A creative liturgy will guide us more deeply into the varied seasons of the
Christian year and the truth they proclaim.

Liturgy, joy and pain
Have you noticed how in moments of heightened joy and pain our way of
speaking becomes more liturgical, repeating particular phrases over again?
This is a natural way of expressing what is heightened and important.

Liturgy today – a spiritual health warning

We have never had such a variety and richness of liturgical resources available for shaping our praying, personally and corporately. But we now need
to re-learn the skills of praying and worshipping well with it. In this
respect there are signs we are suffering from a liturgical loss of nerve. Out
of a concern perhaps to be relevant, easily understood and informal, the
public leading of liturgical worship is too often punctuated by chatty
asides or introductions. It means that rather than establishing community
prayer in familiar and sustaining rhythms our worship reflects the jerky
restlessness of the world outside. Liturgy is good for you.

Form and improvisation

Christian liturgy has been following the worlds of theatre, music and even
comedy in the way it now leaves spaces within structure. Many artistic disciplines have been dominated by controlling form and order. Order and
improvization are now becoming partners again.

Jazz has long understood this relationship. Jazz works through a very
precise relationship between order and spontaneity. On the surface it can
sound wildly disordered and chaotic. But it can only do that because at its
centre it respects a very disciplined beat that holds the music together.
Without that beat the result would be chaos. If it was only the beat the
result would be stifling conformity. Each must honour the other.

Certain Christian liturgical traditions developed precisely as an expression of this insight. In Byzantine liturgy of the fifteenth century, the choir
held a single bass note while the cantors improvized songs of worship and
prayer on behalf of the people. Theologically that bass note represents the

song of God that holds all things in being. Because that ground bass is there and utterly reliable, all other songs become possible. Dietrich Bonhoeffer called this divine song a *cantus firmus*. He spent the last years of his life as a prisoner of the Nazis before his execution in 1945. The idea of the *cantus firmus* was his expression of hope and security as he wrestled, wrote and prayed in the darkness of the terrible evils and suffering that were engulfing the world (see Alves, 1990, p. 129).

So at the heart of what we call spiritual life and liturgy is the task of weaving our song around the *cantus firmus*, the song of divine love. Learning to hear it is the priority for what our age calls spirituality. Sustained on that deep ground bass all the music of life is free to develop without limit or end, as it was in the beginning. Wandering this strange land, we are learning to sing, even as we are sung.

A prayer for times of boredom

Creator God,
whose gift of life is found as much in tedium as in glory,
teach us to be faithful in the most ordinary tasks of life,
and to consecrate our boredom to your service
lest, in mistaking dullness for your absence, we lose heart;
and in confusing excitement for your presence, we lose faith.
For the glory of your name
in all the world.
Amen.

For thought, prayer and activity

1   What has been the place of liturgy in your own spiritual life and patterns of prayer?

2   (a) What non-religious liturgies and rituals do you see in your own life?
      (b) Can you explore their value and the functions that they perform for you?

3   (a) Does your prayer and meditation life need some scaffolding to support it?

(b) There are many different liturgical prayer patterns available. Would it be helpful to go exploring and try out something different?

4   If you haven't already, start a prayer scrapbook of meditation, liturgies and pictures you have found helpful along the way.

Further reading

Bradshaw, Paul, *Two Ways of Praying: Introducing Liturgical Spirituality* (London: SPCK, 1995).

Guiver, George, *Company of Voices: Daily Prayer and the People of God* (London: Canterbury Press, 2001).

Headley, Caroline, *Liturgy and Spiritual Formation* (Cambridge: Grove Books, 1997).

White, Susan, *The Spirit of Worship: The Liturgical Tradition* (London: Darton, Longman and Todd, 1999).

18 In the life of the Word

Ignatius, the Bible and prayer

Around the year 1520, a badly wounded soldier, Ignatius Loyola, was convalescing in his family home in Spain. Recovery was slow and he was bored. To pass the time he read two books he had found in the family library. The first was *Romances of Chivalric Knights*, a collection of heroic sagas very popular in his day. The second was *The Life of Christ*. The soldier became a Christian, sold his possessions and (with typical thoroughness) began to plan out a disciplined pattern for his discipleship for Christ. In 1536, at the age of 45, he founded the Society of Jesus (hence 'Jesuits'), for which he wrote a kind of spiritual military training programme. It was published in 1548 as *The Spiritual Exercises*. They have been widely used ever since.

Two vocations come together in Ignatius' writings – those of soldier and disciple. In this sense he was a product of his time. This was at the high point of medieval chivalry in Spain – full of exploits for God, heroic endeavour, battles for honour, struggles between good and evil. Ignatius saw himself as a spiritual knight for Christ. Christian life is active service. The battle is fierce, and requires rigorous training. So there is a strong emphasis on spiritual warfare, discernment, the need for personal discipline and constant vigilance. The Spiritual Exercises offered a sixteenth-century kind of rigorous Roman Catholic Alpha course – though probably without the supper.

The impact of his teaching in his day was considerable. Along with Teresa of Ávila (1515–82) and St John of the Cross (1542–91) Ignatius was a leader in a deep spiritual awakening in sixteenth-century southern Europe.

Today, under the influence of such writers as Gerard Hughes and Margaret Silf, Ignatian spirituality is a popular approach to prayer, meditation and spiritual direction. Its strength does not lie in any unusual features to its spirituality – the value of the imagination in Bible meditation, for example, is now affirmed in many approaches to Christian spirituality. But in the present climate of spiritual hunger it offers a distinctively integrative approach to the task of spiritual and life formation that many find helpful. Ignatian retreats are widely available for the traditional 30 days, adapted to eight days or reworked in various ways for use by busy people in daily life. The Jesuit website <www.sacredspace.ie> offers short patterns of prayer that are used by thousands of people daily.

Features of Ignatian spirituality

A *spirituality for the* active person
The Ignatian approach has much in common with charismatic renewal with its emphasis on direct encounter with God and living radically under the guidance of the Holy Spirit.

Relating to God is two-way and deeply personal. We expect to hear God speak in prayer, in the silence, in the reading of the scriptures and when we allow the time for them to be digested into our whole beings. It is a non-pietistic, renewal spirituality.

A *spirituality for* active service
Ignatius was not founding a contemplative community but an apostolic one. The vision was for a renewal of vocation in the world. This is a *missionary* spirituality. Three early Jesuits were radical, pioneering and sometimes controversial missionaries in different parts of the world – Francis Xavier in Goa, Robert Nobili in South India and Matteo Ricci in Macau and Beijing.

A *spirituality of* regular self-examination
At the heart of the Exercises is something called the 'Examen'. This is central to the Ignatian discipline of prayer. Each evening we are to ask ourselves two questions:

1   What opportunity or experience of God's grace and love have I missed today?
2   How have I experienced God's grace and presence this day?

Notice how these questions lead to both repentance and a deeper awareness of God's grace. We learn to pray as sinners who are held in God's continuing mercy.

A spirituality of the renewed mind

There is a strong commitment to learning and education. Ignatius himself actually went back to school and sat among children in class to learn Latin. There is therefore no split between prayerful devotion and intellectual rigour.

A spirituality centred on disciplined Bible meditation

This is particularly centred on the Gospels and the life of Christ. The aim is threefold:

- The purpose is the transformation of character (Heb. 4.12).
- The process is through the renewal of our minds (Rom. 12.2).
- The method is by digestion and absorption of God's word (Col. 3.16).

The goal is not to read and apply the Bible to make it relevant to our world and needs. The Word of God introduces us to God's own world and the vision for what he makes possible (Barth).

A goal-centred spirituality

The language of battle and struggle predominates. In the traditional 30-day retreat the retreatant would be guided through four stages of prayer and meditation:

- purgative – leading to repentance, examination, confession and amendment of life;
- elective – deciding for a new way of life; converting;
- illuminative – sealing our conformity in Christ;
- unitive – sharing in the glory and love of Christ.

A masculine spirituality?

The language is dominated by images of military service, heroic endeavour, wars and battles – traditionally a male domain. But interestingly today many women are very drawn to this Ignatian spirituality. At the risk of generalizing, this may in part be because it is a spirituality that is comfortable with feelings and the senses. For men in the culture of Ignatius's day this would not have been as embarrassing or off-putting as it remains for much male culture today. It may also reflect the way the traditional worlds of men and women now overlap considerably.

A *spirituality with a* strong affective dimension

It is an approach to prayer and biblical meditation that engages all the senses and the emotions. It is far removed from any detached intellectualism. You are expected to meet God in direct encounter and sense his presence. The use of the imagination is of fundamental importance in leading us to a meaningful, decisive prayer. We would be expected to use our senses when meditating on a biblical passage. After reading a Bible passage you would be encouraged to ask yourself:

- What can I hear?
- What can I see?
- What can I smell?
- What can I touch?
- What can I taste?

You would also be encouraged to have a conversation with people in the Gospel stories, or with Jesus himself.

A *vision for human* vocational integration *through prayer and retreat*

The Exercises are actually the Director's handbook for leading someone through a 30-day silent retreat. These retreats effectively provided vocational guidance through spiritual formation. Their aim was to train people severely and hard as soldiers for Christ. Rigorous application, discipline and obedience are essential in pursuing the Exercises. The daily pattern on retreat would include:

- daily eucharist;
- meeting with a personal spiritual director (who would guide the retreatant and offer them a Bible passage for meditation for that day);
- passage for meditation;
- five hours personal prayer a day.

This is still a requirement in some traditions for people training for ministry. Although the practice of the retreat is growing again in our day there is still much to be learned from this approach. From my own experience in ministry training, for example, I observe that for many ordinands in the Church of England the three-day pre-ordination retreat is the first experience of sustained silence and reflection that many have had. Needless to say it not the ideal place to start.

So what we have here is a vision and method for the transformation of the whole of life through deep immersion in the life of the Word. For all his military-mindedness, Ignatius never expected his Exercises to be imposed as a system or 'method' on people. It was to be an individually led journey under the guidance of the Holy Spirit. No one posture or method of praying was required. The pace at which each person could travel was to be respected. I remember making an Ignatian retreat where my retreat conductor realized that I was stuck on a particular issue. I was pleasantly surprised and enormously strengthened when she insisted on going no further until I had been helped to work through the issue and was ready to pick up the journey again.

Thinking and feeling

Some people can be uneasy about Ignatian spirituality. This may be because its origins are Roman Catholic, or because of its stress on imagination and feelings as a way of meditating on scripture. It may help to note that from a very different tradition of the church, the saintly puritan pastor Richard Baxter advocated precisely the same approach.

However, it is a matter of observation that some contemporary devotional books based on the Ignatian approach are very weak on offering a thoughtful reading of scripture on its own terms and over-emphasize 'me, my imagination and my feelings'. By contrast some approaches that claim to pay closest attention to the study of scripture can tend to use it in a very prescriptive and directive way. Attention to feelings is discouraged as being merely subjective and suspect. Ignatius insisted on holding the two together in a disciplined and life-transforming relationship. We need to hear what God's Word can bring to us. But we also need to discern the mystery of our own wants and passions if we are to make a faithful response. Here is a vision for a relationship with scripture that involves our whole being in response to the whole of God's Word.

Support for this Ignatian conviction comes from an unexpected source. Brain research shows that our common assumption about the difference between thinking and feeling is actually wrong. Most of us grew up being taught that thinking is rational and objective and feeling is emotional and subjective. Of the two, rational thought was considered superior and more reliable. But the evidence shows that when we are thinking the brain is stimulated in the same way as when our feelings are stimulated. In other words there is no thinking that is not also emotional and no feeling that is not thoughtful. They are not opposites. It is more accurate to speak of the 'emotional mind'.

For thought, prayer and activity

An Ignatian-style Bible meditation
Mark 5.1–15, the Gerasene demoniac
(Some of the notes that follow are suggestions to give the flavour of an Ignatian guided meditation. They are not otherwise intended to be directive.)

Read the passage slowly, perhaps several times.
What in the details of the story do you particularly notice?
He lived among the tombs (verse 3).
Chains could not hold him (3, 4).
No one had the strength to subdue him (4).
Night and day among the tombs (5).
He ran and fell before Jesus (6).
Sitting clothed and in his right mind (15).

Take a moment to think through the background situation of the passage you have read.
What information do you need to appreciate the full context?

Picture the place in your imagination and seek to enter into the story yourself.
In your imagination, see the tombs and the person in torment.
What torments you – what conflicts, accusations, anxieties, fears, temptations or fantasies arise for you?

Seek to listen to what God is saying to you through the scripture passage and your entry into it.
You see Jesus come out of the boat to the man in the tombs.
He runs and falls at his feet.
He had no idea what Jesus could do. He was not programming the outcome.
He left the action to Jesus.
The results? He had to allow God to work that out.

Can you bring some of your own confusion/chaos/noise to Jesus?
Approach the Son of the Most High.
You can't imagine what he will do.
You're not trying to programme the outcome which God will choose.
You are giving yourself now to Jesus because you want him to choose the way.
You want him to show you the way forward.
You want to break through into a new ability to be with him in the stillness.

Stay there at the feet of Jesus for a while.
Picture yourself before him, wanting, waiting.
Then receive the touch of Jesus.

What is God asking you to do, showing you, or teaching you?
You may or may not understand the implications of it immediately – if so, hold it in your mind and ponder it, or preferably check it out with your director, spiritual friend, prayer partner etc.

Respond in prayer.
What would you like to say to God in the light of what you have seen, heard, learned?
What confession, intercession etc. is God asking of you?
Is there some specific direction in your life which God is giving you?

(You may find it helpful to talk and/or pray through your responses to this meditation with a wise friend or pastor.)

Further reading

Baker, Jonathan, *Attending to Scripture* (Cambridge: Grove Books, 2002).

Hebblethwaite, Margaret, *The Way of Ignatius* (London: Fount, 1994).

Hughes, Gerard, *God of Surprises* (London: Darton, Longman and Todd, 1996).

Hughes, Gerard, *God in All Things* (London: Hodder and Stoughton, 2004).

Silf, Margaret, *Landmarks: Exploration of Ignatian Spirituality* (London: Darton, Longman and Todd, 1998).

IN THE MIDST OF LIFE

Spirituality in a real world

19 Every bush is burning

Creation and spirituality

I grew up in the Far East just before air flight took over from ocean liners. By the age of eight I had sailed round the world twice. I remember, day after day, looking out over the vastness of the sea under the wide, endless sky. It gave me a deep sense of the life and power of creation. It was vibrantly alive and in some deep and wonderful way God was alive in it all. That conviction has stayed with me ever since.

Some years later, when Christian faith came alive, I became aware that the simple conviction of a child was actually more complex. The relationship between church, spiritual life and the created world has always been an uneasy one.

Faith in creation

The Christian Church has had a bad name among environmentalists, ecologists and emerging creation-centred spiritualities. Although its popular art shows a warmly sentimental attachment to creation – from cute kittens to beautiful mountain lakes – Christians stand accused of encouraging a number of destructive assumptions about our relationship to the natural world.

1   Christianity is an anthropocentric religion. Human life is firmly the centre of interest and humanity tends to be interested in creation only for its own ends and on its own terms.
2   The relationship with creation is expressed in terms of 'power over', control and 'having dominion' (Gen. 1.26). Creation is treated as a resource to be exploited. It is seen in terms of its usefulness for us.
3   Christian faith emphasizes the importance of the spiritual at the expense of the material world. It has therefore tended to treat the physical world as irrelevant, inferior or a dangerous distraction.

4   A faith that emphasizes sin and the need for salvation has sometimes
assumed the physical world to be 'fallen' and therefore suspect.

There is truth in these accusations but they are also examples of a distorted
understanding of Christianity and creation. Christian teaching has a great
deal to offer a world that is growing in its awareness of this fragile planet
and its responsibilities towards it.

> There is, in all created things, an inexhaustible sweetness and purity, a
> silence that is a fount of action and joy. It rises up in wordless gentle-
> ness and flows out to me from the unseen roots of all created being,
> welcoming me tenderly, saluting me with indescribable humility.
>
> (Thomas Merton in de Waal, 2000, p. 21)

Creation and theology

Medieval theologians described creation as the 'first Bible', in that it was a
revelation of God long before there were any words to speak. We must
learn to read it alongside the written word of the scriptures. And what
insights might we find there if we do?

Creation has its own life in God

The universe was around for countless millions of years before human
beings appeared. The Bible pictures the life of creation as a joyful
celebration in God, a continuous outpouring of speech beyond words.
'The heavens are telling the glory of God' (Ps. 19.1). The assumption has
long been that creation was cursed, along with Adam and Eve, in what we
call 'The Fall'. But is it true? At heart, creation never seems to be anything
other than what God intended. Have you noticed the response of
creation at key points in the earthly life of Jesus – the star at his birth, the
light at his transfiguration, the darkness at his cross, the earthquake at his
resurrection and the cloud at his ascension? Something more original
than sin is being affirmed here. In spite of sin that so distorts our existence and leaves creation groaning and sighing (Rom. 8.22), the world
is still a vast theophany (revelation of God). 'Heaven *and earth* are full
of your glory' (my italics).

Creation is useless

I mean this in the sense that it is not necessary. God did not need to create anything. He was not lonely or lacking in any way. He does not need our love or attention. Creation is not here to make a point or achieve anything. This world exists simply because God takes pleasure in it. It is free gift sustained in divine delight – a work of boundless imagination. The evidence for this is everywhere. For one thing there is too much in this world that is simply unnecessary. Does this universe look like the work of a divine industrialist who has created a machine to carry out tasks efficiently and economically? We are still discovering how intricately it does all work together, but it is shot through with wasteful flourishes of beauty. In this world you never turn a corner and see where the plaster or paintwork has stopped, just out of sight. Instead this universe never ends. Far out of sight it is still emerging.

Within a technological, consumer-driven society where things are only valued for their usefulness or purpose, this is a subversive insight. It invites us to contemplate a wholly different way of understanding why we, or this world, are here at all.

The universe as worship leader

The participation of all of created beings in the worship of God is a constant theme in the Bible. Mountains, trees, animals, moon and stars all join in the praise of God. The sheer wonder of what is made awakens awe and prayer. 'The heavens are telling the glory of God', declares Psalm 19. Creation is pouring out a torrent of secret praise, night and day, never heard, 'yet their voice goes out through all the earth' (19.4). For Jesus too the created world around him constantly revealed his Father's love and character. 'Look at the birds of the air . . .' (Matt. 6.26). This world is a place of immanence where even a desert thorn bush can burn with the holy presence of God and not be consumed (Exod. 3.2).

Creation and redemption

Creation is as much the work of Christ as our re-creation through him. This truth is often missed. The incarnate Jesus is none other the eternal 'Word' who has always been the creative source of all life. 'All things came into being through him, and without him not one thing came into being' (John 1.3). 'In him all things in heaven and on earth were created, things visible and invisible . . . all things have been created through him and for him ... and in him all things hold together' (Col. 1.16–17). And he still 'sustains all things by his powerful word' (Heb. 1.3). In the joyful celebration of Christ in the first chapter of Ephesians the work of creation and of redemption are hardly distinguished. Jesus said, 'Whoever has seen me has seen the Father' (John 14.9). If the creator God is Christlike, what do we learn from Jesus about the way God creates and sustains this world?

Contemplating creation

Sacred and secular

We all make assumptions about where in this world we are likely to meet God and where we are not. But we need to question them. For example, does the Bible really suggest a world in which God is closer to us in church than in the supermarket, or at worship rather than at work? Does God really prefer natural beauty spots to the inner city? Of course there are moments when God is more real to us than at others. There will be times and places where God meets us in special ways. We must constantly resist the suggestion that he is 'here' and not 'there' – a kind of spiritual apartheid that separates our 'holy places' from the rest of life.

After I was ordained I worked in a parish in north-west London. My Sunday routine meant an early walk to the church down the deserted high street. It took me under a grimy railway bridge, past a pub and a rather drab row of shops. The pavement was filthy with litter.

But one particular Sunday I turned into the High Street, and knew it was a holy place. It was the same old road, but God was there. I stopped in my tracks and slowly drank in the realization that all this dirt and drab greyness was soaked in something holy. It was so improbable. In that Presence everything felt infinitely loved – and infinitely lovable. I wanted to laugh and cry and stay silent all at once. I wanted to dance for joy and hide in fear. But perhaps the most abiding sense of that vision was the realization that this was no 'special' visit. What I glimpsed in that moment was the longing, abiding Presence that

> Mummy, can you hear the wind in the trees?
> *Yes, dear.*
> That is the sound of God talking.
> *Is it? What is he saying?*
> *(pause)*
> He is saying, 'Love one another.'
> (6-year-old child)

held all of life through its mad, headlong flight – the Presence that we would soon drown out again with the roar of traffic and trampling humanity. It was new to me because previously I had neither the eye nor heart to perceive it. 'Surely the LORD is in this place – and I did not know it! . . . This is none other than the house of God' (Gen. 28.16–17). (See Runcorn, 1990, p. 135.)

Seasons and rhythms
We can learn from the seasons of creation. Human life is seasonal and rhythmic too but in contemporary living we all too easily lose sight of this. We have daily and weekly patterns to our living. We try to balance work and rest. But the signs are that we are driven to destructive patterns of living. A world which emphasizes material security and where we are encouraged to expect to have what we want whenever we want it does us no favours. We become stressed and dis-eased. It is like trying to live constantly in the intensity and fruitfulness of summer. We need to honour all the seasons of life with their distinctive pace and task for our overall flourishing and well being. Does winter feel guilty for not being summer? Does autumn look at spring and feel it is failing by dying when it ought to be springing into new life?

Compassion and healing
While on a walking holiday with friends in North Cornwall we stopped for lunch in a deserted cove. We later commented on the sense of sadness and depression that seemed to have soaked into that place. The next day we returned and prayed there for the blessing of creation and its healing. Only later did we discover that years before almost the entire male population of the small fishing community that lived there had drowned at sea in a storm. The last remains of their cottages could just be seen in the undergrowth. St Paul speaks of creation groaning with humanity for all that is yet to be fulfilled and healed (Rom. 8.20–22). The early Christian teachers insisted that Christian love is a compassionate longing that longs after all created things. It flows out of a deep sense of interdependency and shared vocation in the creating gift of divine love.

A common feature of many of the spiritualities and lifestyles outside traditional Christian faith is their sensitivity to creation and a concern to live in right relationship with it. Without accepting the underlying philosophy behind feng shui, for example, the vocation to live in discerning, creative partnership with the surrounding world, sensitive to and respectful of its own rhythms and needs, has long been part of Christian teaching. But like all humanity we can be forgetful and need reminding.

For thought, prayer and activity

1   An Awareness Walk – an exercise for groups or individuals
You might try this walk in two contrasting places to walk – for example, in countryside and in a built-up area. Decide your route beforehand so that you don't have to think about it as you walk. Pray for God's blessing and discernment.

Jesus said, 'follow me'.
(a)   Walk slowly, deliberately. You are going to use all your five senses as you walk, so start by being aware of the light, the warmth of the sun, the touch of the air, the colours around you.
(b)   Begin to notice greater details in patterns, shapes, thickness, the shades of colours, the contrasts and juxtapositions and how things relate.
(c)   Touch and feel, pick up stones, twigs, earth, leaves and hold them gently. If appropriate, take off your shoes and walk barefoot. (Try to receive without censoring or rejecting. Pavements, buildings, machines, people are all part of your walk and world.)
(d)   Try to stop thinking and simply to be. Let everything drop away and instead try to be totally present to what is reaching you through your senses.
(e)   Begin to notice more acutely the scent of growing things, of the earth itself. Listen to the range of sounds, far-off distant sounds, those which are close, your own breathing.
(f)   Where appropriate you may bring something back that you have particularly noticed or enjoyed as you have walked. Take some time at the end to gather impressions.

2   Write your own prayer or meditation making full use of natural imagery. Try to include weather, seasons, plants, animals, planets and stars, growth and decay – as many of the rich and varied offerings of the natural world as you can.
What is your favourite season?
What is its gift to you?

3   What is your least favourite season?
What is its burden for you?

4   Imagine you are one of the seasons. Write a letter to your opposite season.
(a)   What would you want to say?
(b)   Write the reply you think you might receive.

5   'We must constantly resist the suggestion that he is "here" and not "there"'. Take some objects that are not normally expected to reflect God's creative goodness: empty cans or bottles, or stained or broken things. Use them to contemplate God's life in all creation.

Further reading and resources
Berry, R. J. (ed.), *The Care of Creation*, (Leicester, IVP, 2000).
Jones, James, *Jesus and Creation* (London: SPCK, 2003).
Osborn, Lawrence, *Meeting God in Creation* (Cambridge: Grove Books, 1990).

www.arocha.org
www.christian-ecology.org.uk

20 Praying in whirlpools and rapids

Spirituality in times of change, uncertainty and transition

'I don't like new places. You have to notice everything. Sometimes when I am in a new place it is like a computer crashing and I have to close my eyes and put my hands over my ears and groan so that I can remember what I am doing and where I am meant to be going.'

Christopher is a 15-year-old boy who has Asperger's Syndrome. He expresses very vividly what life can feel like when it all becomes simply overwhelming. His way of coping is the psychological equivalent of shutting down a computer – like pressing Ctrl, Alt, Del and re-booting himself.

(Haddon, 2004, pp. 174–8)

How do you live with change? You may be someone who finds it exciting, or you too often want to put your hands over your eyes and groan. Change is fact of life. Human living and development involves negotiating continuous and often demanding change (see Chapter 13). But there is at least a recognizable continuity about that kind of change. One of the most destructive features of the kind of change our society now endures is that it is continuously *dis*continuous. It is not allowed to bear any relation to what has gone before. 'White water change' is another way of describing it. It can feel like trying to negotiate rapids – without the right equipment or experience. Stress-related illness is now one of the most common causes of health breakdown. But switching off and re-booting does not solve the problem. We need ways of understanding and managing what life is loading on to us.

What spiritual resources help us in such times? Part of the trouble is that many of the traditional sources of nurture and stability are themselves caught up in the same changes. This includes the Church. A faith that for so long has identified itself with all that is unchanging and permanent is struggling to respond in a culture that requires constant creative adaptability. The crisis is very real. All the signs are that unless it can establish fresh expressions of its life and mission the Christian Church will cease to be an effective presence in large parts of the Western world.

Change and transition

Think of an experience of change in your life. It can be very significant or very ordinary. What feelings were associated with it? In discussion groups the commonly chosen words include 'excitement', 'renewing', 'buzz', 'fearful', 'anxious', 'energized', 'bewilderment'.

But these words do not describe change but *transition*. Change is about the outer, practical task of moving house, office or job from A to B, for example. Transition is the inner psychological, emotional, relational and spiritual adjustments that I must make in order to live well with the outer change. Change is about where we are going. Transition is about what we are leaving. Change is about beginnings. Transition is about endings.

Many organizations are good at making changes and poor at giving space for the transitions those changes require. While people are still carrying the pain of loss they will not find it easy to embrace strategies for change and transformation. Change will not be achieved until transition has been managed successfully.

It helps to realize that in even the most chaotic change there are always three basic stages to be lived through. Firstly, there will be the task of letting go – of leaving and making endings. There will be the final hope and longing of arriving somewhere new. And between these two is a place that is neither one nor the other. It has been called the 'neutral zone'. Books on managing change often turn to the biblical wilderness stories to illustrate the kind of place it is (Bridges, 2003).

These are not neat stages. Human becoming is never a tidy process. We can get stuck, take long detours, get lost or give up and try to turn round and go 'home'. We will rarely manage these stages in the right order. In fact we can be living in all three stages simultaneously to some degree. But they offer a way of understanding the demands of the task and what they require of us.

Ending, leavings and letting go

This stage involves our capacity to face death and loss. One appropriate response to death is grief and mourning. These changes may not have been chosen or looked for. We may be very angry. But some endings come as a relief. We may have waited a long time for this moment. We feel we escaped. This loss is something to celebrate. For many it will be a bit of both, so this stage is marked by some ambivalence and uncertainty.

At this stage it will be important to consider:

- What precisely is coming to an end? Name it.
- How does it feel?
- What must I leave behind?
- What can I take with me?
- Are there important ways to mark and honour what is ending?

This needs time and care. It should not be hurried – but it usually is. How long does it take to leave somewhere? We are often required to arrive and begin somewhere new before we have completely left the old. Family life may reflect this tension. For example, the whole family often uproots in order that one member may begin a new job. That member may be excited and already deep into the new life while the others are still grieving for what they have left behind.

Entering the new

Arrivals and new beginnings may be marked by feelings of new energy, direction and vision. But they may also be a bit unsettling and frightening. It is still an unknown. A lot is at stake. Will it be what I hoped for?

It was said of Abraham and Sarah that they obeyed the call, journeyed without knowing where they were going and when they reached the place they pitched their tent and lived as strangers in the land of promise (see Heb. 11.8–9). That beautifully expresses the highly paradoxical mixture in this stage.

At this stage it may be important to consider:

- What precisely is new for me in this place?
- How long will I need to *really* arrive?
- What am I feeling about what is now beginning?
- How do I now relate to what I have left behind?
- What resources do I need to live with what is unfamiliar but demanding?
- Are there helpful ways I can mark or celebrate this new beginning?

Wandering in the neutral zone

This is the stage between the old and the new. It is a vital stage to live in faithfully if we are to be able to let go of what must pass and to embrace the new.

But the neutral zone is an uncomfortable place. It feels like a wilderness. No one wants to be there any longer than they have to be. It can feel directionless, restless and barren. There is no clear direction because the final destination may not yet be in sight. Leaders in the neutral zone will easily feel like failures because it is not clear what they should be *doing*. It is a waiting time that can feel like a wasting time. We are told that the people of Israel spent 40 years in the wilderness before reaching the Promised Land. A glance at the map will show that they took an amazingly rambling route by any standards. The neutral zone is a vital place of preparation and spiritual development. This is the place where we complete our leavings and are made ready to enter the new. It must not to be rushed or cut short. (See Chapter 1.)

At this stage it may be important to consider:

- What does this place look and feel like?
- Do you know where you are going to?
- Confusion and anxiety are natural at this time – normalize the neutral zone. There is nothing wrong with you.
- What resources do you need to live in this place?
- This place offers a chance to be aware of questions or issues that there hasn't been space to listen to before. Do any come to mind?

But we must beware of two particular temptations in this stage. One is to try to return to the 'old life'. This is not always a rational longing. Even the return to abject slavery in Egypt felt attractive to the wandering Israelites when they were longing for a decent meal (Num. 11.4–6)!

The other temptation is to 'fanaticism' (Bridges, 2003, Chapter 6). An important task in this stage is to explore new vision and direction. But simply because the wilderness leaves us feeling so out of control and vulnerable we will be tempted by any packaged solution that promises 'the Promised Land'. We will apply it with uncritical certainty. This is the way we must go! Christian and secular bookshops alike cater well for the temptations of the neutral zone.

Spirituality in transitional times

What understanding of God do we turn to in times of change and transition?

God is our creator and sustainer

This is God's world. He created it out of the formless void and he holds it in being moment by moment. He will not let it slip back into shapeless chaos. Nor is he threatened by the powers that threaten us. He can speak to the wind and the waves and their tumult ceases (Matt. 8.23–7). He can be known as shelter, refuge and rock when all else is threatening.

God is unchanging

There is an ancient Christian prayer that asks of God that 'we who are wearied by the chances and changes of this fleeting world may rest upon your eternal changelessness'. Down the centuries the eternal trustworthiness of God and his promises has been a source of comfort and strength to people in the midst of troubles.

God the changer and transformer

If we only expect God to be a tamer and calmer of the things that trouble us we are missing something. In the Bible God himself can be the provoker of turbulent and uncertain change. He is a disturber as well as a comforter. Someone once said that 'change is the angel of the changeless God'. The three stages of transition are found again and again in the life of God's people in the Bible. Walter Brueggemann (1984) describes this as a journey from orientation (the familiar, inherited ways), through *dis*-orientation ('where are we?', 'where is God?' – the neutral zone) to *re*-orientation (the place of God's deliverance, a new beginning). This is God's way of jolting and provoking his people into new growth, deeper trust and maturer faith.

In the Gospels the ministry of Jesus has a similar impact. His presence is a catalyst for change – but it feels radically discontinuous. The common response to his teaching was amazement and the sense of hearing something completely new. 'What is this? A new teaching – with authority!' (Mark 1.22, 27).

The same three stages are even found in the very place you expect confident faith and vision to have finally emerged. For the first disciples the experience of Easter was traumatic and disorientating. There on the day of Christ's resurrection a woman weeps by an empty tomb. 'They have taken away my Lord' (John 20.13). He was dead but at least they knew where to find him. Resurrection life asks us to endure the radical loss of all that is familiar and secure and journey through profound transition.

After Easter day there is a period of 40 days before Jesus physically ascended to heaven. It reads as a curiously understated time. There is no obvious purpose or direction. There are no dynamic programmes of training or mission strategies. Instead there is a lot of space interspersed by encounters with the risen Jesus in unexpected moments and places, often unrecognized.

It was a time of continued bewilderment for the disciples. Even the evidence we would expect them to find convincing apparently is not. The empty tomb itself does not reassure them. Even after Jesus has appeared to Peter and others they are still to be found trying to return to the old life. 'I'm going fishing', said Peter. But they catch nothing. There is no way back (John 21.3–4).

This vividly expresses faith in the neutral zone. They are caught between old and new, between death and life and are at home in neither. There is nothing they can *do*. They must allow themselves to be acted upon. Something bigger is going on that intimately involves them and that is the secret of their life and vocation. But they are not in any place to see it. The vision is not given.

And where was Christ in all this? He was there in the neutral zone of bewilderment and confusion. The whole ministry of the risen Jesus seems to be ministering and reassuring with the gift of his presence. So he meets Mary in her grief, Thomas in his doubts and Peter in his need for reconciliation. He comes as pure gift to that locked in, uncertain, paralysed community and leads them surely from the old to the new.

What if God's presence in this world is altogether more vigorous, energetic and risky? Where is the God to be found who rides the wings of the winds and who delights in watching the chaos monsters playing in the deep (Job 41)? What if he is not primarily concerned to calm and subdue but is deep in the midst of the raw uncertainties of life, working through them to fashion something new? What if God is choosing not to dam the river but actually wants to teach us to ride rapids with him? How do we pray to such a God in a world like ours (Runcorn, 2002, Chapter 4)? I remember the shock and excitement when I once came across a prayer that began: 'Lord, I'm praying for storm tonight – your very *wildest* kind.'

For thought, prayer and activity

1 Where would you place yourself in relation to transition at the moment: are you letting go, in the neutral zone or arriving somewhere new?

2 The chapter suggests key questions with which to try to understand each stage in times of transition.
   (a) Think back to the major transitions in your life so far or reflect on what is happening to you now.
   (b) Using the questions in the chapter, allow yourself time to reflect on each one in turn. Consider how the experience changed/is changing you and what you have learnt/are learning from it.

3 (a) What are your expectations of your spiritual life and the reality of God in times of difficult change?
   (b) If you were counselling or praying with someone undergoing a difficult life transition, what words of support and comfort could you offer from your own experiences?

Further reading

Bridges, William, *Managing Transitions: Making the Most of Change* (Cambridge, Mass.: Da Capo Press, 2003).

Mursell, Gordon, *Praying in Exile* (London: Darton, Longman and Todd, 2005).

21 Peace be with you

Praying in a world of violence and division

'We pray for peace in the world'. Is any prayer prayed with more frequency and longing in a world like ours? But in the face of the violence and sustained suffering that is the experience of millions on the planet these words quickly feel empty and powerless to change much. For Christians living in more affluent nations there is a further issue. The economy that sustains our living standards is made possible by privileged trade agreements, military superiority and a system of global financial controls that leaves the greater part of the world population living in poverty and debt.

So when we pray for peace what are we actually asking for?

'Shalom' in the Bible is concerned with peace at all levels of life including international relations and within societies and communities. At the heart of this is the reconciliation, through Christ, of humanity to God and the establishing of Christ's rule of justice and mercy. Though 'shalom' may include particular feelings or a tranquil state of mind this is not the primary meaning of the word or a measure of its presence.

When we try and imagine what the peace of God must be like we tend to start from our best experiences of earthly peace. Surely it must be a bit like that – only much deeper and more lasting? But that is precisely what Jesus said it is *not*. He said, 'My peace I give to you. I do not give to you as the world gives. Do not let your hearts be troubled'. (John 14.27).

Not only is the peace of Jesus not like the peace of the world, he was very often a peace-breaker. His presence led to furious conflict. He himself said, 'I have not come to bring peace, but a sword' (Matt. 10.34). The Prince of Peace confronts the peace of this world. He stands in judgement over all our attempts at living in peace. It seems that the peace of God can only be received after the peace of this world has been shattered and exposed as false. In this world the peace of God is to be found in the midst of strife and division, not as an absence of it. This is very good news in a world like ours. If peace is only available where there is no conflict, then only the privileged few who can afford to live there will enjoy it.

Searching for meaning

There are places in the Gospels where Jesus makes very unexpected responses in the presence of violence, injustice and suffering.

On one occasion some people came to Jesus and reported an atrocity to him that they had witnessed. 'At that very time there were some present who told him about the Galileans whose blood Pilate had mingled with their sacrifices. He asked them, "Do you think that because these Galileans suffered in this way they were worse sinners than all other Galileans? No, I tell you; but unless you repent, you will all perish as they did"' (Luke 13.1–3).

Nothing else is known about this incident. It concerns the victims of a barbaric, evil, earthly ruler. There is something very contemporary about that. The audience expects Jesus to take sides and pronounce God's judgement on the oppressor and the vindication of the victims. Isn't it clear who is good and who is bad? But Jesus expresses no pity or judgement. He offers no comment on Pilate, the victims or God. He refuses to takes sides at all. Instead he issues this blunt call to repentance.

He underlines his point by reminding them of another local disaster. This tragedy involved no immediate human agency, good or bad. A tower had collapsed in a town, killing 18 people. His response is the same. He seems quite unmoved by the actual events, the suffering of the victims or any question of where God was in it all. Instead he repeats the same warning: 'unless you repent, you will all perish just as they did" (Luke 13.5).

This apparent indifference surfaces again as Jesus was leaving the Temple with his disciples on one occasion. One of the disciples is moved by the sheer scale and magnificence of this holy place of prayer. 'Look, Teacher, what large stones and what large buildings!' But Jesus replies, 'Do you see these great buildings? Not one stone will be left upon another; all will be thrown down' (Mark 13.1–2).

He has responded to natural disaster and human oppression with apparent indifference. Here he is responding in the same way to the central symbol of the religion of his people. He refuses to treat the Temple as theologically important or its destruction as a meaningful sign of the times.

How would we react if Jesus spoke to us in this way? Imagine him sitting with us now. Perhaps we have just watched the news with him. We tell him stories of suffering in a recent natural disaster. Perhaps he meets victims of a dictator's brutality. We share our vision for the Church in our land. But he doesn't seem moved by all this. He doesn't treat these events as offering any sign of the times or carrying divine meaning. He doesn't warn us against Islam or Western consumerism. He attaches no special value to the church as an institution in our midst. He refuses to involve God in the discussion at all. But the warning is the same. 'Unless you repent you will all perish.'

Repent of what, exactly?

In Chapter 15 we suggested that sin is not primarily about wrong doing so much as wrong *being*. Jesus clearly saw human living as characterized more than anything else by a profound blindness – an inability to see with truth what we are part of and therefore why we are acting as we do. Because we cannot see we profoundly misinterpret what is going on around us, God's ways within it and how we should respond to it. In Chapter 22 we explore an understanding of prayer as the healing of sight. Jesus reserves some of his toughest condemnation not for those who are blind, but for those who are blind but claim they can see (John 9.40–1).

What do we learn from these teachings of Jesus?

First, to be very careful before making assumptions about where God is to be found in this world, whose side he is on and how much he shares our sense of what is important.

Second, to be very cautious therefore about where we seek 'meaning' in the events of the world. In our self-interest or insecurity there is a real temptation to shore up our own place and significance in the world by claiming God's special protection and attention.

In particular we must beware of making assumptions about good and evil. In the response of Jesus, the people who are 'good' or 'innocent' are in just as much peril as people who are 'bad'. Both are called to repentance. The language used in the present 'war against terror' is an example of this. All too easily Western values are presented as uncritically and universally 'good' for everyone. The 'enemies'' beliefs are all bad and evil.

But in these teachings being 'good' is no more significant than being 'bad'. Jesus refuses to even enter the debate on those terms. Elsewhere he even refuses to allow himself to be called good (Luke 18.19). For Jesus 'good' and 'goodness' were words whose meaning had become so polluted as to be unusable. While this is our standpoint on the world we are in as much peril as anyone else.

If we get caught up in a world of giving sacred meaning to our hopes, longings and struggles we will remain trapped in the world of deadly rivalry and reciprocal violence. 'Unless you repent, you will all perish as they did' (Luke 13.3).

Of course we need to look for meaning and purpose in the events of life – and we are right to. Of course we seek the presence of God. But in a complex world the issues are too easily oversimplified. Jesus is warning us about where we look and the conclusions we will be tempted to draw. It is revealing that after his comments on the Temple he goes on to teach at length about misinterpreting the signs of the times and following false messiahs.

If this is true, then an important part of what we need to repent of is our praying and spirituality. 'Our religious talking, seeing and knowing needs a kind of cleansing' (Rowan Williams).

The violent peacemaking – a parable

Of all the terrible images from the international conflicts of recent years one picture keeps returning. In the middle of the night of 6 April 2003 a bomb landed in a civilian area of Baghdad and destroyed the home of 12-year-old Ali Ismaeel Abbas. His father, pregnant mother, brother, three cousins and three other relatives were killed. Ali lost both his arms and suffered 60 per cent burns over his body.

He is propped up on a hospital bed. His head is heavily bandaged above his tearful face. The stumps that were his arms form a cruciform shape. The arms of Jesus on the cross have always moved me. But this child, crucified across the horrors of modern warfare and political strategy, has no arms at all.

A cross with no arms. What if this is a picture of where our attempts at enforcing peace bring us to? An act of violence that actually further disables and leaves us helpless before the forces we have unleashed. And what of our good intentions and our hope of change? 'I wanted to be a soldier', said Ali. ' Now I want to be a doctor – but how can I? I don't have hands'.

What if this is a picture of where we have come to?

Some marks of Christian prayer for peace

Struggle

Christian prayer is more often marked by conflict than by feelings of peace. The Christ we seek is in the midst of life not some privileged escape from it.

Caution

The deeper conflicts and violence of our own lives or of our world are not to be spoken of lightly or entered carelessly. Praying for peace not only means seeking God but requires us generously and imaginatively to enter the world of our enemies. This is not a place for good intentions or heroism. It needs the shared wisdom, discernment and support of a praying community.

Tears

'Blessed are those who mourn', said Jesus (Matt. 5.4). Peacemaking requires a willingness to feel pain. Tears have an important place in Christian prayer. They express an involvement and discontentment with the way life is for so many. There is comfort for such people, said Jesus. The church in the world is to be a community of blessed mourners.

Truth

Praying for peace needs a careful commitment to truth. Hurt people do not fight fairly – even Christians. We will be tempted to distort the issues in our favour. We misrepresent our enemy's case and motives. Praying for peace requires careful listening and research. We must choose with great care the words we pray with.

Anger

The late anti-apartheid campaigner Archbishop Trevor Huddleston once startled a group of trainee ministers by insisting, 'I want to impress on you the importance of learning how to hate. We have forgotten how to hate. We must hate what is evil.'

Christian faith is so accustomed to thinking of anger as something to be controlled that its spiritual life offers little positive use for it. We think our problem is that we lose our tempers but actually many of us have yet to find them in the first place. Our capacity for anger is God-given. The trouble is that it doesn't do what it is intended to do. It is huge imaginative energy within us and praying and working for peace needs all the energy it can get.

Hospitality

There can be no peacemaking without actual meeting with those we are divided from. Praying must lead to action. One of the most moving books to come out of the conflicts in Israel in recent years is by a Jewish journalist, Yossi Klein Halevi (2002). He came to the conviction that peace would not come through setting religion aside. Spirituality was at the heart of it and he must draw near rather than avoid it. So he spent months visiting Christians and Muslims, often at some personal risk, talking and praying with them. He closes with these words:

> It is precisely times like these that the beautiful teachings of the faith become either real or mere sentiment. More than ever the goal of a spiritual life in the Holy Land is to live with an open heart at the centre of unbearable tension.

This has been vividly described as 'living with a heart close to cracking' (James Allison). Peacemaking is prayer in action.

Christ is our peace

The epistles often speak of the death of Jesus as breaking down a dividing wall, a wall of hostility (Eph. 2.14). The cycle of violence and revenge has been broken into. Something has been done for us. There is somewhere we can bring all the pain and violence of our divisions. A work of reconciliation has been achieved. Some experience it as a sudden freedom to think and act in quite new ways. More often it is the daily grace to turn from conflict, to bind up wounds again and reach out again in peace.

At the end of Christian worship we are often sent out with the words 'Go in peace'. We are not being urged to leave 'feeling peaceful'. We are being invited to enter. Go *into* shalom. That is what it means. Go into the place where Christ's reigning love is making possible a new way of living together, where there will be unexpected possibilities for responding differently, for conversion of life – however hesitantly – to ways of peace and reconciliation.

Go in peace.

For thought, prayer and activity

1   Imagine that you are to lead prayers for peace in church this week. In the congregation are victims of torture, someone who has been maimed by terrorist action and a family left parentless by disease. Can you write a meaningful prayer of peace for all of them?

2   Write your own dictionary definition of 'peace'. Can you make it positive, not just a lack of conflict?

3   'We must beware of making assumptions about good and evil.' What assumptions of this kind do you make? What unthinking prejudices do you carry with you?

4   Try to imagine being part of the discussion with Jesus on page 176. What would you want to ask or say to him?

Further reading and resources

Allison, James, *On Being Liked* (London: Darton, Longman and Todd, 2003). The Bible exposition in this chapter draws on Chapter 3, 'Contemplation in a world of violence'.

Halevi, Yossi Klein, *At the Entrance to the Garden of Eden: A Jew's Search for Hope with Christians and Muslims in the Holy Land* (San Francisco: Perennial, 2002).

Patterson, Colin, *How to Learn Through Conflict* (Cambridge: Grove Books, 2000).

Raven, Charles, *Conflict and Growth* (Cambridge: Grove Books, 1998).

Williams, Rowan, *The Truce of God: Peacemaking in Troubled Times* (London: Canterbury Press, 2005).

Mennonites Conflict Mediation resources
www.menno.org.uk

22 That I may receive my sight

Contemplating the world

Jesus raised the dead, cast out demons, healed the paralysed and opened the ears of the deaf. But in the records of his teachings and ministry, twice as much prominence is given to the themes of blindness and sight. For him it illustrates the most central need of our disordered world. Nothing is more central than the way we see things. 'Your eye is the lamp of your body,' said Jesus. 'If your eye is healthy, your whole body is full of light; but if it is not healthy, your body is full of darkness' (Luke 11.34). Only one thing is worse than being blind. It is to be blind but think you see (see John 9.41).

'What do you want me to do for you?' Jesus asked the blind man by the side of the road. 'Lord, let me see again.' And Jesus restored his sight (Luke 18.41). But this is clearly a parable about a different kind of seeing. In this world to have open eyes is no guarantee of clear sight. This is a world of distorted vision. True seeing does not come naturally. It must be received through a gift of healing.

I see

Early biological theories of sight were mechanistic. The watcher was passive in the process. The image was thought to enter through the eye like a pinhole camera, to be projected onto the brain as a visual statement of fact. We now know that it is a much more subtle and complex process. As you look at this page, astonishingly little is received with real sharpness of image – just a few letters in fact. The brain uses this small area of clarity to make sense of the image as a whole using a mixture of memory, guesswork, experience and intuition. We interpret and decode what we see and so we encounter it in terms of a *meaning*. Seeing is much more than a physical reflex. Our whole beings are involved in the task of living by sight. And even then it is an act of vulnerable trust. Living by sight is an act of faith.

Seeing comes before words in our experience and for that reason sight remains the most powerful of all our senses. It is the most significant way in which we seek to discern our sense of our place in the world. Our language reflects this. When we understand, we say 'I *see*'. The old name for a prophet (one who hears God's Word) is 'seer' – literally see-er. So seeing is intimately related to knowing. Just as seeing is more than a physical process, so knowledge is more than gathering facts. Knowing involves the whole of our being. We seek *in*sight. The Hebrew verb 'to know' reflects this. In Genesis it is used both of knowing good and evil and of the intimacy of love-making between Adam and Eve (Gen. 3.5, 7; 4.1).

It is also used interchangeably with the word for 'wisdom'. The Latin word for this kind of knowing is *contemplatio*. It has long been the name for a particular approach to prayer.

Wondering

Contemplative prayer has too often been regarded as something for spiritual specialists – monks and nuns in enclosed communities. But rather than involving the mastery of spiritual techniques it begins with nothing more than a capacity for wonder. It is not a method of prayer so much as a way of looking, listening and considering. It is best illustrated by the capacity of children to be totally absorbed and give their full attention to what is before them. Children are natural contemplatives and Jesus calls grown-ups to that childlike quality if we are to enter the life of the kingdom (Mark 10.13–16).

'Contemplation' and 'meditation' are sometimes used interchangeably. They are closely related but different. In the Bible, meditation is a disciplined mental attentiveness and delight in God's Word. One illustration of the Word comes from actors repeating and rehearsing their words until they become so much a part of them they do not have to think about it. That is the point at which meditation becomes contemplation. It is the difference between thinking *about* love and being *in* love, for example. Contemplative writers often use the language of love and lovers.

Contemplating the world

Christian contemplation is not an inward withdrawal from the world into God. It does involve a detachment. But this is not an abandonment so much as a re-engagment in the world in the love of God.

Thomas Merton, contemplative monk and social critic, taught that the Western world had become radically alienated from its own spiritual life by technology, materialism and the pursuit of power. He believed that this was a sickness that only the renewal of contemplation could heal. He noted how repressive governments instinctively recognized the threat posed by contemplatives – artists, poets and writers as well those from the praying traditions. In Christian history the contemplative tradition has close links to the awakening of conscience and to resistance movements.

Kenneth Leech urges that the church itself needs to urgently rediscover the contemplative life. Without the contemplative dimension religion becomes activist, task-driven and pragmatic and lives its life in competition with the spirit and powers of the age rather than offering an alternative. A contemplative church will help lead people away from a religion of easy answers, from false certainties, the idolatry of consumer spirituality and the temptation to fundamentalism of all kinds (Leech, 1992).

The Canadian Catholic writer Ronald Rolheiser (1998) summarizes our age above all else as 'non-contemplative'. Like Merton and Leech, he sees this as a deep sickness that is revealed in a number of destructive symptoms. A non-contemplative world is one in which reality holds no mystery any more. It is a culture driven by an aggressively technological, problem–solution mindset in which everything must be controlled by having an explanation.

There is a loss of the sacred, of boundary and respect for the 'other'. There is also a loss of symbol and sacrament. Everything is measured by its purpose-driven usefulness and profitability. If it is not immediately relevant it is thrown out. This approach can be as evident in church life as outside it.

There is a loss of transcendence – the loss of any higher point of reference for life. There is no place for honour or worship. A non-contemplative world is a rampantly individual one. 'Me' and my 'self' is the measure of what is real and what really matters. There is therefore a collapse of communities and the institutions that have traditionally given shape to our social world.

There is a loss of celebration. This is such an anxious and stressed world. By contrast, Jesus again and again told stories of parties and weddings feasts to describe the life of the Kingdom. In those stories the invitations went out widely, but have you noticed that those who didn't come were the ones who had important work to do (Luke 14.16–24)?

Finally, while claiming to increase personal choice and freedom, this non-contemplative world actually ends up requiring a narrow conformity. It becomes trapped in addictive patterns of behaviour and lacks the imagination and will to address the scandal of the gross inequalities that are the consequence of its own greed.

By contrast, contemplation enlarges our view of reality by leading us more deeply into God, ourselves and our world. Contemplation changes the subject away from ourselves and insists on recognizing the 'Other'. The shift is from wondering how/if/about, to wondering *at*. It restores our capacity for astonishment. Contemplation restores to us our own distinct individuality through revealing to us our sense of belonging to the greater whole. It leads us into the mystery of things (and so is experienced as both light and darkness). Above all else, contemplation restores us to our primary relationship with God in the midst of all life.

Steps into contemplative prayer

If what we have been saying is true, this contemplative life is already alive in us, natural to us and even restless in us – though it may be very deeply buried. We are not trying to discover something new so much as seeking what we have lost.

Finding a place to be still
Thomas Merton once said that the reason we don't get anywhere in prayer is because we don't start some*where*. So where will it be? It may be a favourite chair or corner of a room. It may be a nearby retreat house. Geography is important. We need somewhere we will be undistracted. We may not spend long there at a time, but ideally it will be a place we visit regularly. (For helpful guidance on becoming still, see Nash, 2005.)

Focusing
After taking time to settle we may find it helpful to have a focus for our attention. One approach is to take a short passage of scripture. Read it slowly, perhaps several times. Now choose one word from the passage – like 'God' or 'love'. Fix this word in your heart. Repeat it gently but firmly in your depths (this is not unlike the approach of the Jesus Prayer in Chapter 3). In the process the mind becomes *inactive* in prayer. It is not abandoned or emptied in any way, but in this work of prayer it is not central.

In the Orthodox tradition the gift of icons is significant here. Through disciplined, steady attentiveness to these gospel images, our eyes are 'washed clean by contemplation' (Seddon, 1999). We are such a visually promiscuous age and live at high levels of sensual stimulation all the time. The greatest obstacle in a non-contemplative world is sheer over-familiarity. Our spiritual and psychological task is to learn to look at things that are familiar until they become unfamiliar again.

Waiting and watching

Holding the word or image we are waiting on God. Like everything else in the spiritual life, this must be a gift of God. We can do nothing to demand or manufacture it. Picture it as like going on safari to see wildlife. Lacking all sensitivity to the world we are entering, we crash in excitedly, scarcely aware of the disturbance we are causing and the threat we pose. There may be tantalizing glimpses of the backs of things fleeing in the distance, then nothing. It all seems empty. What we seek stays hidden. We begin to doubt if there is anything there to be found. Contemplative insight is elusive and shy. It is not for taming. We must just sit still and wait. While we carry any hope of capturing or using what we seek, it will remain out of sight. We have to let go of any hope of possessing as a way of knowing anything.

Darkness

The beginnings of contemplative prayer may be marked by a disturbing sense of loss and darkness. Familiar words and images may lose their meaning. We may well think our prayer life has collapsed. In the first instance we are entering into our own darkness. We may even think of this as a tough but merciful detoxification of our own promiscuous senses. This is where that word becomes important. With this word we cry out in faith and longing. We use it to beat upon the cloud and darkness. The apophatic (hidden) tradition in the Orthodox church stresses the importance of darkness for keeping us from idolatry. The true God is always much more than our words or pictures of him. This darkness is a sanctifying corrective to those times when we claim vision or understanding of the living God – who is always beyond sight and mind.

Conversion to the world

Contemplating the love of God will draw us into a new contemplation of all that he has made. In fact this is a test of Christian prayer. And in this world, 'to contemplate the smallest object is to experience the Trinity' (Olivier Clément).

When Thomas Merton entered an enclosed contemplative monastery in America it felt like the completion of his conversion to Christ. He longed for nothing else than to pour his life into the love of Christ and, as he put it, 'to disappear into God'. Like all fervent converts he was very dismissive of the world he had left. Some years later he had to go back into that world for a hospital appointment in a nearby town. There something happened to him that was like a second conversion.

> In Louisville, at the corner of Fourth and Walnut, I was suddenly overwhelmed with the realisation that I loved all these people, that they were mine and I was theirs . . . It was like waking from a dream of separateness . . . to take your place as a member of the human race in which God himself became incarnate. If only everybody could realise this. But it cannot be explained. There is no way of telling people they are all walking round shining like the sun.'
>
> (Merton, 1977, pp. 153–4)

This contemplative quest may begin with our own hunger or curiosity. We reach out in faith and longing love. In any way we can, we make ourselves open and available. But this love cannot be compelled or demanded, even where it is promised. It can only be freely given. We must wait on the gift of the Beloved. And in that freedom he will come with the gift of his presence. This is sometimes described as 'infused' contemplation – the response of the Beloved to the lover. It may be experienced as a loving and joyful consummation, or in tears and deep darkness. But the experience of God is not what we seek. It is God – and God alone.

For thought, prayer and activity

1   (a)   What is the heart of the challenge in this chapter for you?
    (b)   How does it leave you wanting to act or pray?

2   (a)   Watch television with the sound turned off, treating the pictures as material for contemplation.
    (b)   What does this 'window on the world' show you?

(c) Choose one image and use it as the basis for further thought and prayer.

3   'To contemplate the smallest object is to experience the Trinity'.
(a) Pick out a small, routine detail of your life to contemplate – perhaps something from your journey to work or a well-known picture in your home.
(b) Look at it until the familiar begins to become unfamiliar and the possibility that this is all part of something much greater and deeper starts to become apparent.

4
He himself is my contemplation
he is my delight
him for his own sake I seek above me
from him himself I feed within me
he is the field in which I labour
he is the fruit for which I labour
he is my cause
he is my effect
he is my beginning
he is my end without end
he is for me
eternity.
(Isaac of Stella, c. 1100–1169)

Further reading

Borst, Jim, *Coming to God in the Stillness: A Method of Contemplative Prayer* (Guildford: Eagle, 1992).

de Waal, Esther, *Lost in Wonder: Rediscovering the Spiritual Art of Attentiveness* (London: Canterbury Press, 2003).

Leech, Kenneth, *The Eye of the Storm: Living Spiritually in the Real World* (San Francisco: HarperCollins, 1992).

Merton, Thomas, *Contemplation in a World of Action* (New York: Doubleday, 1971).

Rolheiser, Ronald, *Seeking Spirituality: Guidelines for Christian Spirituality for the Twenty-first Century* (London: Hodder and Stoughton, 1998).

23 On being spies of God

Spirituality beyond religion

Not so long ago this would have been an unexpected chapter in a book like this. Like most religions Christianity liked to think that spiritual life, prayer and life in God was its own property, only available to the initiated – to people who are followers. The appropriate starting point for relating to those who are outside the Church was therefore seen not as prayer or spirituality, which of course they couldn't understand, but evangelism. But one of the features of a contemporary culture increasingly distanced from any organized religion is the sheer creative variety and seriousness of interest in spirituality.

Spiritual life in a post-Christian culture

Research shows that a majority of the population admit to having had significant experiences of 'spiritual' life. Compared to a survey done a decade earlier, there was a significant increase in the number who said that:

- they sensed a benevolent patterning in events – life was not random;
- they had had experience of answered prayer;
- they had experienced an awareness of evil;
- they felt moments of awareness of 'God's' presence;
- they were aware of the 'sacred' in nature.

These results could suggest that spiritual experiences are on the increase. It is more likely that they reflect a culture that is increasingly open to speaking about spiritual experience. What is worth noting is that during this same period church attendance has declined very significantly (see Richmond, 2005, pp. 8–15).

The results support the evidence of the Alister Hardy Institute and other researchers who have spent time encouraging people to share specific stories of spiritual experiences. The great majority of those questioned had no contact with church. They preferred to describe themselves as 'spiritual' rather than 'religious'. Many of the stories shared go back to childhood, never forgotten but never shared before. The experiences were always in very ordinary times and places. They were unsought and unexpected; they had a sense of being 'given'. A consistent feature of these stories is the sense of the unity of everything. Here is one example, an experience vividly recalled 60 years after the event.

> I was three years old. I crouched down, as children do, very close to the ground. A black slug moved across the path, very slowly, silently, leaving a shiny trail, and I sat back on my haunches to watch it. My cotton print dress circled the ground around me. Overhead the sky was blue, the sun shone . . . a tune was in my head and I hummed it . . . There was a movement among the trees. Not the movement made by someone passing through, but an overall rustle of attention as in a crowd before the arrival of royalty. Each leaf was aware, expectant. Each blade of grass alert. God was everywhere. I felt secure; held; at one with everything around me.   (Taylor, 1992, p. 38)

Sir Alister Hardy was an eminent biologist who died in 1985. He pioneered research into spiritual and religious experience by inviting people to share their personal stories of spiritual awareness or encounter. The Institute that bears his name has a collection of over 30,000 stories. Hardy concluded that spiritual awareness was so natural and innate to human beings that it could be described as part of our biology. Research on the spiritual awareness of children strongly confirms this but also suggests that Western society has been destructive of spiritual awareness and discourages a continued sensitivity to it. But it does not go away. It is simply driven underground and remains intensely private.

What is going on?

Human and spiritual
The first conclusion to be drawn from these experiences is that life is spiritually porous: spiritual experiences seep into our lives unasked (though

not unwanted). To be spiritual is therefore not about being religious in any particular sense. In fact you don't have to be religious at all. It is a characteristic of being human.

The searching Spirit

But these stories take us one step further. They suggest that something spiritual is seeking us. Psalm 139 is a meditation on such an experience. 'Where can I go from your spirit? Or where can I flee from your presence?' (v. 7). This searching God is most fully revealed in the coming of Jesus, living in our midst and sharing our nature.

Surprised by faith

One of the features of the stories of Jesus in the Gospels is how often faith and spiritual understanding keep appearing where they are not expected, and not appearing where they should be expected. Spiritual life keeps falling into the wrong hands. Examples are Jesus meeting with the centurion (Matt. 8.5–13) or his conversation with the Syro-Phoenecian woman (Mark 7.25–30). Jesus was clearly surprised by the faith of these outsiders. The parable of the tax-collector and the Pharisee makes precisely this point (Luke 18.9–14). So Jesus says to the religious people of his day: 'the tax-collectors and the prostitutes are going into the kingdom of God ahead of you' (Matt. 21.31).

The same happens in the experience of the early church community. The story of Peter and Cornelius is perhaps the best known (Acts 10). The effect was to shock the Christian community into an awareness of the sheer wideness of God's activity and presence in the world.

Finding a place to meet

Places of welcome and listening

Many of those who shared their stories with the researchers admitted they had never told anyone before. One person specifically thanked them, saying that ever since the experience he had lived with a sense of regret that he had not found anywhere he could share the experience or begin to discern its meaning for him. You might think that the church is an obvious place to start. But there is one obstacle to overcome first. I remember talking with a woman who had obviously felt she could trust me enough to share a story that had been very important in shaping her spiritual understanding. But she could only start by saying, 'Of course, I know you won't agree with this, vicar, but . . .' Her assumption is not untypical. Many people fear that official religion will stand in judgement of their most formative and deeply help convictions and experiences of life and God.

John V. Taylor notes that the church has done a much better job of being open to hearing stories of human sin.

> How regrettable it is, how unnatural in fact, that through the cen-
> turies the confessional stalls around the walls of many churches have
> received the secrets of so many sins, and not been equally available to
> the confidences of men and women and children who have been
> overtaken by the ecstasies or insights or consolations that declare the
> reality of God! Had this other side of personal experience been
> invited it might have redressed the balance and made the churches
> everywhere as mindful of divine initiative as of human failure.
>
> If it could become normal for people to know that a church was
> the place where confidences of that sort could be shared and under-
> stood; where they could be helped to reflect upon the experience and
> grow by responding to it; where they could learn that, just as they
> have known the approach of God in the strength of a tree or the
> swelling tide of music, others have known it in a bush lapped in flame
> or the action of a potter at the wheel; where they could find that the
> church itself was living and growing by such experiences . . . then I
> believe that the Christian community might rediscover the more
> dynamic exploratory view of the knowledge of God which its own
> scriptures display.   (Taylor, 1992, p. 56)

Seeking a common language

Steve Hollinghurst (2003) trains Christian teams to run stalls at New Age festivals. He says that Christians need to understand how to communicate faith in radically unchurched contexts. What we think we are saying is not necessarily what people are hearing. He contrasts what he calls the trad-itional 'Christendom' approach with a 'fellow explorer' approach. However well intended, he knows from long experience how the first is experienced as directive and giving answers. It tends to use methods or techniques to achieve its end, correcting other people's views because they are wrong, and requiring others to enter a Christian culture as an unspoken condition of conversion. It is experienced as prescriptive, authoritarian and lacking any expectation that there might be things to learn or receive from others. In a highly individualized culture where 'my truth' is as valid as yours and there is no expectation of one overall truth or belief, such an approach just alienates the listeners.

The 'fellow explorer' approach is more interested in relationships than methods. A fellow explorer will be open to the possibility that both sides will be learning as they go. In fact unless we are open to this possibility then we will not be listening at all. The very act of listening makes possible new understanding and appreciation and therefore requires an openness to change. This requires a willingness to enter and inhabit the culture of those you listen to. In this meeting Christian convictions are not denied or left unspoken. What is important is how they are shared: 'I am interested in what you believe. Here is what I believe and these are the reasons it is important to me.' For Henri Nouwen this openness to others expresses the heart of Christian hospitality towards the world. But being receptive to others does not mean becoming neutral. It is neither polite nor respectful to just sit agreeing with everything your guest says. We are to offer a real articulate presence, sharing our own beliefs, opinions and lifestyle clearly and distinctly. 'An empty house is not a hospitable house,' he says. 'Real receptivity asks for confrontation' (Nouwen, 1980, p. 92).

Agnostics Anonymous

One church ran a Christian enquirers' group with the 'fellow explorers' approach. They agreed two rules at the start. No question would be laughed at or treated as unimportant and you did not have to become a Christian by the end of it. What was striking was how liberating and energizing people found this format. It released an exciting sense of the naturalness of spiritual life and the vitality of going searching. It also led to profound exploration of Christian faith and the experience stood in marked contrast to the more traditional 'confirmation classes' that they replaced.

Spaces to pray

In a house of suitable size, quiet mornings were held. Among those invited were parents who were being helped to prepare for the baptism of their children. Many people find the moment of bringing a child into the world awakens a spiritual longing within themselves as well as a desire to offer something spiritual to their child. But they have often never learned to pray before becoming parents and certainly have little time to start now!

A brief introduction was offered, a verse from the Bible to focus on. There were practical suggestions about becoming still and receptive. Coffee and tea and someone to talk to were available throughout the time. In the stillness, a number of people had quite deep spiritual encounters. They became curious about coming to church or joining a home group just to find out more about the presence they had begun to be aware of.

Exploring and discerning

It has been said that evangelism today needs all the gifts traditionally associated with spiritual direction. At the heart of that ancient ministry is the concern to listen and discern the ways of the Spirit in a person's life. For the Church today that means taking the faith into the spiritual market place where people are already talking and questioning and wondering – and searching for wisdom. The stories that are around will be unusual, often confused – perhaps even dangerous at times. But they are signs of life not death. And the vocation of the Christian community is to be a hospitable place in which all the life of the scriptures, the shared wisdom of fellow-travellers, and the discipline of prayer and worship offer the space needed where people may come to discern the life and call of this mysterious searching Spirit.

For thought, prayer and activity

1   'I thought of this: I thought of how every day each of us experiences a few little moments that have just a bit more resonance than other moments – we hear a word that sticks in our mind – or maybe we have a small experience that pulls us out of ourselves, if only briefly . . . a stranger gives us a piece of bread to feed to the ducks, say; a small child starts a conversation with us. And if we were to collect these small moments in a notebook and collect them over a period of months we would see certain trends emerge from our collection, certain voices would emerge that have been trying to speak through us. We would realise that we have been having another life altogether, one that we didn't even know was going on inside us. And maybe this *other* life is more important than the one we think of as being real – this clunky

day-to-day world of furniture and noise and metal. So just maybe it is these small silent moments which are the true story-making events of our lives.'   (Coupland, 2002, pp. 105–6)

(a) Do you carry any stories of unexpected encounters – moments when God was very near and real?

(b) How have you responded to them?

(c) How have they fitted in with your understanding of Christian faith and teaching?

(d) Do they leave you with questions or tensions?

(e) Would it help to find someone you could talk them through with?

2 'Evangelism today needs all the gifts traditionally associated with spiritual direction.'

(a) What gifts do you think are being referred to?

(b) How might this insight change the way we approach people to share our faith?

3 Are there people you could ask to share with you their spiritual journey and experiences? All you have to do is give to them the gift of listening.

4 A mission statement?

> . . . live,
> And pray, and sing, and tell old tales and laugh . . .
> And take upon's the mystery of things,
> As if we were God's spies.
>
> (Shakespeare, *King Lear*, V.iii.11–17)

Further reading and resources

Clifford, Ross and Johnson, Philip, *Jesus and the Gods of the New Age: Communicating Christ in Today's Spiritual Supermarket* (Oxford: Lion, 2001).

Equipping your Church in a Spiritual Age (London: Church House Publishing, 2005).

Frost, Rob, *Essence* (Eastbourne: Kingsway, 2003).

Hollinghurst, Steve, *New Age, Paganism and Christian Mission* (Cambridge: Grove Books, 2003).

Nouwen, Henri, *Reaching Out: The Three Movements of the Spiritual Life* (London: Fount, 1992)

Richmond, Yvonne (ed.), *Evangelism in a Spiritual Age* (London: Church House Publishing, 2005).

www.rejesus.co.uk

Further reading and resources

The following books and websites have either been referred to directly in this book or have provided significant source material. The website addresses are correct at the time of publication.

Introductory books on spirituality and prayer
Leech, Kenneth, *True Prayer: A Study of Spirituality* (Harrisburg, Penn.: Morehouse, 1995).
McGrath, Alister, *Christian Spirituality* (Oxford: Blackwell, 1999).
Mursell, Gordon, *The Story of Christian Spirituality* (Oxford: Lion, 2001).

Other books
Allison, James, *The Joy of Being Wrong: Original Sin through Easter Eyes* (New York: Crossroad Herder, 1998).
Allison, James, *On Being Liked* (London: Darton, Longman and Todd, 2003).
Alves, Rubem, *The Poet, The Warrior, The Prophet* (London: SCM Press, 1990).
Barrington-Ward, Simon, *The Jesus Prayer* (Oxford: Bible Reading Fellowship, 1996).
Barrington-Ward, Simon and Brother Ramon SSF, *Praying the Jesus Prayer Together* (Oxford: Bible Reading Fellowship, 2001).
Begbie, Jeremy (ed.), *Beholding the Glory: Incarnation Through the Arts* (London: Darton, Longman and Todd, 2000).
Belton, Neil, *The Good Listener: Helen Bamber, A Life Against Cruelty* (London: Weidenfeld and Nicholson, 1998).
Berry, R. J. (ed.), *The Care of Creation* (Leicester: IVP, 2000).
Bloom, Metropolitan Antony, *The Essence of Prayer* (London: Darton, Longman and Todd, 1989).
Bonhoeffer, Dietrich, *Life Together* (London: SCM Press, 1981).
Borst, Jim, *Coming to God in the Stillness* (Guildford: Eagle, 1992).
Bradshaw, Paul, *Two Ways of Praying: Introducing Liturgical Spirituality* (London: SPCK, 1995).
Bridges, William, *Managing Transitions: Making the Most of Change* (Cambridge, Mass.: Da Capo Press, 2003).
Brueggemann, Walter, *The Message of the Psalms* (Minneapolis, Minn.: Augsburg Fortress, 1984).
Bryson, Bill, *A Short History of Nearly Everything* (New York: Doubleday, 2003).
Bunting, Ian (ed.), *Celebrating the Anglican Way* (London: Hodder and Stoughton, 1996).

Chan, Simon, *Pentecostal Theology and the Christian Spiritual Tradition* (Sheffield: Sheffield University Press, 2001).

Chittister, Joan, *The Rule of Benedict* (New York: Crossroad, 2001).

Clarke, Clifton, *Introducing Black Pentecostal Spirituality* (Cambridge: Grove Books, 1997).

Clément, Olivier, *On Human Being* (London: New City, 2000).

Clément, Olivier, *Roots of Christian Mysticism* (New York: New City, 1995).

Cockerton, John, *The Essentials of Evangelical Spirituality* (Cambridge: Grove Books, 1994).

Conway, Stephen (ed.), *Living the Eucharist: Affirming Catholicism and the Liturgy* (London: Darton, Longman and Todd, 2001).

Cotter, Jim, *Prayer at Night* (Sheffield: Cairns Publications, 1989). Revised edition, *Prayer at Night's Approaching* (Sheffield: Cairns Publications, 2001).

Cottrell, Stephen, *Sacrament, Wholeness and Evangelism* (Cambridge: Grove Books, 1996).

Coupland, Douglas, *Generation X: Tales for an Accelerated Culture* (London: Abacus, 1996).

Coupland, Douglas, *Life After God* (New York: Scribner, 2002).

Covey, Stephen, *Seven Habits of Highly Effective People* (New York: Simon and Schuster, 1992).

Craig, Yvonne Joan, *Peacemaking for Churches* (London: SPCK, 1999).

Culling, Elizabeth, *Making the Most of Communion* (Cambridge: Grove Books, 1998).

de Waal, Esther, *A Seven Day Journey with Thomas Merton* (Guildford: Eagle, 2000).

de Waal, Esther, *Lost in Wonder: Rediscovering the Spiritual Art of Attentiveness* (London: Canterbury Press, 2003).

Drane John, *What is the New Age Saying to the Church?* (Grand Rapids, Mich.: Zondervan, 1999).

Dudley, Martin and Rowell, Geoffrey, *Confession and Absolution* (Collegeville, Minn.: Liturgical Press, 1990).

Ford, David, *The Shape of Living* (London: Hodder and Stoughton, 1997).

Foster, Richard, *A Celebration of Discipline* (London: Hodder and Stoughton, 1998).

Foster, Richard, *Prayer: Finding the Heart's True Home* (London: Hodder and Stoughton, 1992).

Foster, Richard, *Streams of Living Water: Celebrating the Great Traditions of the Christian Faith* (San Francisco: HarperCollins, 1998).

Fowke, Ruth, *Finding Your Prayer Personality* (Oxford: Abingdon, 2002).

Fowler, James, *Stages of Faith* (San Francisco: Harper & Row, 1980).

Frost, Rob, *Essence* (Eastbourne: Kingsway, 2003).

George, Timothy and McGrath, Alister (eds), *For All the Saints: Evangelical Theology and Christian Spirituality* (Louisville, Ky.: Westminster John Knox Press, 2003).

Giles, Richard, *How to be an Anglican: Let Me Count the Ways . . .* (London: Canterbury Press, 2003).

Gillett, David, *Trust and Obey: Explorations in Evangelical Spirituality* (London: Darton, Longman and Todd, 1993).

Gordon, James, *Evangelical Spirituality: From the Wesleys to John Stott* (London: SPCK, 1991).

Grubb, Norman, *Rees Howells: Intercessor* (Cambridge: Lutterworth Press, 1991).

Guiver, George, *Company of Voices: Daily Prayer and the People of God* (London: Canterbury Press, 2001).

Haddon, Mark, *The Curious Incident of the Dog in the Night-time* (London: Vintage, 2004).

Halevi, Yossi Klein, *At the Entrance to the Garden of Eden: A Jew's Search for Hope with Christians and Muslims in the Holy Land* (San Fransisco: Perennial, 2002).

Hay, David, *Religious Experience Today* (London: Cassells, 1990).

Hay, David and Nye, Rebecca, *The Spirit of the Child* (London: Fount, 1998).

Hebblethwaite, Margaret, *The Way of Ignatius* (London: Fount, 1994).

Hollinghurst, Steve, *New Age, Paganism and Christian Mission* (Cambridge: Grove Books, 2003).

Hoste, A. and Salet, G. (eds), *Isaac de l'Étoile: Sermons 1* (Paris: Sources Chrétienes, 1967).

Howard, Geoffrey, *Dare to Break Bread: Eucharist in Desert and City* (London: Darton, Longman and Todd, 1992).

Hubbard, Keith, *In the Name of Jesus* (Cambridge: Grove Books, 2000).

Hughes, Gerard, *God in All Things* (London: Hodder and Stoughton, 2004).

Hughes, Gerard, *God of Surprises* (London: Darton, Longman and Todd, 1996).

Ind, Jo, *Memories of Bliss: God, Sex and Us* (London: SCM Press, 2003).

Innes, Robert, *Personality Indicators and the Spiritual Life* (Cambridge: Grove Books, 1996).

Jones, James, *Jesus and Creation* (London: SPCK, 2003).

Keirsey, David and Bates, Marilyn, *Please Understand Me: Character and Temperament Types* (Del Mar, Calif.: Prometheus Nemesis Books, 1984).

Leach, John, *The Spirit Comes* (San Francisco: HarperCollins, 2001).

Leech, Kenneth, *The Eye of the Storm: Living Spiritually in the Real World* (San Francisco: HarperCollins, 1992).

Leech, Kenneth, *Soul Friend* (Harrisburg, Penn.: Morehouse, 2001).

Leech, Kenneth, *True Prayer: A Study of Spirituality* (Harrisburg, Penn.: Morehouse, 1995).

Louth, Andrew, *The Wilderness of God* (London: Darton, Longman and Todd, 1991).

Mayne, Michael, *This Sunrise of Wonder* (London: Fount, 1995).

Metz, Barbara and Burchill, John, *The Enneagram and Prayer* (Denville, NJ: Dimension Books, 1987).

Merton, Thomas, *Conjectures of a Guilty Bystander* (London: Sheldon Press, 1977).

Merton, Thomas, *Contemplation in a World of Action* (New York: Doubleday, 1971).

Merton, Thomas, *New Seeds of Contemplation* (London: Continuum, 2003).

Michael, Chester P. and Norrisey, Marie, *Prayer and Temperament: Different Prayer Forms for Different Personality Types* (Charlottesville, Va.: Open Door, 1991).

Miller, Charles, *Praying the Eucharist: Reflections on the Eucharistic Experience of God* (London: SPCK, 1995).

Miller, Harold, *Finding a Personal Rule of Life* (Cambridge: Grove Books, 1983).

Mitton, Michael, *Wild Beasts and Angels: Remaining Human in the Healing Ministry* (London: Darton, Longman and Todd, 2000).

Moreton, Mark, *Personal Confession Reconsidered* (Cambridge: Grove Books, 1994).

Morley, Janet, *All Desires Known* (London: SPCK, 2005).

Morley, Janet (ed.), *Bread of Tomorrow: Praying with the World's Poor* (London: SPCK, 2004).

Morrison, Toni, *Beloved* (New York: Vintage, 1997).

Mursell, Gordon, *Out of the Deep: Prayer as Protest* (London: Darton, Longman and Todd, 1989).

Mursell, Gordon, *Praying as Exile* (London: Darton, Longman and Todd, 2005).

Nash, Wanda, *Simple Tools for Stillness* (Cambridge: Grove Books, 2005).

Nelson, James, *Embodiment: Approaches to Sexuality and Christian Theology* (Minneapolis, Minn.: Augsburg Fortress, 1979).

Nelson, James, *The Intimate Connection: Male Sexuality, Masculine Spirituality* (Louisville, Ky.: Westminster John Knox Press, 1999).

Nicholl, Donald, *The Testing of Hearts* (London: Darton, Longman and Todd, 1998).

Nouwen, Henri, *Reaching Out: The Three Movements of the Spiritual Life* (London: Fount, 1992).

Nouwen, Henri, *The Way of the Heart* (London: Darton, Longman and Todd, 1999).

Osborn, Lawrence, *Meeting God in Creation* (Cambridge: Grove Books, 1990).

Packer, James, *Knowing God* (Downers Grove, Ill.: Intervarsity Press, 1998).

Parsons, Tony, *Man and Boy* (San Francisco: HarperCollins, 2000).

Patterson, Colin, *How to Learn Through Conflict* (Cambridge: Grove Books, 2000).

Ramsay, Michael, *The Anglican Spirit* (New York: Church Publishing, 2005).

Richmond, Yvonne (ed.), *Evangelism in a Spiritual Age* (London: Church House Publishing, 2005).

Rolheiser, Ronald, *Seeking Spirituality: Guidelines for Christian Spirituality for the Twenty-first Century* (London: Hodder and Stoughton, 1998).

Rowell, Geoffrey, Stevenson, Kenneth and Williams, Rowan (eds), *Love's Redeeming Work: The Anglican Quest for Holiness* (Oxford: Oxford University Press, 2004).

Runcorn, David, *Choice, Desire and the Will of God* (London: SPCK, 2002).

Runcorn, David, *The Creation of Adam: Seven Guided Reflections from Genesis* (Cambridge: Grove Books, 2001).

Runcorn, David, *Rumours of Life: Reflections on the Resurrection Appearances* (London: Darton, Longman and Todd, 1996).

Runcorn, David, *Space for God: Silence and Solitude in the Christian Life* (London: Darton, Longman and Todd, 1990).

Sakharov, Archimandrite Sophrony, *The Monk of Mount Athos* (New York: St Vladimir Press, 1983).

Seddon, Deborah, *Gospel Icons* (Cambridge: Grove Books, 1999).

Seddon, Philip, *Darkness* (Cambridge: Grove Books, 1983).

Seddon, Philip, *Gospel and Sacrament: Reclaiming a Holistic Evangelical Spirituality* (Cambridge: Grove Books, 2004).

Silf, Margaret, *Landmarks: Exploration of Ignatian Spirituality* (London: Darton, Longman and Todd, 1998).

Skeats, David, *Experience of Grace: Aspects of Faith and Spirituality in the Puritan Tradition* (Cambridge: Grove Books, 1997).

Smail, Tom, *The Giving Gift: The Holy Spirit in Person* (London: Darton, Longman and Todd, 1994).

Stackhouse, Ian, *The Gospel-driven Church* (Milton Keynes: Paternoster, 2004).

Stockitt, Robin, *Open to the Spirit: St Ignatius and John Wimber in Dialogue* (Cambridge: Grove Books, 2000).

Suurmond, Jean-Jacques, *Word and Spirit at Play: Towards a Charismatic Theology* (London: SCM Press, 1994).

Taylor, John, V., *The Christlike God* (London: SCM Press, 1992, reprinted 2004).

Taylor, John, V., *The Go-between God* (London: SCM Press, 1972, reprinted 2004).

Tutu, Desmond, *No Future Without Forgiveness: A Personal Overview of South Africa's Truth and Reconciliation Commission* (London: Rider, 2000).

Vanier, Jean, *Community and Growth* (New York: Paulist Press, 1989).

Ward, Pete (ed.), *Mass Culture* (Oxford: Bible Reading Fellowship, 1999).

Ward, Benedicta, *The Lives of the Desert Fathers* (London: Mowbray, 1981).

Ward, Benedicta, *The Sayings of the Desert Fathers* (London: Mowbray, 1981).

Ware, Kallistos, *The Orthodox Way* (New York: SVS Press, 1998).

Watts, Fraser (ed.), *Perspectives on Prayer* (London: SPCK, 2002).

White, Susan, *The Spirit of Worship: The Liturgical Tradition* (London: Darton, Longman and Todd, 1999).

Whyte, David, *Crossing the Unknown Sea: Work as a Pilgrimage of Identity* (London: Penguin Putnam, 2001).

Williams, Rowan, *Ponder These Things* (London: Canterbury Press, 2002).

Williams, Rowan, *Silence and Honey Cakes* (Oxford: Lion, 2004).

Williams, Rowan, *The Truce of God: Peacemaking in Troubled Times* (London: Canterbury Press, 2005).

Williams, Rowan, *The Wound of Knowledge: Christian Spirituality from the New Testament to St John of the Cross* (London: Darton, Longman and Todd, 1990).

Journal articles

Cocksworth, C., 'Holding Together: Catholic Evangelical Worship in the Spirit', *Anvil Journal*, Vol 22:1 (2005).

Endean, P., SJ, 'Embodiment', *The Way: Review of Contemporary Christian Spirituality*, Vol 35, Number 2 (April 1995). The whole issue is on the theme of 'Embodiment'.

Websites

Christian environmental issues
www.arocha.org
www.christian-ecology.org.uk

Charismatic renewal
www.new-wine.org

Church of England
www.cofe.anglican.org

Ignatian
www.sacredspace.ie

Liturgy
www.praxisworship.org.uk

Peace and conflict: Mennonite Conflict Mediation resources
www.menno.org.uk

Spirituality and mission
www.rejesus.co.uk

Index

Abraham and Sarah 170
Acts of the Apostles 67; healing 81; hour of prayer 144; Peter and Cornelius 191; the Spirit 138
Adam 90–1, 162
Alister Hardy Institute 189–90
Allison, James 128, 180
Alves, Rubem 96
Antony of the Desert 9

Bamber, Helen 98
Barratt, T. B. 33–4
Barth, Karl 10, 153
Benedict, St 59
Bible, the: Ignatian approach 153; liturgy and 146; sacraments and 69–70; *see also under individual books*
Boddy, Alexander 33–4
Bonhoeffer, Dietrich 52, 53, 54, 148
Book of Common Prayer 146
Broken Wall, Community of the 55–6
Brueggemann, Walter 172
Bryson, Bill 88

Catholic Church: communion and 69; Ignatian approach 155
Celtic spirituality 144
change: living with 168–71; spirituality in 172–4
charismatic movement *see* Pentecostal spirituality
Church of England: theological history of 17–20; worldwide community 18
churches: exploration and 191–4; liturgy and 147
Clément, Olivier 187
Colossians, letter to the 55, 153, 164
communion: preparing for 73–5; understanding 67–71
communion, sacrament of: contribution to spirituality 71–3

community: communion and 71; confession in 130–2; the creatures of 77–83; of the Holy Spirit 137–9; meeting places 191–4; rule of life 64–6; sexuality and 105–6; spirituality within 51–7
Community of the Broken Wall 55–6
compassion 165–6
contemplation 183–8, 185–8; Ignatian retreat 154–5
Corinthians, letters to the 27, 44, 97; on communion 70–1, 73; a new creation 45, 53; the Spirit 138
Cotter, Jim 100, 107
Coupland, Douglas 104, 195
Covey, Stephen 61
Cranmer, Thomas 21
creation 19–20, 68, 138–9; communion and 71; contemplation of 164–7; faith in 161–2; theology of 162–4

Daniel, book of 143–4
desert/wilderness: test of the 11–12; three essentials of 13–14; understanding: 9–13; in the world 14–16
Dillard, Annie 146

Eastern Orthodox churches 25–31, 133, 186
Eliot, T. S. 115
Ephesians, letter to the: husbands and wives 106; the Spirit 139; violence and revenge 180
evangelical spirituality: affirmation across differences 40; features of 44–6; historical view of 41–3
Eve 162
exile 23
Exodus, book of 163
Ezekiel, book of 97, 122, 125

faith: assurance 45–6; life stages of 109–17; prayers of 27–8
Ford, David 58, 65
forgiveness: confession 130–3; fore-giving 128
Fowke, Ruth 76
Fowler, James 109, 110

Galatians, letter to the 64, 140
Genesis, book of: Adam and Eve 102, 183; community 51; God's house 165; human beings 90–1
Gerasene demoniac 156–7
Gillett, David 76
God: creation 161–7; liturgy and 146; the Spirit and 137; Word of 153
good and evil 176–8

Haddon, Mark 168
Halevi, Yossi Klein 180
Hardy Institute *see* Alister Hardy Institute
healing 35, 165–6
Hebrews, letter to the 46, 153, 170; God's word 164; intercession 121
Heschel, Abraham 37
Hillesum, Etty 96
Hollinghurst, Steve 192
Holloway, Richard 45
Holy Spirit: community 137–9; fire of 141; Ignatian approach 151–2; living in 139–42; presence of 135–7
Holy Trinity *see* Trinity
Howells, Rees 126
Huddleston, Archbishop Trevor 179
human beings: body, flesh and spirit 95–100; the Fall 162; personal identity 86–94

Ignatius Loyola, St: approach to spirituality 151–7

intercession 121–7
Iona community 64, 144
Isaac of Stella 188

Jeremiah, book of 10
Jesuits 151–2
Jesus Christ: blindness and sight
    182; breaking bread 67, 71;
    brings transition 172–3;
    devotion to 45; goodness
    177–8; as meeting place 122–3;
    Orthodox prayer 25–31, 185;
    prayer and 126–7; resurrection
    97, 173; and the Word 70
Joel, book of 33, 135
John, Gospel of 97; following
    Jesus 115; human beings 92;
    love 54; Peter in transition
    173; redemption 164; the Spirit
    138; the unknown 53
John of the Cross, St 115, 151
Jung, Carl G. 82
justice 71, 175–8

Keble, John 22

Lavelle, Louis 103
Lee Abbey community 54–5
Leech, Kenneth 184
Leviticus, book of 143
liturgy: definition and source
    143–5; features of 145–8; forms
    of 148–9; modern concerns
    148; natural to man 145
love: within community 54; peace
    and 180–1; sexual passion
    103–5
Luke, Gospel of: Bible study 70;
    on breaking bread 67, 70–1;
    celebrations 184; goodness
    177; justice 35, 176; the lamp
    of your body 182; on mercy
    26; playful wisdom 36; prayer
    123; shepherd and lambs 128;
    the Spirit 138; unexpected
    places 191
Luther, Martin 69

Mark, Gospel of: call to follow 9;
    the Gerasene demoniac 156–7;
    Jesus as new 172; justice 176;
    like children 183; unexpected
    places 191
Marshall, Michael 20
Matthew, Gospel of: creation 163;
    on doubt 21; God as shelter
    172; living by the words 13; the
    meek 35; peacemaking 175,
    179; prayer 123, 125; the Spirit

139; unexpected places 191
men and women 153–4
mercy 25–9, 175
Merton, Thomas 162, 184, 185,
    187
miracles 35
mission 70–1
Morrison, Toni 95
Mursell, Gordon 19

Nouwen, Henri 54, 193

obedience 13–14

pain 98
Parham, Charles 33
Parsons, Tony: Man and Boy 114
Paul, St: communion 70–1; on
    flesh 97; gratitude 55; sexuality
    105; the Spirit 137, 140
peace: meaning in the world
    176–8; praying for 175
Pentecostal spirituality 135;
    characteristics of 34–7; from
    the Gospels 138; history of
    32–4, 37–8
Peter, St 81, 173; letters of 64
Philippians, letter to the 64
prayers and praying: within
    Anglican tradition 20–3;
    contemplative 185–8; creatures
    of 80–2; intercession 121–7;
    the Jesus prayer 25–31, 185;
    liturgy and 146, 147; for peace
    175, 179–81; personal
    confession 132–3; physical
    being and 95, 96; ropes 29;
    together 29
Protestantism 69
Proverbs, book of 36
Psalms, book of: the body 99; the
    desert 10; exile 23; faith 115;
    glory of God 162, 163;
    searching spirit 191; worship
    144

race and ethnicity 32–3, 35–8
Ramsey, Michael 122
reconciliation: communion and
    73; in community 54–5;
    physical being and 98–9
redemption 19–20, 163–4
repentance 129–30; confession
    130–3
resurrection 97, 173
Revelation, book of: creation 71;
    glimpse of heaven 76; singing
    without ceasing 29, 144
Ricci, Matteo 152

Rolheiser, Ronald 184
Romans, letter to the 71, 97, 153,
    162; creation 165–6;
    intercession 121; the Spirit
    137, 139, 140
rule of life 58–60; community
    64–6; personal 60–2, 62–4

sacraments: marriage 106; the
    Word and 69; see also
    communion
salvation 162
Savage, Sara 98
Scriven, Joseph 45
searching for spirituality 189–95
Seddon, Philip 92
seeing 182–3
sexuality 97; abuse 105–6; in
    Christianity 103–8; human
    need
    102
Seymour, Bill 32–3
silence 13
Simeon, Charles 46
sin 129, 162; confession and
    forgiveness 130–3
Society of Jesus 151–2
Song of Solomon 103, 115
stability 13
Staretz Silouan 29
Suurmond, Jean-Jacques 36, 38

Taizé community 64, 144
Taylor, John 190, 192
Temple, William 19
Teresa of Ávila, St 151
test of the desert see
    desert/wilderness
Theophan, St 29
Thessalonians, letters to the:
    praying without ceasing 27
Tilby, Angela 107
time and rhythm 165
Timothy, letters to: Jesus the
    mediator 130
Torah, the 68
Trinity, the 51

Vanier, Jean 52–5

Weil, Simone 23
Wesley brothers 42–3
Whyte, David: Crossing an
    Unknown Sea 89
wilderness 11–12; see also
    desert/wilderness
Williams, Rowan 21, 92–3, 178
wonder 183
Wren, Brian 72